1969

This book may be kept

FOURTEEN DAYS

The French Novel

Winfried Engler

THE
FRENCH NOVEL

from Eighteen Hundred
to the Present

Revised and enlarged by the author

Translated by
ALEXANDER GODE

FREDERICK UNGAR PUBLISHING CO.
NEW YORK

Translated from the original German,
Der französische Roman von 1800 bis zur Gegenwart,
by arrangement with Francke Verlag, Bern, Switzerland

INTRODUCTION

꽃 Throughout the nineteenth century—and continuing in the twentieth up to the present—the literatures of the world have been undergoing a characteristic process of increasingly manifest deconfinement. In matters of form this has involved a breakdown of the conventional definitions of genres, while the traditional subjects and themes have been enriched by the addition of more and more authentic—and less and less restrained—disclosures about the worldly realities of human existence which the past had all too often passed over in silence. Everywhere the new writers appeared determined to tolerate no longer any kind of taboo; they postulated ever more emphatically that truth rather than fiction must be the concern of the novel, even of the fantastic novel. Parallel to this, however, the lines of thought of eighteenth-century enlightenment did continue on—particularly so in France where the Revolution of 1789 had been a politically unique manifestation of them.

The Revolution marked the beginning of an age of politics intent upon displacing the old order, the *ancien régime*, in all its functions. The Revolution gave the writer, who had been relieved of his duties as a paid court poet almost a century

v

before, a new set of creative freedoms. These were guaranteed, as it were, by the revolutionary *liberté*; but contained in them —as in the area of politics—lay the dangerous germs of anarchy and chaos.

Here lies the link between revolution and literature which has been the determining characteristic—not only in France— of the more than a century and a half gone by since the year 1800.

For the organization of a work on the novel of modern times it follows that we cannot begin with Restif de la Bretonne or with the Marquis de Sade. Their works manifest at most a partial deconfinement—in the inherent principles of ethics and morals—while in terms of literary art they belong to the eighteenth century even more typically than do the novels of Diderot, Voltaire, or Rousseau, although these latter are earlier in time. Furthermore, if we were prepared to go that far afield, the sentimental novel of the English eighteenth century, the impact of young Goethe, and the endeavors of the early romanticists in Germany—these latter through their concept of the novel as the "universe of poesy"—might prove much more informative. However, the orientation of our study is consciously national both as to its continuity and its inception, and its chronological baseline shall be the year 1789 or at least the turn from the eighteenth to the nineteenth century.

This is simultaneously a requirement imposed on the present study by the objectives it wishes to serve. To be sure, it would be foolish to claim that in the realm of the novel things began with a "clean slate" in 1789 or in 1800. ... But, if we think of the reader who, as a student or otherwise, wishes to obtain an introductory survey of what there is by way of French novels from 1800 to 1960, in order, presumably, to single out preferred areas as the topics for a more thorough subsequent preoccupation, it means more to him if he is given a systematic outline than if he is presented with a much more comprehensive and much more detailed account which omits nothing and in which he must know himself how to visualize structural patterns.

In practical terms this means that our study is bound to turn out quite different, for instance, from René Lalou's very successful book, *Le Roman français depuis 1900* (Fourth

Edition, Paris, 1960), for Lalou was concerned with presenting as complete a roster as possible of all modern novelists, without highlights and without points of emphasis. On the other hand, Pierre-Georges Castex of the Sorbonne, in his handbook for French students, *Manuel des études littéraires françaises* (Volumes V and VI: Nineteenth and Twentieth Centuries, Paris, 1950 and 1953), was guided by a pedagogically sound principle of selection which made him choose a limited number of samples for the purpose of showing what was typical of a particular epoch or a particular form, but which also—in many cases—made him overlook the existing historical continuities, with the result that the student gets the impression that the history of literature is a random medley rather than a harmonious texture of human achievement in the realm of the spirit.

This, however, is precisely what the present author regards as the special function of the study of literature. By noting continuities—reflected in his text in prospective and retrospective references—he wants to show how a particular author stands on the shoulders of his predecessors, while nonetheless the truly original contribution always goes far beyond that which precedes it. Where a contribution fails to do so, there is nothing the historian of literature can do but to record that this or that form has been taken over or that this or that subject has been imitated.

But the study of literature which strives to be more than the garnering of information implies something else. It must lead to an early respect for critical research, more specifically, for detailed studies of the kind found in journal articles and monographs. Without this—just as without the more obviously necessary study of manuals and surveys[1] (which may indifferently precede or follow the meticulous scrutiny of the texts themselves)—there can be, for the student, no awareness of highlights and of a proper distribution of emphasis. The limitations in space imposed upon the present work make it impossible, of course, to provide extensive bibliographies for each individual chapter. Selective references are all we can offer. But the student will have no difficulty in finding what is needed by consulting the well-known bibliographies.[2] The principle of selection which has guided us throughout this work will guide him too.

While we must have the courage to omit, we also must find ways and means of escaping the dilemma of distortion which could easily result as we try to present so many-faceted a picture within so narrow a frame. We cannot, in all cases, justify our value judgments in greater detail, but we may hope that these will not appear glaringly prejudiced, thanks to our principle of organization and thanks to the division into chapters, in which we have used a combination of the chronological approach with the technique of presenting the material in structurally crystallized units.

In other words, we have divided the history of the novel since 1800 in groups by authors, avoiding overlappings as far as possible, with the objective of showing that the historical continuity in literature is more than a random sequence of chance, and we have then presented those groups in the form of more or less autonomous chapters of which each one is held together by a guiding theme. This implies that the conventional categories of the history of literature have been abandoned. There are sound reasons for doing so, among them—in our case —the fact that the so-called *nouveau roman* of Robbe-Grillet or Butor, treated in Chapter XIV, casts an entirely new light on the earlier novel. This is a point which Henri Peyre, for instance, could not possibly appreciate when he wrote, as recently as 1955, that from Marcel Proust and James Joyce on, the novel has been the literary form with the fewest experimental products. The names of Robbe-Grillet and Butor and their like were not even mentioned by Peyre.

Of course, it would be a dubious venture to interpret the entire modern novel in the perspective of the *nouveau roman*. Indeed, our concluding chapter deals critically with this "novel of objects" which has already ceased to be an acute problem. But it remains a fact that this form of the novel—however protean it may have turned out to be—strove to express the very opposite of what the "novel of individualism" from Senancour to Gobineau and the "psychological novel" from Gide to Sagan hoped to achieve. It wanted to remove man as the moving principle from the center of events. The result was a completely shifted picture of man, one requiring in its artistic precipitate radically new resources of language. And the procession of the fourteen chapters of this work must supply the reader with an answer to the basic question—a question with which every literary investigation cannot but be concerned—of the connection between meaning and form, between content and configuration, paying due heed as well to the role of the spirit of the age and of the world as to the ever-changing ambience of social realities. It must be possible to recognize at all times the connection of epoch and art form as clearly as it can be recognized for instance in the case of Zola and his age. Thus, the historian of literature recasts chronological categories in aesthetic terms, and indeed, such recasting is the primary object of his historical interest. As a result, all sorts of catchwords—especially those of the "istic" variety—fall by the wayside, and this the more readily the more clearly a precise knowledge of the texts enables us to see that "romanticism" or "realism" or "surrealism" are terms which indifferently stand for an epoch or for a style.

All this needs to be stressed the more insistently since the recognition of the functional interdependence of meaning and form, as the exclusive principle of critical evaluation, is more difficult in the novel than in lyrical genres such as the sonnet or the sestina. It is an open secret that in our days numerous attempts are afoot to apply extraneous criteria in matters of literature. A case in point is the intolerable notion that writers should be evaluated—that is, should be down- or up-graded—in terms of their "positive" outlook on life or in terms of an ethical norm which in this day and age it seems absurd to regard as universally binding. In concrete terms, such an approach may possibly be adequate to help the newcomer appreciate Saint-Exupéry, while the real need would rather seem to be to guide him in his effort to learn how to read Martin du Gard, Julien Green, or Jean-Paul Sartre properly. How bad this situation is was recently shown in a paper by Jauss.[3]

On the other hand it seems irresponsible to abandon the modern novel exclusively to the critical care of the daily press just because it is contemporary literature, just because the authors are still alive and are still writing. Indeed, the historian of literature can profit from an almost personal contact with the creative process, can derive from it otherwise unattainable insights. When the workroom of the poet and the writer and the study of the critic and the historian belong to the same intellectual and spiritual realm, the consequences for the humanities and specifically for the learned pre-occupation with the world of letters can only be wholesome.

Zola and the brothers Goncourt tried hard to impose upon their time—and on ours—the prophesy that the novel had come to be the only form of writing commensurate with the present and, specifically, that lyrical poetry had fallen behind. But the novel of the *fin de siècle* and the works of numerous novelists from 1900 to 1960 disprove that thesis. In Genet or Beckett, the line separating narrative prose from lyrical poetry appears to be still more obscured, and the novel moved into a border region not unlike that tentatively assigned to it in the late eighteenth century. In fact, the modern novel has come to be able to take in any kind of theme, invading in the present the stylistic domain of the drama, of lyrical poetry, and of the philosophical essay and providing with its many-faceted *gestalt* a new version of the idea of a "universe of poesy."

What can be expected from the novel—in terms of both form and subject matter—has never been summed up in a strict canon of rules, except with respect to a few basic modes of narration (such as those conditioned by reporting in the third or the first person or from a neutral point of view), and this may well account for the endeavor of modern novelists to qualify their works as "drama," "study," "account," "chronicle," or "portrayal of manners." In any event, the appeal of the novel lies now in the virtually unrestricted range of what it may set out to achieve, that is, in the creation of a myth, the teaching of science, the exemplification of a moral lesson, or the purveyance of plain entertainment. It no longer holds true that a particular type of subject matter favors a particular mode of narration as was still postulated by Otto Ludwig (1813–65) in his *Formen der Erzählung*. As recently as 1927, Karl Vossler, in his work, *Der Roman bei den Romanen*, regarded the luxuriant growths in content and form of the novel as a loss in terms of the standards of high literature. We cannot agree with him, for it seems to us that no other literary genre is apt to be more strikingly enriched by the attenuation and the removal of the restrictive confines of the genres than is narrative prose.

Introduction

I cannot let this book appear in published form without expressing my sincere gratitude to my wife, Dr. Eva-Maria
Engler, who critically read the manuscript, as well as to Dr.
Helmut Bender, Reader-in-Chief of the Francke Verlag, and
to the editorial staffs of the Francke Verlag and the Frederick
Ungar Publishing Co. who gave me the benefit of their expert
advice and obliged me by their cooperative attitude throughout the technical phases of the publication.

To Dr. Alexander Gode-von Aesch—"als hochbegabtem
Ubersetzer"—I owe the possibility of establishing contact with
a new and wider circle of readers. I cannot overrate the value
of his congenial effort to re-create, instead of merely rendering,
my book in its new form.

Dr. Winifred Engler

Berlin
Fall 1968

All

French quotations in the text

have been translated into English

from the original sources

by Alexander Gode.

For those quotations followed by an asterisk,

the original French is given

in the Appendix of French Quotations.

CONTENT

The French Novel

I

THE NOVEL OF INDIVIDUALISM

Etienne Pivert de Senancour, Germaine de Staël, Benjamin Constant,
François-René de Chateaubriand, Charles-Augustin Sainte-Beuve,
Alfred de Vigny, Alphonse de Lamartine, George Sand,
Stendhal (Henri Beyle), Joseph-Arthur de Gobineau

The French nineteenth and twentieth centuries belong together, constituting in the history of ideas and culture a single
epoch of high tension. The superficiality of Voltaire had been
replaced—since Rousseau and, indirectly, since Goethe—by a
vibrating unrest which pervaded the subsequent literary production. This was in no small measure the unrest of the individual in confrontation with the variously conceived challenge
of things transcendental. We think of it routinely as characteristic of Chateaubriand, Hugo, Sade, Vigny, and Nerval, but
it likewise flares up in Flaubert's novel of the temptation of the
hermit Anthony. By the turn of the century, Friedrich
Nietzsche epitomized, both in his person and in his work,
this generally European complex of problems and handed it
back, as it were, especially impressively, to the French novel.
Gide would be unthinkable without this concatenation.[1]
Simultaneously the hypochondriac spleen, the *ennui*, of the
René generation was divested of its romantic garb to show
up in Sartre as "disgust."

The beginning of this epoch may, for the present, be compre-
hended conveniently under a single catchword: that of deconfinement—in politics, religion, philosophy, ethics, aesthetics,

3

and (concretely) in terms of geographical space. In other words, we are now dealing with a *homo politicus* who has come of age; we encounter an increasingly intense hatred of dogmatism coupled with an increasingly intense religious quest, a growing syncretism, the concept of moral autonomy for the genius, the literary struggle against confinement and against rules, the first manifestations of a global trend in literary thought, and finally the strong romantic longing for the exotic and faraway.

It would be wrong to regard these phenomena as marking an absolutely new beginning in the history of literature. The individualism manifesting itself here on the level of the epic had significant premises of which W. P. Friederich has given us a list.[2] It had its precursors in the humanism of the Renaissance and in the Protestant uprising. The might and the right of the individual are additionally derivable from the philosophy of Descartes, with a simple shift from "I think, therefore I am" to "I *feel*, therefore am *I*." The grandly prophetic bearing of individual novelists—of Madame de Staël, for instance, or of Hugo, but subsequently of Zola, too—echoed the conviction of the age of enlightenment that the outstanding individual could better the world. In any event, at the beginning of the nineteenth century, the writer claimed for himself a special rank backed by Platonic conceptions, and it was only temporarily that the late nineteenth century was able to depose the *poeta vates*.

It is a remarkable fact—particularly significant for the onset of the new orientation in the novel of individualism—that Rousseau's dreaming and the sentimentalism of the English eighteenth century, along with the impact of Goethe's *Werther* from 1774 on, exerted at first a stronger formative influence on narrative literature than the political events in France after 1789. Except for an episode in Vigny's *Stello*, it was only in a novel by Hugo, *1793*, and in Anatole France's *Les Dieux ont soif* that the events of that age of political upheaval attained poetic reality in the novel. What does characterize the initial phases is much rather a deconfinement of the individual tending toward the narcissistic dream and also toward the Promethean posture of challenge. Madame de Staël and George Sand displayed their ability to assume such a challenging posture in their programs of emancipation. This shuttling to and fro between the extremes of passive endurance and the active will to achieve characterizes certain novels up to the time of Stendhal. In them the stress shifts from the picture of Narcissus to that of an enterprising Prometheus and back to a hero in chains. This inner process, borne by the strong individualism of modern writers, can hardly be expected to be cogently clarified in terms of categories such as Rousseauism, romanticism, or the like, and the utilization of these will always require the foregoing qualification.

In his newly achieved posture, the novelist was ready to accept suggestive stimuli from all sides. He managed to develop for himself a distinctive physiognomy, particularly through his knowledge of Goethe, Byron, and Scott[3] but also through the "Italian myth," as in the case of Madame de Staël and Stendhal, and later through the fascination of things Spanish, as in the case of Hugo, Nodier, and Mérimée, and finally through the germanophile complex, as in the case of Nerval. The contemporary historian of literature recognizes these dovetailing relationships in their full significance.[4] The controversy of pro and con triggered by the antiromantic campaigns of the Xavier de Maistres and the Nisards has been lessening in intensity in the years since 1925.[5]

In historical terms, the significance of the novel of individualism lies—additionally—in the fact that it contributed the first move toward establishing the novel, which had not been held in particularly high regard, as the most essential literary form of the nineteenth century and possibly of the twentieth as well. This does not mean that the output of novels had been insignificant. On the contrary, the figures are quite substantial. But in quality most of the works were at best on a par with today's mass production. A. J. George[6] lists 230 titles of novels for 1821, 320 for 1824, and 330 for 1825.

The transition was accomplished by the French novel in the works of Etienne Pivert de Senancour (1770–1846). Senancour's life[7] was one of misery, isolation, and physical ailing. At the age of nineteen he fled from Paris to Switzerland because he did not want to become a priest. At the age of twenty he married out of a false sense of honor. From 1800 on he suffered from severe manifestations of a paralytic disorder.

His two novels in letters, *Aldomen* (1795) and *Oberman* (1804), reflect the vissicitudes of the author's personal life. The two ideological essays, "*Sur les générations actuelles*" (1793) and "*Rêveries sur la nature primitive de l'homme*" (1799), appear to have taken their cues from the early writings of Rousseau and Bernardin de Saint-Pierre. They strongly suggest that Senancour's narrative prose as well as his analytical essays may be viewed as prematurely published fragments—differing in the degree of their mimetic affiliation—of a grandly conceived ideological work with which Senancour occupied himself from 1789 to 1804. In this comprehensive frame there is room, too, for Senancour's draft of 1802 of a Swiss constitution, "*Enoncé rapide et simple de quelques considérations relatives à l'acte constitutionnel.*"

A good way of appreciating Senancour is to begin with his *Oberman*, although his characteristic form was fully established in the earlier work, *Aldomen*. In her preface to the third version of *Oberman* in 1840, George Sand wrote that the hero of this work was the embodiment of "a clear, pronounced, unassailable, persistent, avowed awareness of inadequate faculties." Senancour was, George Sand continued, like a bird "to whom nature denied wings," and nothing was left him but melancholy.

The action of *Oberman*[8] is placed for the most part in Switzerland, in localities which Senancour knew well (the cantons of Vaud and Valais and the Bernese Oberland). Written "at the whim of the pen" [*au hasard de la plume*], with Montaigne—as the author explicitly stated—as his model, this novel in letters was meant to be "the history of his endeavors and not that of his intellect." The hero's discomfort in the face of the prevailing social order, which appeared to him as much at odds with nature as it had to Rousseau, his discomfort in an urban environment, his world-weary savoring of the ephemerality of all things human, and his enlightened fault-finding with the God of the Christian churches urge and compel him—as he measures himself by the standards of the "man of action" [*homme du jour*]—to search for the reasons for the loss of paradise which Saint-Martin's *De l'Esprit des choses* (1800) could not explain to his satisfaction and to imagine in his dreams a way to recover the primordial state of intact integrity: "All is cold, all is empty: aimlessly we live in a place of exile, and our hearts, heavy with loathing, long to escape from this pit of distaste to establish themselves in an imaginary homeland." (Letter xxx)

Senancour saw through the illusion and yet clung to this irrational solution. Deconfinement and failure, hyperalert and hypersensitive intelligence, and nihilistic outbursts of emotions are symptomatic of the critical situation from which the novel of the nineteenth century was born, even though in matters of form it was not yet ready to break with the past.

That the French novel stayed on this course was the doing of Germaine de Staël (1766–1817) who, furthermore, was possessed of incomparably stronger magnetic powers of appeal than Senancour. An external condition shared by her and Senancour was that Switzerland came to be for both a refuge in exile. Germaine de Staël's father was Jacques Necker, known through his role as Director General of the Finances in France, whose policies over and beyond the reform measures of the physiocrats took the *ancien régime* a big step closer to its collapse and whose dismissal precipitated the events of the 14th of July, 1789.

Germaine grew up and intellectually came of age in the atmosphere of enlightenment of the salon of her parents. In 1786 she married the Swedish diplomat von Staël-Holstein. Her maturity as a woman and her training as a woman of letters were to a large extent determined by her relationships with the Count Narbonne and with Benjamin Constant. But there was in her to begin with an unquenchable thirst for knowledge. In 1803 and 1807, after Napoleon had expelled the troublesome woman from the country, she traveled—by way of her Swiss estate of Coppet—to Germany and, in 1812, to Russia, Sweden, and England. Her most important work was *De l'Allemagne* (Paris, 1810; London, 1813). In it she presented to her countrymen a picture of Germany and simultaneously a poetic concept which came to be important for the continuity of modern literature[9] by reason of its emphasis on enthusiasm, local color, and the Christian principle of the search of conscience, impelling the individual to keep looking and to keep probing inside of himself. She thus supplied a theoretical substructure for the first-person novel of which she herself produced two specimens: *Delphine* (1802) and *Corinne ou l'Italie* (1807).

These works—depositories of the author's ideas, manifestos of feminism—were written by an emancipated woman. They are a plea for womanhood, its distinctive inner life, and every line in them betrays the autobiographic presence of the author. This was expressly stated in the foreword to *Delphine*. Furthermore, the author defined the idea of the novel as follows:

"The events occurring in a novel should merely provide an opportunity to develop the passions of the human heart.... Those novels which will forever claim our admiration—*Clarissa, Clementina, Tom Jones, La Nouvelle Héloise, Werther*—serve the purpose of disclosing or delineating the welter of feelings of which, in the depths of the soul, the happiness or the unhappiness of existence is constituted. These are the feelings which we never state because they are linked to our secrets or to our weaknesses and because men live their lives among men without ever confiding in one another what they experience." Here the afore-mentioned English and German affiliations—Richardson and Goethe—are referred to explicitly.

Delphine d'Albémar, like Madame de Staël herself, is an exceptional person. Corinne, like the author, suffers through love a deprivation greater by far than any lasting fulfillment she might derive from it, for her ecstatically inspired individualism interposes between her and the mediocrity of her partner a barrier of forces that cannot be crossed. Replete with tragic passion, she is a woman who stands sky-high above the humdrum of everyday life. Thematically, *Corinne* is important, in particular, because with it, French literature rediscovered Italy, which was to play so significant a role in the works of Stendhal and Gobineau.

Germaine de Staël's life was itself a novel. This is additionally apparent from the works of Benjamin Constant (1776–1830) who for many years was her companion. He was born in Lausanne of a family of Hugenot émigrés and at an early age proved himself skilled in the ways of the world. From 1787 to 1794 he lived in Brunswick and subsequently stayed with Madame de Staël, first at Coppet and then for seven years at Paris (1795–1802). When Napoleon forced Madame de Staël to go into exile, Constant went with her. He died in Paris in

1830, having become a liberal deputy in 1819. His two novels, *Adolphe* (1816) and *Cécile* (written in 1813 at Göttingen, discovered in 1948, and published in 1951), show clearly the extent to which Constant remained indebted to the eighteenth century. The cold psychology and the lack of "local color" are cases in point. What is new is that in *Adolphe* the "woman of thirty" makes her début in the novel and that the cosmopolitan character of the work reflects the author's Europeanism. Both novels—*Adolphe* and *Cécile*—share the trait that they arose, as did in a later period the works of André Gide, from the author's will to achieve self-knowledge. Thematically they are closely allied to the diary.

Adolphe is an autobiography in disguise. The twenty-two-year-old son of a minister of the Prince Elector, having just completed his studies at Göttingen, is introduced at a party to the beautiful Polish woman Ellénore and playfully tries to win her for himself. She does in fact abandon her lover for his sake, and Adolphe—though already beset with qualms—follows her to her estates. More and more at odds with himself, he decides to break with her but keeps postponing the moment of decision. When Ellénore learns about his plans, she collapses. Now Adolphe is free. He turns to politics, but the adventure which had begun so pleasantly leaves behind an unpleasant taste.

If Ellénore in *Adolphe* represents Madame de Staël, the heroine of *Cécile* is Charlotte von Hardenberg, while Germaine appears in this latter novel under the name of Madame de Malbée. The hero stands undecided between the two women. There is again no doubt about his being Constant himself. What draws him to Cécile is the charm of her girlish innocence, while Madame de Malbée holds him with "the most beautiful eyes the world has seen" (Part VII) and a promise of marriage. When she leaves him in disillusionment, he notes : "She was the tyrant but also the goal of my life. . . . Meanwhile Cécile was awaiting me, sweet, good, angelic Cécile." But the longed-for encounter occasions new unhappiness. The novel ends without a solution. "Madame de Malbée is the cross you must bear."

All this was put down with the greatest economy in the use of words. *Adolphe* abounds in paratactic constructions, and the three most frequent sentence openings are "I . . .," "She . . .,"

and "We . . ." Metaphors and similies, which even the naturalistic novel of Zola was to find itself unable to dispense with, are
used sparingly or not at all, and yet this diagnostic style is
somehow extremely lively. A minimum of devices serves to
produce a maximum of effect. Here we sense the continued
hold of Choderlos de Laclos, of the moralists, and of the
memorialists. After a declamatory interlude, represented
especially by the novels of Hugo, this sober style was to be
taken up again by Stendhal, Mérimée, and Flaubert. However,
the figure of Adolphe and that of the male hero in *Cécile*
breathe a new atmosphere, arising from a psychological mixture of sentimentalism and egocentricity, of fear of decisive
action and ethical boldness. From case to case these principles
cancel each other out and thus occasion the world-weary
pessimism of their protagonists, the unfathomable sensation
of vacuity and incommensurateness.[10]

Oberman, Adolphe, and *Cécile*—and also, next to them, the
novel in letters by Ugo Foscolo, *Le Ultime lettere de Jacopo
Ortis* (1802), in which the influence of *Werther* is particularly
apparent (as admitted by the author in his correspondence with
Goethe under the date of January 16, 1802)—stand at the beginning of the nineteenth century as representatives of one and
the same generation. *René* (1804) completes and confirms this
impression.

François-René de Chateaubriand (1768–1848) is the most
important of the authors listed so far. His creative versatility
made Victor Hugo, who in terms of form was the greatest talent
of the nineteenth century, express the wish to become a
Chateaubriand or nothing. And on *René* we have the emphatic
verdict of George Sand who identified herself completely with
its hero. Among Chateaubriand's first-person novels it is precisely *René* which had the strongest impact throughout
Europe. The traces of this novel of world-weariness have been
pursued all the way to Russia, to Pushkin and Lermontov.[11]
In *René* the romanticist Chateaubriand reworked in a new
way the lesson of *Werther*. We know from the *Mémoires
d'outre-tombe* (1848; first critical edition by Levaillant, 1948)
that *René* was written against Goethe in the name of Christianity, albeit a Christianity which—in the wake of Rousseau
and a misunderstood Pascal—hoped to reach God through the

emotions and was taken as an aesthetic principle of the first order.

Of Chateaubriand's three novels,[12] two came to be important specifically as exemplifications of the principles of local color and of the romantic nostalgia for distant lands. *Atala* (1801) continued the line of Bernardin de Saint-Pierre's *Paul et Virginie* with its theme of immortal love in an exotic setting. It is a story of Indians, with a setting in Louisiana, Kentucky, Florida, and Canada. The Natchez Indian Chactas, now an old man and blind, tells the young Frenchman René, whom he has adopted as his son, the story of his unhappy love for Atala. During a warlike expedition of his tribe, Chactas had lost his parents. In the course of the ensuing flight he spent some time in a settlement of white men, but this failed to arouse his enthusiasm for occidental culture and mores. He then tried to find his way back to his tribe, but the enemies of his father caught him and condemned him to death. Atala, the christened stepdaughter of the chief, freed Chactas and fled with him. As the two pursued their adventurous wanderings through the forests, the girl related to Chactas how her mother had dedicated her to the Virgin Mary and had vowed to have her enter a convent. Chactas's impetuous wooing aroused in Atala a tragic conflict of conscience from which she escaped by killing herself.

This melodramatic action was imbued by Chateaubriand with an idea upheld at that time by Madame de Staël too, that is, the idea that the passions of the individual must of necessity be transmuted through the restraint imposed upon them by the Christian dogma of morals. In addition, Chateaubriand worked into the novel his own unhappy experiences in love. He did the same in *Les Aventures du dernier Abencérage* (written, 1809–10; published, 1826)[13] in which he treated the Spanish romancical motif of the love of a Moor for a Christian. Allusions to the race problem can be found in *Mathilde* by Madame Cottin (1805) which centers around the love of an Arab for an Englishwoman. This theme goes far to meet the demands of the romantic emotions, for it involves insoluble conflicts and situations from which there is no escape. The fable of *Les Aventures du dernier Abencérage* is as follows: More than twenty years after his family has been expelled

11

from Granada through the final consummation of the *recon-quista*, Abn Hamet returns to Spain where he falls head over heels in love with the Christian Spaniard Blanca. The pair suffer from being separated in religion, race, and clan, the latter by reason of the sworn enmity between Blanca's and Abn Hamet's families, of which the hero learns only toward the end of the novel. So the last male scion of a formerly great family returns to North Africa while the girl, consumed in the fire of love, mourns for him by the seashore.

Such extremes are typical of the early nineteenth century. In French literature they were prepared by Sébastien Mercier, though the German Storm and Stress contributed essentially to their subsequent development. But there are also the fasci-nation of the motif of the last scion of a social organism (still felt by Montherlant in his *Maître de Santiago*), the elabora-tion of religious contrasts, and medieval local color. To be sure, elements of classicism can likewise be discerned, as in the person of Blanca's brother Carlos which is reminiscent of the figure of the Cid. So we have in this novel an historically inter-esting mixture of ethos of Corneille, of local color, and of storm and stress. It is the element of picturesque versatility which distinguishes *Atala* and *Les Aventures du dernier Abencérage* from *Oberman, Adolphe,* or *Cécile.* In *René* Chateaubriand dispensed with it at least in part, for in this novel the Indian forests of North America are not the setting of the action but only the place where the story is told.

René, just as *Atala,* reveals a didactic link to Chateaubriand's apologia, *Le Génie du christianisme,* in that it illustrates the thesis of the melancholy nature of the passions that have come to the fore in modern man. René's world is full of questions and crises, and the solution proposed in the end is not in keeping with their urgency. This justifies leveling the reproach at Chateaubriand that he gave greater literary weight to the diagnosis of the negative which he set out to cure than to the therapeutic proposal itself. The hero of the novel is en-dowed with a remarkable propensity for being preoccupied with the unharmonious side of things. And the spiritual re-orientation which does eventually occur means that René be-gins to derive pleasure from this painful deconfinement in his inner as well as his secular life and to make his disharmony an object of pride.[14] What this means in psychological terms becomes clear when we recall that *"ennui,"* the key-word of the entire novel, is derived from Latin *"inodiare,"* to inspire odium and disgust.

The title hero of *René* is the young Frenchman we know from *Atala,* where his role was to listen to Chactas. He now tells the Indian and Father Souël the story of his own life. He had spent a lonely childhood in France, brightened somewhat by the tender affection of his sister Amélie. He tried in vain to derive satisfaction and inner gain from travels reminiscent of a grand tour. After his return he was struck by the strange behavior of his sister who appeared more and more to avoid him. His sadness and the melancholy mood of a desolate landscape in autumn drove René to the verge of committing suicide. Amélie, informed of his plans, hurried to his side. Days of overwrought affection of brother and sister followed. Then, of a sudden, the girl entered a convent. During the ceremony, while she took the veil, René overheard her murmuring a terrible confession. She asked God's forgiveness for her criminal passion which, however, her brother had not reciprocated. Deeply shaken, René saw no way out but to flee to the world of savages in order to regain his inner composure in the setting of life still imbued with the simplicity of paradise.

Chactas consoles him while Father Souël strives to make him understand that he shares the guilt of his sister's spiritual incest and advises him to dispel his *ennui* and hypochondriac *mal de siècle* by sharing the constructive work of a community of human beings as one of its members.

Many elements in this account can be elucidated through biographical references on the level of "poetry and truth." In 1791 Chateaubriand spent five months in America; in 1793 he went to London; and in 1803 he held the post of secretary to the ambassador in Rome. The grand tour undertaken by René through the eastern Mediterranean became a personal experience of Chateaubriand, it is true, only in 1806 and 1807. His relationship with his sister Lucile and its poetic precipitate will concern us in another context. At the beginning of René's account there is a passage which perfectly illustrates the tenor of his self-analysis.

"As I begin my story, I cannot repress a feeling of shame. The peace in your hearts, worthy elders, and the serenity of nature all around us make me blush at the troubled and agitated state of my soul.

"How you will pity me! How my unceasing worries must seem wretched to you! You who have known all the ultimate cares of life, what must you think of a young man without strength and virtue who finds his torment within himself and can hardly complain but of ills which he has inflicted upon himself? Pray, do not condemn him; his punishment—even so —is all too severe!

"In being born into this world I took away my mother's life; I was taken from her womb by blades of steel. I had a brother on whom my father bestowed his blessings since he regarded him as his first-born son. As for myself, delivered early into the hands of strangers, I was raised far from the paternal hearth.

"I was impetuous of temper; my nature was erratic. Merry and boisterous and in turn somber and brooding, I gathered around me my youthful companions, only to leave them again abruptly, sitting down by myself to stare into the fleeting night or to listen to the rain falling on the foliage."*

On first reading this text with its abundance of oratorical elements of exclamation, interrogation, parallelism, and anti-thesis, one is truck by the distinct prevalence of negative evalu-ations and verdicts. Together they provide a representative impression of the structure of René's thought which, in the work as a whole, appears differentiated in four fairly distinct complexes. These are discernible in part in the foregoing ex-cerpt. We have here the weariness with culture and civilization, which—opposed to all the tenets of enlightenment—discovered its ideal in a Rousseauistically conceived existence in harmony with nature as exemplified by the lives of Chactas and the priest. This topic of the primordially paradisiac, in contrast to the decline of modern times, which was employed in *Atala* too, assumed new timeliness at the turn of the eighteenth century. Rousseau and the Swiss idylist Gesner provided the essential first impetus. It is an ideal which shines the more brightly when set off against the somber background of René's solitude and ambivalence with which he appears afflicted from birth as with a congenital defect. Nothing is more romantic than this patently or surreptitiously savored stigma which imparts to an exceptional individual, by his very nature, a fatalistically somber aura. From Schiller's *Räuber* to Nerval's *Desdichado*—and in Byron in between—we encounter this self-imposed black curse. Seen in the perspective of Senancour and Constant, it is something new. Musset, later on, was to sum up this "standing and living apart" in the metaphor of the white merl.

Toward the end of *René* we note that the tenor of the work undergoes a change. The hero speaks of the "burden of existence" and expresses his awareness of his human situation between the all and the nothing in the phrase "the abyss of my existence" [*l'abîme de mon existence*]. And now the element emerges which is specifically characteristic of *René*. In our excerpt it is alluded to in the words: "What must you think of a young man without strength and virtue who finds his torment within himself and can hardly complain but of ills which he has inflicted upon himself?" In this we recognize the many different things which the romantic hero is simultaneously capable of being: the accused, the judge, and the executioner to boot. These are, in many cases, anabaptist ideas, fragments of a black mysticism: The concept of man in Kafka is but one step away. Ultimately René reaches a point where he derives from his *mal de siècle* a kind of voluptuous exaltation: "In the plenty of my sorrow I actually found an unexpected satisfaction." Or: "There is pleasure for us in what is out of the ordinary, even when this something out of the ordinary is a misfortune." This is the title of nobility of the romantic soul.

Essential traits in the figure of René stem from its creator, as we have pointed out before. But this approach in the interpretation of the work goes too far when it derives—as Moreau[15] had to do—the motif of incest from Chateaubriand's relationship with his sister Lucile. The motif occurs much too frequently in the literature of the eighteenth century to restrict us to this autobiographical source. It appears in M. A. de Roumier, Constant d'Orville, Restif de la Bretonne, and Baculard d'Arnaud. A work by Mercier, *L'Homme sauvage* (1767), comes especially close to Chateaubriand's way of dealing with the motif in *René*. But beyond all biographical promptings and all documented precedents, Chateaubriand was able to create a new literary type whose autonomous integrity places it on a par with Don Juan, Molière's Tartuffe, and Gide's Lafcadio.

We already know what George Sand thought of *René*. Lamartine confessed in 1809 that he had been able to read these revelations only with tears in his eyes, and Sainte-Beuve, at the age of sixteen, recognized his own self, as did George Sand, in the hero of the novel. The first English imitation was published as early as 1808.[16] Almost three decades after the publication of *Werther*, Chateaubriand returned to European letters, in an accentuated form, the figure of the tragic young hero whom, in *René*, he vested with new attributes: the awareness of being misunderstood and of being different, the lust for life, and the existential failure as well as the remorse of conscience. Baudelaire was to take up, most particularly, the last-named. In Chateaubriand's work as a whole, we note the continuation of Rousseau and of the night-thought poetry of the English eighteenth century; we are impressed by Chateaubriand's emphasis on historical elements and on the emotionally religious as well as by the achievements of his rich, suggestive prose. But beyond all this, it is the creation of the figure of René which will remain one of Chateaubriand's lasting accomplishments.

While discussing *René*, we mentioned the name of Charles-Augustin Sainte-Beuve (1804–69). He is known especially as a critic of literature and as a writer of lyrical poetry. That he was also a novelist is all too often overlooked.[17] The work here to be mentioned bears the ill-chosen and certainly misleading title of *Volupté* (1834). In it Sainte-Beuve presented neither more nor less than a moralistic autobiography with a setting in a circle of characters reminiscent of that of Constant's *Cécile*. The hero, Amaury, is placed, however, in a triangle of women. Long passages of the novel consist in the analysis of passions. Here the continuity of action comes to an almost complete standstill. By this procedure we are to be initiated step by step into the mysteries of voluptuousness. We are given a lesson in sensualism, although the taboo of things sexual is still strong (as it will continue to be to the time of the Goncourts and of Zola). In *Volupté*, the novel of individualism takes on a new generic feature of which preparatory phases can be traced in England and Germany. It is an educational novel of the kind referred to in German criticism as a *"Bildungsroman."* To be sure, in *René*, too, the hero grew and matured in the course of the events of the novel, but the primary accent in the narrative lay elsewhere.

Amaury owes his first experience of voluptuousness to his classical schooling. As he grows older he begins to look at women with the interest of an enlightened youth. But he finds no satisfaction. This is a parallel to the development of Sainte Beuve's relationship with Madame Hugo (which represents both a premise and prerequisite for the work). The figure of the Marquis de Couaën may be taken to be Victor Hugo, seen here as the politician who so often manages to side with the wrong cause. The hero's contact with women increases in intensity, and his attitude evolves to the point of his cursing "voluptuousness" and the female sex as a whole (Chapter 11). Yet, in true romantic indecision, the mood changes again: "When voluptuousness declines, pride and the triumphant joy of satisfaction rise correspondingly." Here we have not only a repetition of the libertinistic moralism as found from the end of the seventeenth century on and hence a dismissal of Christian ethics but also an ebbing away of the tides of storm and stress. Man's ethos consists accordingly in a leveling of all the forces in his soul and not in the repression of any one among them. It would seem that the lack of spirit which is so evidently characteristic of Sainte-Beuve's *Volupté* in comparison with *Corinne* or *René* is in large part a consequence of this ethical conception. It also reflects, on the other hand, the simple fact that Sainte-Beuve was not a born novelist. Had he been one, he would have shown how voluptuousness generates in the hero a process of deconfinement. Instead, the high points of the novel are found in portrayals of interiors and still lifes (as for instance the description of a castle in Chapter 4).

Truly romantic and truly characteristic of the novel of individualism of this era (which extends to Stendhal) is the ultimate failure of the hero. Sainte-Beuve's characters are weighed and judged by lost standards, that is, the standards of their unimpaired but distant youth, with the result that the *mal de siècle* of Amaury in *Volupté* derives from the fact that the gulf between the lost intact world and the humiliation which is associated with old age becomes unbearable.

Thus all the theses are belied which tend to regard the early nineteenth century as a period emphasizing, to the exclusion of everything else, a progressivistic, future-oriented form of thought, a period which had done with "looking back." Such an approach may be tenable in the case of Hugo's *Légende des siècles*. In the novel of individualism, in any event, the tenor of pessimism and tragedy prevails, oppressing the hero increasingly as he grows older.

We have come to regard Alfred de Vigney (1797-1863) as one of the most somber protagonists of this attitude. The corpus of his highly personal novels diffused the early nineteenth century with a pessimistic atmosphere that was perhaps unequaled in oppressive weight.[18] We shall have more to say about the narrative work of this writer in the next chapter, in connection with the school of Sir Walter Scott. It would seem that Alfred de Vigny meant to link his *Stello* (1832), his *Servitude et grandeur militaires* (1835), and his *Emmanuel* (1837, incomplete; published in part in 1912 as *Daphné*) as a trilogy of ideas. Vigny's literary position and posture are easily understood as reflecting the attitude of a disenfranchised aristocrat toward the revolutionary *égalité*.

Stello is a philosophical dialogue of sorts. In the course of it, Dr. Noir relates three anecdotes teaching the same lesson. Through the illustrative examples of Gilbert, Chatterton, and André Chénier—victims, respectively, of royal absolutism, of British constitutionalism (1770), and of the French Revolution (1794)—Stello is to be shown how harmful a man's political involvement may turn out to be for him. Some critics have regarded this narrative technique of the dialogue as a reflection of Vigny's inner disharmony, which is indeed a state of mind most commensurately to be represented in that literary form. In this perspective, Dr. Noir embodies the awareness of the necessity of the powers of the state and the understanding of the individual's collision with the realities of politics, while Stello is armed for such a fatal confrontation with nothing but his longing for the ivory tower.[19]

No less "excluded" than the poet, no less a romantic pariah, is the soldier. That is the message of the three short novels combined in *Servitude et grandeur militaires*, for modern warfare, with its "people's armies" as they have arisen since the time

of the Revolution, deprives the soldier of his dignity and re-
duces him to the status of a tool in the deployment of mass of
men against mass of men. By virtue of its form, this is probably
Vigny's most timeless book. Its language is simple. The use of
figures of style is restrained. The introduction of the device
of regular leitmotifs—a sealed letter, a cane—has resulted in
a masterly tightening of the continuity of action.

The poet in *Stello* and the soldier in *Servitude et grandeur
militaires* are joined by the "theosopher," a term by which the
central figure of *Daphné* may aptly be designated. Here the
mouthpiece for Vigny's ideas is Emperor Julian the Apostate,
whose syncretistic project of reconciling paganism and Christianity with Plato came to naught when his death in an engagement with the Persians terminated his policies. Julian strove to
deconfine the dogmatism of the Christian religion but he failed
no less as a theosopher than as an anti-Constantinian politician.
Like Oberman, Corinne, or Amaury, Julian set up for himself a
great goal whose significance in the end is manifest only in the
excessive weight of the tragic burden crushing him.

Alfred de Vigny's narrative prose is not the most powerful
product of his art, though it does represent an extrapolation of
the pessimism of his lyrical poetry. This same observation holds
true, perhaps to an even greater extent, for Alphonse de
Lamartine (1790–1869). His achievement was that around 1820
he carried Rousseauism into the realm of French lyrical verse.
In his inmost being Lamartine was a lyric poet, a singer of
melancholy and of the occult bonds that interlink nature and
the soul. The prose publications of this sensitive Burgundian
diplomat do not in any way modify that characterization.[20]

Most of Lamartine's works in prose are occasional compositions. The later ones were written and published, in part at
least, for material reasons. Very few ever came to be known,
even by name, to a wider reading public. We list *Les Confidences* (1849), *Raphaël* (1849), *Geneviève* (1850), *Le Tailleur
de pierres de Saint-Point* (1851), *Les Nouvelles confidences*
(1851), and *Graziella* (1852). The time of action in the short
novel *Graziella* is the Napoleonic era, the place somewhere
along the Gulf of Naples. It is a story of overly abundant emo-
tionalism reminiscent of Bernardin de Saint-Pierre's *Paul et
Virginie*. It presents two eager young Frenchmen bent on im-

proving their minds first in Rome and then in Naples where, however, they come to know—and to appreciate—the simple life of fishermen whose closeness to nature makes them appear a part of it. When one of the young men is obliged to leave sooner than originally planned, a romance evolves between the other and the fisherman's daughter Graziella. In the course of time this relationship grows, on Graziella's part, into a great and all-pervading love. She survives the unavoidable separation for only a short time. A melodramatic conclusion, to be sure, but even Stendhal in *Le Rouge et le noir* could not dispense with the like of it. Madame de Rênal does not survive her separation from Julien either.

This touching portrait of a woman's life, this tragic song of songs of love serves aptly as the transition to a woman writer whose novels of individualism take up once again, in modified form, the feministic theses of Madame de Staël. Graziella might very well be one of the early works of George Sand (1804–1876)—stemming from the epoch during which she composed her passionate romantic novels of theses and didacticism. George Sand in her time exerted, next to Chateaubriand, the greatest influence throughout all of Europe. It is traceable as well in the works of the Spanish woman novelist Gertrudis Gómez de Avellaneda as in *Wally, die Zweiflerin* (1835) by the "Young German" Gutzkow.

George Sand was born in Paris in 1804 as Aurore Dupin, a remote descendant of King Augustus II of Saxony. Her mother was a milliner and dressmaker. The psychological complex conditioned by this background was in no way less problematic than that in the lives of Vigny and Nerval. We witness a painful awareness of inborn stature which finds itself disregarded by the realities of the individual's undeserved social position. This sensitive ego-awareness of George Sand then merged with the ideas of Madame de Staël. In 1822 George Sand married the Baron Dudevant whom she left in 1830. This marriage broke up for the simple reason that George Sand was imbued with the knowledge that as a woman she was an exceptional being. She went to Paris to live among the romantics, "a true romantic lioness" [*une vraie lionne romantique*], as Moreau put it. When she began to write, she took on the pseudonym George Sand. In her early narratives, for instance in *Le Chêne parlant*—the title of the complete collection, *Conte d'une grand'mère*, was consciously chosen as an allusion to Perrault's fairy tales—a somehow fairiesque tone serves to suggest a magic relationship of men and, in particular, of children to nature. Her later, better-known novels are radically different.[21] They are predominantly portrayals of tragic partnerships (in wedlock and otherwise), reflecting George Sand's own burden.

In *Indiana* (1832), a young Creole woman (whose name gave the book its title) is married to an elderly colonel. She meets Raymond de Ramière, a character reminiscent of Adolphe, who arouses her love, leads her to the greatest renunciation, humiliates her, and deserts her. Indiana discovers in the person of her cousin, Ralph Brown, a good-hearted, uncomplicated human being. Together with him she builds, in a hut in the mountains, a life of simplicity and quietude. Such an edifying conclusion suggests the heritage of Rousseau's eighteenth century. It reveals influences of Dickens's and Richardson's faith in the goodness of man. But this optimism cannot prevent us from recognizing that Indiana, Corinne, and Delphine, and also Ellénore from *Adolphe*, belong together. The motif of the "ill-assorted couple" was handled by George Sand more tragically, and more romantically, than later by Flaubert (in *Madame Bovary*) or by Fontane (in *Effie Briest*) and yet more thoughtfully than by Alexandre Dumas (in his play *Anthony*).

The women in George Sand suffer from the lack of fulfillment in their marriages, and it is difficult for them to decide to regain their freedom. There is, however, a law which, to George Sand, stands above the law of marriage and which, as she sees it, is violated by the latter: the law of passion. *Valentine* (1833) is likewise the story of an "ill-matched woman." When, in this book, a tempestuous young lover comes into the life—and into the marriage—of the heroine, he does so by the right of passion. George Sand's *Jacques* (1834) is psychologically more revealing, for this is a work breathing an atmosphere reminiscent of Racine. Jacques is thirty-five years old. He marries a younger woman. After several months of harmony and happiness, the marriage breaks up, for Fernande's lover Octave has appeared. When Jacques recognizes that Fernande and Octave are truly in love with one another and that he is unable to oppose that love with one of greater strength, he lets the pair stay together, resigns, and puts an end to his own life: "a suicide from duty."[22]

"Right of passion" and "recognition of renunciation" belong together. Why should this be? Because marriage, says George Sand, is a human institution, while eros is a gift of the gods. Here we may see to what extent the nineteenth century was ready to accept Plato. When marriage and eros conflict, marriage is in the wrong. With this, George Sand goes beyond Germaine de Staël, who—in her novels of emancipation—presented above all women of genius. George Sand is ready to plead for any woman, provided she loves unhappily.

With *Lélia* (1833; second edition 1836), a work of which two versions are extant, the first period of George Sand's creative life was concluded. We may take this surprising allegorical novel as a summation of the ideas of romanticism: the struggle of intelligence with sensuousness; the religion of love; a sentimental world pessimism. After *Indiana* and *Jacques*, the book left George Sand's readers perplexed. It disappointed them. It did carry the principle of deconfinement to a logical extreme, but it did not contain anything new. The time had come for a new approach to the psychological novel and the novel of the ego. Henceforth, George Sand was preoccupied with the subgenre often referred to as "the era novel." The time had come, in a sense, for the deromanticization of the novel of individualism.

This development occurred in the work of a man whose manner escapes all efforts to classify it as either romantic or realistic. As was the case with the first phase of the novel of individualism, the new orientation in the novel likewise harks back to the eighteenth century, not, however, to Rousseau and Bernardin de Saint-Pierre, but to Saint-Evremond, Voltaire, Saint-Simon, and Choderlos de Laclos. This new beginning was accomplished by Henri Beyle, among whose numerous pseudonyms that of Stendhal is the best known.

Henri Beyle, or Stendhal (1783–1842), was born in Grenoble as the son of a mother of Italian descent and a bourgeois father of a family of devout mountaineers. He hated in the latter the typically French combination of self-satisfied pride in the possession of monetary wealth with a bend toward clericalistic rigor, while he revered in his mother the Mediterranean heritage, the spirit of the Italian Renaissance, the grandeur and the great. The dualism implied in these simplified terms determined, from the beginning, the life and the work of this novelist. During his formative years he was attracted in particular by mathematics and the natural sciences. In 1799 he became a student at the Ecole Polytechnique in Paris. At the time his subjective philosophy depended on the ideological influence of Condillac, Helvétius, and Destutt de Tracy. Full of enthusiasm he accompanied one of Napoleon's armies to Italy, the homeland of his mother and of his dreams. In 1802 he resigned his military commission and accepted an administrative post.

After the return of the Bourbons, Stendhal went to Milan, where he devoted himself to studies in the history of art. It was not before 1821 that he returned to Paris. In 1830 he was appointed consul in Trieste, but only four years later, by reason of his connections with the *carbonari*, the Hapsburgs declared him *persona non grata*. Now his government transferred him to Città Vecchia in the Pontifical State. In 1842, while on leave in Paris, he collapsed in the street and died shortly thereafter. For his gravestone he had himself provided the inscription: "Arrigo Beyle, Milanese. He lived, wrote, loved."

Italy, to which he paid tribute even in death, is the theme which runs as a continuous thread through all of Stendhal's works, which include seven full-length novels and twenty novellae. In the concept of Italy, Stendhal—whose physical appearance was plump and suggestive of the petit bourgeois— revered the dynamic powers of man and man's grandeur.

His first novel, *Armance*, appeared in 1827. This was still a work of romanticism, as is abundantly clear when one studies the somber and pale figure of Octave in love with the Russian woman Armance in Paris. *Le Rouge et le noir*, with the publication date of November 13, 1830, was Stendhal's first great success. The skeleton of action, as is often the case in Stendhal, was taken from a written document—in this instance a criminal-law case. Stendhal was interested in the character of the young seminarian who, while supporting himself as a resident tutor, starts an affair with the mother of his wards and shoots the woman to death when she asks him to leave the house. The seminarian is condemned to death.

The ambition of this individual, his determination to arrive, coincided at least in part with Stendhal's own motivations. From this evolved *Le Rouge et le noir*,[23] the story of Julien Sorel, the son of a saw-mill owner in Verrières in Burgundy. He is chosen by the local mayor, M. de Rênal, to fill the position of tutor to his children. Mme. de Rênal discovers too late how dangerous Julien really is, despite the fact that he is a seminarian preparing for the priesthood. When the affair becomes the subject of rumors, Julien, who has definitely turned his back on the seminary in Besançon, goes to Paris. Here M. de la Môle makes him administrator of his estate and is instrumental in providing him with a title of nobility. The daughter of the family, Mathilde, falls in love with him, for she sees in him an exceptional being, socially her inferior, to be sure, but in no sense servile. (Strindberg was to take up the motif in *Miss Julie.*) But anger and disgust take hold of her once she has given in to him. She becomes pregnant. After a first outburst of wrath, her father obtains for Julien a lieutenant's commission. Then Madame de Rênal unmasks him in a letter. Forthwith Julien travels to Verrières and shoots his former mistress in church. She is not dead. In the ensuing court proceedings, however, Julien confesses to premeditated, albeit unsuccessful murder. He is executed.

Julien Sorel can hardly be fitted into the line of heros of novels we have followed so far, beginning with *Oberman.* Nothing links him to the resignation in George Sand's *Jacques.* At no time does he, like René, display his innermost self in world-weary pessimism or accuse himself of weakness. The novel of individualism is enriched in Stendhal's work by a new dimension, the will to achieve personal greatness and power. This is an artistic principle. Seen thus, it is correct to consider Stendhal—as was done by Kurt Wais[24]—a "pioneer outdoing his predecessors."

But before we can go along with Wais in calling Stendhal the creator of an "ethical novel of heroism," we need to clarify and redefine the concept hero. Stendhal's hero derives his strongest impulses not from religious ardor, as did the heroes of the *chansons de gestes,* but from his craving for a position of importance, the urge to self-glorification, and the quest for love. With all this, the element of self-adulation is no less pronounced than in Chateaubriand or Sainte-Beuve, and Julien too is a man who obstinately refuses, or rather, who is unable to take his place in the established order. He rebels against the world around him, not like Oberman or René, because he wants to pursue his melancholy or his mystical interests, but because his ambition drives him out of the milieu of the saw-mill and also out of that of the seminary. In his ambition he realizes himself instead of losing himself in impotent plaints and vain endeavors like Amaury. This is a declaration of war against *René, Paul et Virginie,* and *Rêveries d'un promeneur solitaire.* The fact that Sorel fails in the end, that he fails tragic-ally, implies no compromise with these conclusions.

"I see nothing but the death sentence to distinguish a man, thought Mathilde. It is the only thing that cannot be bought."[*] While stated in admiration of the revolutionary, Count Altamira, these words may be taken as a prophetic evaluation of Julien Sorel. They also reveal the equality in stature of his mistress. To achieve the objective of self-awareness, Stendhal's characters—especially Julien and Mathilde—frequently in-dulge in inner monologues. Yet the total setting of the narrative presupposes and requires omniscience on the part of the author.

Lucien Leuwen was published only in 1894. It is chronologi-cally a sequel to *Le Rouge et le noir* which played during the years from 1815 to 1830. In the new work, Stendhal—who hated everything to do with money—presented a sarcastic portrayal of a plutocratic society, in the center of which he placed the banker's son Lucien Leuwen, a sensitive, reform-minded indi-vidual, an enthusiastic disciple of Saint-Simon. Once again we are confronted with Stendhal's problem of problems: the re-sistance of an individual against a hostile environment. The novel unfortunately remained incomplete.

In the course of the following years Stendhal wrote his auto-biography, *La Vie de Henri Brulard* (published from 1890 to 1927). The fascination of it lies in the interplay of masquerade and revelation. The writing of Stendal's eight *Chroniques italiennes* belongs to the same period. These are mostly stories of criminals from the Italian sixteenth century. They were in-spired by a chronicle which Stendhal had discovered in Italy and of which he had had a copy made. The copied volumes are preserved in the Bibliothèque Nationale in Paris. *Vittoria Accaramboni* plays in the family of the Orsinis. *Les Cenci* pres-

25

ents in the person of François an ideal type whose energy and unrestrained instincts make him characteristically Stendhalian. The work reflects simultaneously Stendhal's weaknesses, such as his unwarranted tendency to generalize both sociologically and in terms of national psychologies. The *Abbesse de Castro* belongs in the wake of Dumas. How closely Stendhal followed his model is strikingly illustrated by the story of adultery, *La Duchesse de Paliano*. The *Chroniques italiennes* serve to round out the image of Stendhal in that—apart from the "myth of Italy"—they postulate the author's creed of amoralism. In any event, Chateaubriand's preoccupation with remorse is a matter of the past.

The same tendency is apparent in Stendhal's least-known novel, *Lamiel* (written during the years from 1839 on), of which Martineau prepared a critical edition only a decade ago. Here the idea of a full-blooded animality is embodied in the person of the peasant girl Lamiel. The narrative technique is unsentimental in the extreme. The fact, for instance, that Lamiel gave herself to a man, is made known to the reader in a subordinate clause. The role of Stendhal in the novel of individualism of the early nineteenth century is strikingly illustrated by *Lamiel*. In the third chapter, "weariness" [*ennui*] has truly the functions of a *mot-clé* or key word. Lamiel, at the age of twelve, experiences the weariness of a romantic heroine. In the fifth chapter she falls ill from that same "weariness." The physician, Dr. Sansfin, succeeds in curing her by arousing her curiosity about the things of the world. "I want to know what this thing called love is like," she says insistently to a young abbé. Because this abbé forbids her to think of such things, she takes adolescent boys out into the woods. She confesses having done so, just in order to learn more. In the ninth chapter, the characteristic statement occurs: "Lamiel knew no pleasure other than that of giving orders."

Lamiel's leading emotions are her fear of being despised and her conviction that magnaminity will not pay. There are in her traits of Nietzsche's beast. Stendhal's cult of the ego is exemplarily embodied in this figure. The earlier cult of lamentation and melancholy has here turned into a cult of strength. The figure of Lamiel stands halfway between Julien and Fabrice del Dongo in *La Chartreuse de Parme*, for she no longer needs mask and simulation since she is, in her very substance, superior to her environment. She derives her strength from her rural existence. She heeds no rules of etiquette, as Julien still did, but follows unrestrainedly her inner urges.[25] She is one of the "happy few." This concept was taken over by Nietzsche from Stendhal who applied to it standards of aristocracy and derived it primarily from Italy.

In *La Chartreuse de Parme* (1839) the scene is placed in the homeland of Stendhal's ideals. To be sure, through its mixture of psychological and picaresque elements, this novel shows up ambivalent tensions in Stendhal's thought and work. The action is more colorful than in his earlier writings. Fabrice del Dongo, born in 1790 as the fruit of the adulterous union of his mother with an officer of the French forces of occupation, grows up in enthusiastic admiration of Napoleon whose army he joins —at the very moment of the Battle of Waterloo. In civilian clothes, he barely manages to escape to Paris and from there to his aunt Pietranera in Parma. He studies theology—coerced to do so rather than from his own free will—and soon rises to the position of coadjutor to the archbishop. When he kills the comedian Giletti in a brawl, the reigning prince has him imprisoned. The commander of the citadel is Fabio Conti, father of the beloved Clélia. She saves him from being killed by poison. He makes her, a devoutly pious girl, his mistress. But she is forced to marry a wealthy man. Now Fabrice's verbal powers, which had made him a brilliant preacher, are put to work in the service of another kind of exhortation, and Clélia again begins to receive him, albeit only at night. Their happiness does not last long. Fabrice's little son dies in the second year of his life, Clélia dies shortly thereafter, and Fabrice himself withdraws to the Charterhouse at Parma.

André Gide listed *La Chartreuse de Parme* among the ten most beautiful works of French narrative literature, and Kurt Wais wrote about it: 'This novel opens up as though in heliotropic orientation toward Italy and the people of Italy, reflecting the longing of a renegade, a French writer who would have liked to be an Italian writer."[26]

The subject matter had occupied Stendhal's thoughts for a while as early as 1832. He sketched out the plan for this work on and about August 15, 1838. In April, 1839, the book was already on sale in Paris. Such speed of work is characteristic of Stendhal, who dictated the whole of the *Chartreuse* down in seven weeks. At each session he would read only the last page of the previous day's text in order not to lose the continuity and would speak on spontaneously. This explains that the style is not rhetorically polished but sprung from the natural flow of speech of a lively individual.

The first half of the novel serves to develop the setting and draw up the dramatic plot. This is climaxed by Fabrice's mortal clash with Giletti. Stendhal's technique of the "snowballing novel"—the technique of Sir Walter Scott (still to be found in Giraudoux)—seems readily compatible with this manner of writing, which is further helped by the picaresque element.

All this taken together suffices to prove that Stendhal's objective was not the creation of an historical novel, although the outline of his theme was taken from his copy of the aforementioned Italian chronicle. One feature of the source that aroused Stendhal's enthusiasm was the biography of Alexander Farnese, a typical full-blooded man of the Renaissance, who rose to the highest rank within the Church when he was crowned Pope as Paul III. In parallel to this, Fabrice del Dongo is made coadjutor to the archbishop.

There is a certain affinity of this historical theme with the Don-Juan motif, but *La Chartreuse de Parme* lacks, nonetheless, the splendor of the Renaissance. Fabrice is not, as Alexander Farnese was, one of fate's favored children. He roams the land, he is pursued and finds himself in prison, and the hours of happiness are slight compared to the burden of suffering. The result is a novel of "happiness lost," the happiness which Fabrice del Dongo sets out to seek. Alexander, with every principle of morality dropped by the wayside, is—in the end—made Pope; Fabrice winds up a hermit. As the events of the story are transposed from the sixteenth into the nineteenth century, the element of disillusionment appears further strengthened. The ideal goes on existing only in the form of an idea.

The implications of this are weighty. They suggest that in Stendhal's scale of human values—and Stendhal did evaluate at all times—Fabrice stands at the top. Julien Sorel was intent on making himself master by all manner of means; Fabrice del Dongo is a master. The "world on high" has been attained; Stendhal's longingly pursued concept of a full-blooded race of princely bearing has been given palpable form. In lieu of Julien Sorel's monstrous "pursuit of happiness" [*chasse au bonheur*], we now have a spontaneously natural enjoyment of the pleasures of life.[27]

We spoke in an earlier passage of the ambivalence of this work. What was meant will be clear from just this brief passage which occurs in the novel when Fabrice has been imprisoned, with Clélia living nearby: "But finally, to his ineffable joy, after so long a wait and so many disappointments, Clélia appeared toward noon to care for her birds. Fabrice stood motionless, holding his breath, as close as possible to the heavy bars of his window. It struck him that she did not raise her eyes in his direction, that her movements reflected the nervous condition of one aware that someone is watching. . . . Although, by all appearances, she maintained the most perfect control of herself, when she walked up to the opening in the gate, she blushed noticeably. Fabrice's first thought, as he stood there close to the iron bars of his window, was to give in to the naive desire to tap with his hand on the bars to produce enough of a noise for her to hear. Then the very idea of such lack of delicacy filled him with horror."*

Here we see a second force determining the behavior of Stendhal's heroes. Francine Albérès emphasized the point in her study on Stendhal as follows: "Thus life in all of Stendhal's communal groupings goes on with a rhythm reflecting that of the communal grouping of Corneille. Every member of the group is subject only to the desire to go on beyond. . . ." Thus, successively, various personages in *La Chartreuse de Parme* assumed a role of veritable "leaders": Mosca, Gina, but above all Clélia and Fabrice. This element of "haughtiness" [*hauteur*] of an élite of the happy few—to allude to the last words of the novel—imparts to Stendhal's work the specific ethos stressed by Kurt Wais, but it imparts to it also much that seems posed and stilted and contrasts sharply with a style which gives "free rein to the pen's every whim," which proceeds "*au hasard de la plume.*"

In Stendhal, deconfinement and constraint are locked in battle. The hero breaks through the confinement of his position

—Julien Sorel is intent upon rising—but his condition determines the demeanor and the attitudes he must assume in order to achieve full control over it. Yet Stendhal reacts against the novel of individualism of the early nineteenth century, against the unrestrained, sentimental, or somehow remote and detached characters of that novel, and against the fulsome sweep of its Rousseauesque style. In terms of world literature, Stendhal may be seen in his time as the polar opposite of Britain's Charles Dickens. To maintain the low temperature of his language, Stendhal would frequently read a few pages in the Civil Code.

In Stendhal's perception, man belongs in society since he needs a field of endeavor in order to "become what he is," in order to prove himself and his pride. In the conception of Rousseau man belongs in nature in order to find himself and to find what links him to the divine cosmos. Stendhal viewed the individual as the French moralists from La Rochefoucauld on had done. His novels turn into behavorial studies of the prime principle of human existence, that is, of "egotism." This implies the fullest realization of the novel of individualism, but it marks simulataneously a transition to the novel of society.

To be sure, in Stendhal's age, this role was not assigned to him, nor was it recognized generally as being characteristic of him. He himself stated, fully aware of his imperfect conformity with his age, that he expected to gain some recognition by 1860 and that *La Chartreuse de Parme* would certainly be read around 1880. This is precisely what happened, despite Balzac's emphatic statement, "*La Chartreuse de Parma* is, in my opinion, for this era—and with the inclusion of all earlier eras—the masterpiece of French literature." (*Revue Parisienne*, 1840)

Not before Paul Bourget was Stendhal characterized as the great "vanquisher." But from then on, men like Barrès, d'Annunzio, Nietzsche, and Gide were thinking and writing in his spirit. Stendhal taught them to strive in virile determination—shunning the self-intoxication of outpourings from the fullness of the heart—to attain selfhood and to establish the human reality of the happy few. The place of world-weary melancholy and of Dionysian passion is taken by sobriety, courage, honor, friendship, and supreme love. The parting of the ways is between self-realization and contemptible weakness.

At the present time, the extent to which Stendhal has been made the object of literary research is comparable only to the learned investigation of Balzac.[28]

Stendhal's ethos of the individual found in the latter half of the nineteenth century a congenial though also problematic admirer in the person of Count Joseph-Arthur de Gobineau (1816–82) who was, around 1840, the leader of a circle of friends calling themselves the *"scelti,"* i.e., the "chosen," with the avowed objective of taking a condottieri-like stand against the middle classes then in the ascendancy. "Decades before writing on the Renaissance, Gobineau thus acted out the role of the man of the Renaissance."[29] In his *Essai sur l'inégalité des races* (1854), he anticipated Nietzsche's idea of the blonde beast and the racial theories of national socialism. His ideology of a master race, which was inspired by Stendhal, found expression in the motif of the royal children as it appears in his principal novel, *Les Pléiades* (1874). In it, distinguished men of the nineteenth century call themselves latter-day Franks, embodying once again aristocratic principles of existence in a setting of democratic mass rule.

Gobineau's idea of free human self-realization was as much out of tune with the times as Stendhal's idea had been, for it was during these years that the novels of Zola or of Anatole France began to show the impact of the determinism of Taine. How painful this loss of substance was to Gobineau is apparent, for instance, from his fresco, *Renaissance* (1877), in which he presented the gradual dying out of men of sufficient eminence to be a law unto themselves. In the age of Pope Julius II it was they who represented society, and society meant a society of the élite. Then the level of society's ethos declined, and in the end Michelangelo stood alone.

The untimeliness of Gobineau's concept of man is further emphasized by the fact that the mainstream of the French novel had long since begun, in the wake of Sir Walter Scott (and also in emulation of the new beginnings in Stendhal), to pursue a very different course. Great creative portrayals of society overshadow, in the nineteenth century, the concluding phases of the novel of individualism with their predication on such aristocratic premises.

II

THE NOVEL OF SOCIETY

Prosper Mérimée, Alfred de Vigny, Alexandre Dumas, Théophile Gautier, Gustave Flaubert, Victor Hugo, Champfleury (Jules Husson), George Sand, Eugène Sue, Louis-Emile-Edmond Duranty, Honoré de Balzac, Guy de Maupassant, Jules Vallès

❦ It was in precisely the years when the novel of individualism, with Stendhal, underwent its inner reorientation that the novel of society appeared. This came to pass, on the one hand, when poets gave way to the romantic longing for the past and transposed historical tableaus into aesthetic realities but it also occurred where the concept of history was expanded and made to take in, through a new appraisal, the most recent past and finally even the present. Thus, by degrees, can the historical novel pass over into the period novel. In contrast to the norm in the novel of individualism, the individual is now viewed in the position he occupies in the social structure. His demeanor is observed by the author in terms of the whole.

Again, however, this form of the novel is initially conditioned by a process of deconfinement. This is palpably evidenced in the cast of two thousand in the *Comédie humaine*. For the novel of society undertakes to depict the immeasurable, the boundless, the total. With the novel of society arises the *roman-fleuve*—the stream novel—as a variant of the form previously conceived by the Germans Schlegel and Novalis as the nearest correspondence to the all. Instead of the universe, the French take the idea of "modern times," which only the novel can possibly master in their totality. Indeed, as is apparent from Beaudelaire's *Petits poèmes en prose,* prose achieves a notable mark-up even in lyrical poetry. Yet, even before Balzac's influence could exert itself fully, the historical novel thoroughly prepared the field both in terms of production and in terms of consumption. As we view the development from this vantage point, we note striking correspondences in the portrayal of historical society as it was handled by Vigny in 1826, by Mérimée in 1829, and by Dumas Père in 1844.

Prosper Mérimée (1803–70) came from a family of artists. In 1834 he was appointed Inspector of Historical Monuments [*Inspecteur des monuments historiques*]. He shared Stendhal's profound dislike of the bourgeoisie, his antipathy against all religion, and his keen narrator's gift of observation. On the other hand, being a welcome visitor at the court of Napoleon III, he was, in fact, the man of the world that Stendhal would have liked to be. In his works, his presence—in autobiographical terms—is incomparably less manifest than holds true in the case of Stendhal. His style was more polished, and his fantastic propensities (See Chapter III) established finally a clear-cut difference between him and Stendhal.[1]

In Mérimée's historical novel, *Chronique du règne de Charles IX* (1829), we find the following starting-point situation: The young Huguenot Bernard de Mergy rides to Paris where he intends to offer his services to Coligny. On his way he meets his brother George whose hate for Condé—aroused by the fact that the latter took away his mistress and called him a coward—has made him a convert to Catholicism. To be sure, his image of the Madonna is now the image of a courtesan and *Pantagruel* is his book of prayers. Bernard achieves a quick success in society, winning in particular the favors of the Countess Turgis for whose sake he has fought a duel. Meanwhile Charles IX has selected George for the task of eliminating Coligny. George refuses and in fact warns the Marshal. He does not, however, succeed in preventing the Massacre of St. Bartholomew. Bernard escapes to La Rochelle. When the Catholics close in, he kills his brother in an engagement, and George, still an atheist, dies in Bernard's arms.

Cinq-Mars, ou une conspiration sous Louis XIII by Alfred de Vigny shows extensive parallels in conception and layout to

Mérimée's work. The opposition of Catholics and Huguenots has a correspondence in the opposition of Louis XIII and Richelieu. The young nobleman Cinq-Mars owes it to his ambition that he is caught between these millstones when he attempts with Spanish help to organize an uprising against the powerful cardinal. His plans become known, and the King drops him.

A third sample is supplied by Alexander Dumas (1802–70) whose play, *Henri III et sa cour*, prepared the way for the success of Hugo's *Hernani* and who, although literary criticism has regarded him on the whole as second or third rate, was exceedingly fertile as a novelist. Dumas was self-taught and his lack of formal schooling enabled him to see history in a light that had to escape the scholarly precision of Mérimée or the philosophical approach of de Vigny. As a man he was a colossus, a grand seigneur with the airs of the *ancien régime*. His novels show this, with their sweeping vitality and their nonchalant display of impossible "realities."[2] *Les Trois mousquetaires* (1844) is his principal work. It begins with the ride of eighteen-year-old d'Artagnan from the Gascogne to Paris where he is drawn forthwith into the conflict of the king's musketeers and Richelieu's guard as well as into that between Queen Anne and the Cardinal. The cloak and dagger novel ends peaceably as d'Artagnan, albeit unintentionally, rids Richelieu of a dangerous female "working for him." The Cardinal decrees that he be commissioned lieutenant of the musketeers.

The foregoing should serve to show the schematic identities of exposition in Vigny, Mérimée, and Dumas. It is a pattern from Sir Walter Scott (1771–1832), who had used it in novels set in the Middle Ages—*Ivanhoe*, for instance—or in the times of the Tudors—such as *Kenilworth*—or under the Stuarts—*Waverley*.[3]

Of course, the presentation of historical material in novel form is not an invention of the nineteenth century. Madame de Lafayette's moorish novel *Zaïde* was based on Spanish romances, and her *Princesse de Clèves* (1678)—a major representative of the classicistic novel, with a setting in the age of Henri II—is unthinkable without the source material of contemporary memoirs. Still, the turn from the eighteenth to the nineteenth centuries was characterized by a more exacting sense of history whose precipitates, as for instance Augustin Thierry's *Récits des temps mérovingiens,* which might have been called "Gregory of Tours Retold"—became extremely popular. A fourth factor was the complex of formal devices developed by Scott, with the frequent feature that the novelist has some individual undertake a trip to some land he does not know. Thus Mérimée's Bernard travels to Paris, Vigny's Cinq-Mars to the royal court in Perpignan and Paris, and Dumas' d'Artagnan likewise to Paris. The traveler then finds himself confronted with two contending parties : Catholics and Huguenots in Mérimée, Louis and Richelieu in de Vigny, and Louis and Richelieu and Richelieu and Anne in Dumas.

The impact of this novel form was immense. Traces of it are found in Spindler, Zschokke, La Motte-Fouqué, Hauff, Raabe, and C. F. Meyer in Germany and Switzerland. Manzoni's *I Promessi sposi, storia milanese del secolo XVII* (1827) in Italy and the Spaniard Benito Pérez Galdós' *Episodios nacionales* (1873) are embued with it. Bulwer-Lytton proceeded in *The Last Days of Pompeii* as Scott might have done, and the same holds true for Thackeray in *Henry Esmond,* Sienkiewicz in *Quo vadis* (1895), and Tolstoy in *War and Peace.*

A requirement of this form of historical novel appears to be the existence of great historical figures who must, however, remain at the periphery of the action, while the central character is freely invented. Among the French authors cited, Dumas is the most typical representative of the school of Scott. He also took over Scott's optimism, allowing it to dictate to him the conciliatory conclusion. In contrast to this, the heroes of Mérimée and de Vigny wind up in failure because they are unable to mediate and to conciliate. A distinctive feature of Mérimée's novel is the close affiliation of the fraternal heroes with events on the great stage of politics. One has the impression that de Vigny and Mérimée were too fanatically involved in questions of politics to dispose of them cavalierly in fictitious terms. Vigny in particular wanted to portray the ills of absolutism which began with Richelieu and show how the nobility was systematically subjected or decimated. In a sense, he wrote the history of his personal bitterness.

Aside from these three authors of the school of Scott we shall mention three others who cannot be associated with it. The first is Théophile Gautier (1811–72), whose contribution to the novel is not on a par with his lyric poetry. Gautier's *Mademoiselle de Maupin*—a novel of art and artists—is, under the surface, clearly and strongly linked to his poetry in verse, a fact particularly apparent in the programmatic foreword. In his *Roman de la momie* (1858), his endeavour is to evoke the realities of Egyptian life, with the mummy representing a symbol of things eternal, things not subject to the laws of the way of the flesh. This extension of the message of Horace passed into the novel via Gautier's poem *"Art"* in *Emaux et camées* (1852). In this work (*Roman de la momie*), Gautier owed much to the descriptive writings of the eighteenth century, in particular to Saint-Amant's *Moïse.* He derived suggestive elements from an art catalogue,[4] from Nerval's *Le Voyage en Orient,* and Rossini's opera *Moses in Egypt* which he had seen in 1852. Stylistically the novel falls off where Gautier took in the events of the Book of Exodus. Here the initial exoticising splendor is replaced by a superficial retracing of Biblical events. This was a concession to the public.

In 1863, Gautier published *Le Capitaine Fracasse,* an imitation of Scarron's *Roman comique.* This work sketched a colorful picture of the seventeenth century in the southwest of France. As Dumas and Vigny had done, Gautier took great interest in the time of upheaval under Louis XIII. (The age of the Sun King appears to be taboo for the historical novel.) Significant too is Gautier's interest in matters of art. Captain Fracasse is a baron who has fallen in love with an actress and tours and plays with her company.

Gustave Flaubert (1821–80; cf. the second half of this chapter), who is so often represented as the realist par excellence, was likewise not immune to the lure of the exotic and historically picturesque, the less so because of the great appeal which aesthetic beauty had for him. His trip to the Orient in 1849 provided for him the requisite first-hand experience. In 1862 he published his *Salammbô,* a vision of Carthage, grouped about the figure of Hamilkar Barkas's daughter and her sacrilegious fondness for the barbarian leader Matho who dares take on the strength of Carthage and pays for it with his life.

In this novel the trend away from the pattern of Scott is

quite striking. Scott's humanitarian tenets were abandoned, for *Salammbô* is full of cruel and ugly scenes of a kind Gautier in his *Roman de la momie* was not yet ready to portray in detail. Religious problems are interpreted in psychological and pathological terms. Salammbô dies because she committed the outrage of touching the mantle of the moon goddess Tanit which Matho had brought to her in secret. We shall have more to say about this theomania of the nineteenth century when we take up Nerval (see Chapter III). The descriptive precision of Gautier is surpassed by Flaubert who freely introduces for the purpose a great many uncommon specialized terms.

Salammbô draws our attention to the complexities in Flaubert who, in a sense, wrote down his works as a self-inflicted punishment. Sainte-Beuve did not hesitate to call his attitude sadistic. Flaubert strove for the impersonal, the non-subjective in his writings and for that reason chose a historically remote subject. He was interested in the hordes of barbarians slowly perishing in their revolt against the strong city. This perspective of a human anthill finds a correspondence in the symbolism of paratactic constructions.

A third author illustrates the transition from the novel of historical scenes to the anthropological novel and the period novel of social criticism: Victor Hugo (1802–85), the most versatile writer of the nineteenth century, of whom, to be sure, it must be said that his lyrical poetry stood the test of time better than either his novels or his dramas. On the stage he was overtaken by Musset with his scintillating plays; his novels were surpassed in colorful variety by those of Dumas and Sue, in historical reliability by Mérimée's, and in mundane comprehensiveness by Balzac's.[5]

Notre-Dame de Paris (1831), with its crowded abundance of material relating to the late fifteenth century, is an illustration of Hugo's poetic conceptions as outlined in the preface to his *Cromwell* (1827). There is the Archdeacon Claude Frollo and by his side his protégé, the Sexton of Notre-Dame, Quasimodo, who is so ugly that on Twelfth Night in 1482 he is elected Pope of Fools. Frollo falls passionately in love with the gypsy girl Esmeralda whose friend Phébus de Châteaupers he tries to stab to death. The attempt is attributed to the girl who is then condemned to death for witchcraft. Quasimodo provides

Esmeralda asylum in the cathedral and protects her against Frollo. But the gypsy, recognized and discovered at the last moment by her mother, still loses her life on the gallows. Bursting out in heinous laughter, the Archdeacon, from the pinnacles of the Church, celebrates his black triumph. Quasimodo pushes him into the depths.

The figure of the Sexton in particular reminds us distantly of the structural scheme in Scott's novels, for Quasimodo plays in a sense a conciliatory role. More clearly apparent is the impact of the Gothic thriller which was destined to exert such a crucial influence on French fiction, especially the *roman noir* in the wake of Charles Nodier. Noteworthy and highly original is the feature that the novel thrives on the local myth of the cathedral, an artistic concept subsequently taken up by Zola in *Le Ventre de Paris*. The action, as planned by Hugo, is a mixture of tragic, grotesque, and comic elements, for life—in Hugo's opinion—recognizes no genres and does not respect their definitions.

In his later narrative prose—the novel *Quatre-vingt-treize* of French royalty or the novel of English feudalism, *L'Homme qui rit*—Hugo moved on to the period novel. This transition is most cogently apparent in *Les Misérables* (1862). The very title, grammatically a plural, suggests that Hugo was not conscerned in this work with the private life of a single individual. Here the most recent past appears as history, and the presentation is replete with problems of immediate timeliness.

Jean Valjean, guilty of stealing a loaf of bread for his sister's hungry children, is sent to the galleys. After his release in 1815 he is hospitably received by a bishop in Southern France, but when he leaves the following day he takes along some silverware. The clergyman protects him against the police. The stigma of the convict, however, is his forever, and Police Inspector Javert sends him back to the bagnio and pursues him after his escape. The political magnanimity which Valjean displays on the barricades in 1830 finally breaks Javert's rigid sense of righteousness with such emotional impact that he throws himself into the Seine. Valjean's adopted daughter Cosette marries Marius Pontmercy who is a lawyer. When, however, the happy couple tries to provide the old man with a harmonious evening of life, he dies. The idea of the novel is clear. Victor Hugo's endeavor is to rehabilitate human dignity. He envelops Jean Valjean with the same love that, as a dramatist, he had felt for the adored Hernani or the courtesan Marion Delorme. Hugo's contemporaries were not slow in noting the social criticism implied in the novel as well as its pleading for legal reforms. In some quarters this led to spirited attacks.[6]

Les Misérables marks a major stage in the development of the period novel, for in it the appeal for reform—a characteristic trait of Vallès and of Zola—seems to be heralded. Since 1836, when George Sand published her *Lélia*, the social novel had indeed come a long way. This is particularly impressive when we consider the thematic knot in *Lélia* and the way it was unraveled. The presentation of themes, the novelist's creative vision as well as his manner of writing have changed and so has the public and the kind of repercussion a novel can evoke. It is an event not previously attested to that a work of fiction came to set off technical discussions among members of the legal profession in France. It appears indeed that literature and social realities have established mutual relations of fertile potentialities.

We shall not—in what follows—try to avoid the use of period designations such as "realism" or "naturalism,"[7] but in adopting such conventions from the familiar histories of literature we proceed with the same reservations as heretofore in the use of the term "romanticism" and the like. After all, the concept of realism is as applicable to Balzac as to Villon and Rabelais and cannot therefore be regarded as typical of a particular genre in literature. Furthermore, it did not originate in the area of literary criticism. It was the painter Courbet (1819–77) who coined the term and who must be credited with having introduced it into the discussion of questions of aesthetics.

Still, we do discern common traits, both in terms of content and of form, in the narrative works of Dickens, Meredith, Gogol, Verga, Galdós, Sand, Balzac, Flaubert, Maupassant, Vallès, Zola, and the brothers Goncourt. These novelists demand and practice a manner of writing which despises rhetorical oratory, and in their statements they violate one taboo after another. It is only the extended range of motifs that makes it possible to treat Zola and the Goncourts in a separate chapter, for much of the *fin de siècle* turns against their work, but we do not find it possible to discern any other difference between the so-called "schools" of realism and naturalism. The new factual objectivity of the authors appears coupled with an increasing preoccupation with scientific disciplines, a term which must be allowed to cover mesmerism, magnetism, and illuminism as well.

Balzac played an eminent role in the beginnings of this trend. But he was not alone to voice such ideas. Henri Murger (1822–61) published in 1851 his *Scènes de la vie de Bohème*. Similarly, Henry Monnier (1799–1877) gave us his *Scènes populaires* (1830) and the novel, *Les Bourgeois de Paris* (1854). Champfleury (1821–89), born in Laon as Jules Husson, retained in his portrayals of morals the common and the vulgar, things actually seen and heard, quite in contrast to the poetizing tendency of Murger. (Puccini appears to have had this impression, too.)

Champfleury's novels *Chien-Caillou* (1847) and *Aventures de Mademoiselle Mariette* (1853) were written expressly in opposition to the prevailing ideas of refinement of taste. In *Les Bourgeois de Molinchart* (1854) and *Les Souffrances du Professeur Delteil* (1855) he dealt with a variant of the Bovary theme. Zola regarded Champfleury as an important precursor who lacked the power and the time to complete the impending breakthrough in the French novel.[8]

A disciple of Champfleury's was Louis-Émile-Edmond Duranty (1833–80) whose theories and novels were so outspoken in their declaration of war against the surviving elements of romanticism, in particular against all stylistic refinement, that Flaubert could state: "I wrote *Madame Bovary* to spite Duranty. I wanted to prove that the piteous woes and the sentimental mediocrity of the bourgeois are compatible with beauty of language."

George Sand, too, must be mentioned in this context. The more she divested herself of the romantic heritage, the more she was drawn into the world of ideas of the younger Saint-Simon (1760–1825), and the more she came under the personal influence of Lamennais and Pierre Leroux. The twenty-year-old proletarian writer Charles Poncy aroused her enthusiasm. This determined as well the future course of her own endeavors. In *Compagnon du tour de France* (1840), George Sand formulated her ideas on labor unions. In the novel *Meunier d'Angibault* (1845), she had a noble lady complain that it would have been better for her had she been born a workman's child. The curse of being rich was exposed by George Sand in *Péché de Monsieur Antoine* (1847), in which a nobleman leaves a fortune to a young couple with the assignment to establish a "kolkhoz."

From now on the rural setting of George Sand's novels became so characteristic that she may well be regarded with Gottfried Keller or Jeremias Gotthelf as one of the founders of the peasant novel.[9] In *La Mare au diable* (1846), a peasant finds the right kind of stepmother for his children. *François le Champi* is the story of a foundling told in the patterns of a peasant novel. The most touching tones George Sand doubtless found in *La Petite Fadette* (1849). In terms of the history of the novel she moved with this work into close proximity with Dickens. This Fadette is the portrait of a child like Oliver Twist, small, ragged, but jaunty and alive. Abandoned by her mother, she tends her grandmother's goats. Her childhood love for Landry Barbeau transforms the ugly duckling into an eye-catching swan, and since her reputation and her material possessions are better than there was reason to suppose, Fadette finally assumes in the eyes of Father Barbeau the qualifications of a good wife for his son.

It is striking that, in George Sand's case, the process of maturation in workmanship ran parallel to a strengthening of her faith in the immutable goodness of man and in his moral perfectibility. These are principles which the other novelists in those years rejected sight unseen. Balzac, for instance, held that French society had been going downhill ever since the great revolution, and in a way we must wait in the French novel for Camus and Louis Aragon before we find again evidence of the acceptance of those principles and that faith. George Sand did not glorify and idealize life close to Nature in factitious enthusiasm, but she was so carried away by Saint-Simonian and Communist ideas that it was impossible for her to relinquish the "principal hope" which to her had reality only in rural life. To be sure, many of her novels exhibit stylistic areas of paper flatness, but with all their tendentiousness, they were unique in those days in terms of the message they conveyed.

We find it incomprehensible nowadays that the contemporaries could prefer Eugène Sue (1804–57) to Balzac, for the colorful variety of action in Sue's works can hardly make up for the black-and-white monotony of their moral portrayals. However, at the time of their publication, the *Mystères de Paris* (1842), *Le Juif errant* (1845–47), or *Les Mystères du peuple* (1849–56) were widely read, and their popularity as works of social criticism often interfered with the dissemenation of Balzac. Dostoevski, for instance, thought highly of Sue and took over from him the figures of prostitutes.

The work of Honoré de Balzac (1799–1850), as that of Flaubert, is more complex than the generally accepted label attached to this writer might let us suppose. It is true, the *Comédie humaine* (1829–49) does represent the center of gravity of Balzac's work, but the realist in him cannot fully overshadow the visionary. Balzac was born in Tours. His father, as the name suggests, came from Southern France. His mother was a Parisian. Honoré attended various boarding schools before taking up the study of law at Paris.

As early as 1819 Balzac had made up his mind that he wanted to be a writer. From 1821 to 1824 he experimented with all sorts of narrative forms. The quantity of his output during these years already bore witness to Balzac's creative frenzy. It is true that there were external factors forcing him to hurry if he did not want to break his contracts with his publishers. It was only through his relationship with the Polish Countess Eva Hanska that his financial and material situation became somewhat regularized. Toward the end of 1832 she had sent him an anonymous letter expressing her admiration for his work. This was the beginning of their acquaintanceship and the first document in their extensive correspondence.

Before this time, Balzac had established his fame with individual novels from the later *Scènes de la vie privée* and especially with *Le Lys dans la vallée* (1830). Although the material success of these works lagged behind the literary recognition they were granted especially by Victor Hugo, Balzac led the life of a grand seigneur. In 1837 he built for himself in Ville d'Avray near Paris the country seat Les Jardies at a cost of a hundred thousand francs of which a mere 17,500 was recovered when the place had to be sold at auction in 1841. That Balzac's collection of antiquities, bronzes, sculptures, and paintings came to represent, by 1848, an estimated value of 350,000 francs was possible only because he drove his taurine constitution to the limit and made of his literary production a gigantic work. Quantity with Balzac is a feature of quality.

In 1841 he had the inspired idea of putting together the greater number of his novels in the *Comédie humaine*: "This idea suggested itself through a comparison of humanity and animality." For, next to the species as a zoological concept, there is the species as a social concept, but "the social situation is beset with hazards which nature does not permit herself. . . . The wife of a storekeeper is at times worthy of being the wife of a prince, and frequently that of a prince is not worth as much as that of an artist." Sir Walter Scott supplied the technical devices for the enormous venture but also the historical and philosophical perspective, while the guiding tenets in Balzac's overall approach are reflected in the statements, "Catholicism and royalty are twin principles" which the electoral principle has come to supersede, and "I reject the exclusivity of elections as a device of social implementation." The French Revolution marked the beginning of the general social decline (Foreword).

In 1843 Balzac undertook a journey to Russia and Germany. He redoubled his literary output in order to be able to offer Madame Hanska, whom he wanted to marry, an existence in material security. That he was able to keep going at this extraordinary pace for three whole decades, that his health did not collapse much sooner can only inspire admiration. In 1847, Balzac did fall seriously ill. A sojourn in the Ukraine with the family of his friend Countess Eva proved more of an ordeal than a recreation, for it was there that he learned how his plan of marrying the Countess was being undermined. To make matters worse, in 1848 he suffered two public defeats, failing in both as a candidate for election into the legislature and as a candidate for election into the Académie Française. On March 14, 1850, he did marry Countess Hanska in the Ukraine. After his return to Paris his heart and lung ailment grew worse. During the night from August 18 to August 19 he died. Victor Hugo delivered the funeral address at his grave in the Père Lachaise Cemetery, famous from Balzac's *Père Goriot*, the place from where Rastignac hurled at Parish the challenge: "You or I now!"*

A work of such magnitude needs to be looked at above all with respect to its evolution and the aspects under which it was composed. We find that the early Balzac does not differ from the later one except insofar as the *Etudes philosophiques* supplied the irrational substructure for his later realism.

The narrative *Les Martyres ignorés* (written in 1836 and 1837) postulates the materialism of thought. Balzac's doctrine of psychic energies appears summarized in the statement: "The term of life is proportional to the force with which the individual is able to oppose thought. . . . Think much and you will live little." The potential of physical destruction inherent in the idée fixe we shall have occasion to observe again in our analysis of the novel *La Cousine Bette*. Physical debility brought on by an idea is likewise illustrated in *Séraphita*. Ideas of Swedenborg as well as of E. T. A. Hoffmann are found in *Gambara* (written in June, 1837) where the musician Gambara gets himself completely wrapped up in the project of a panharmonicum—typically a project of aesthetic deconfinement. *Z. Marcas* (written in May, 1840) was placed in the later organization of the work as a whole among the *Scènes de la vie politique*, but it is full of physiognomonic interpretations, of concepts from the cabala, of mysticism, and of the belief in the materiality of thought which is possessed of lethal powers.

In his *Philosophical Studies*, Balzac undertook to analyze the ultimate bases of human demeanor, and we may well regard these studies as being concerned with the etiology of the portrayals of morals in the *Human Comedy*. Indeed, Balzac used the concept of society with new implications.[10] In the seventeenth and eighteenth centuries, "society" was a juridical, political, and possibly philanthropic entity. Balzac introduced into it a biological element. He examined groups and types of men, forms of action and of being. Humanity appears, by analogy with Linnaeus' vegetable kingdom, subdivided in species, with the sole, albeit essential, difference—subsequently opposed in part by the deterministic novel of Zola—that the limits of the species are not rigid and that social shifts are possible. This introduces a monistic principle into the complex multiplicity of elements in the work as a whole. The creative problem, as seen by Balzac, consisted hence in the need to prevent the portrayal of things typical from obliterating the representation of things individual. Balzac's epic endeavor is sparked by a macabre model: the dynamics of human struggles and of human monomanias in the relentless social decline initiated by the political outburst of the Revolution. Balzac was consciously antidemocratic, for democracy, plutocratic bourgeoisie, and decadence were to him entities interdependent by the necessity of their very nature. That is the grand theme of the *Comédie humaine*. Philarète Chasles, in the introduction he wrote in 1834 to one of Balzac's books, noted that the interest of the writer belonged to "the grand spectacle of the agony of society."

To make quite clear his intent to include all phases of social life, Balzac grouped his novels in *Scènes de la vie privée, Scènes de la vie de province, Scènes de la vie parisienne, Scènes de la vie politique, Scènes de la vie militaire,* and *Scènes de la vie de campagne.* The pseudoscientific encyclopedism of the composition is felicitously compensated for by the fact that individual characters appear in several novels, giving the tremendous opus, with its thousands of characters, a semblance of coherence.

The various divisions were not worked out in the same way. The *Scenes from Private Life* have their center of gravity in *Père Goriot* (1834), a portrait of the monomania of paternal love, of which *Eugénie Grandet* (1833), a novel of the monomania of avarice, may be seen as the counterpart among the *Scenes from Provincial Life.* In both these novels Balzac excels in the character sketches of old and passion-ridden men. The same point will be stressed again as the distinguishing mark of *La Cousine Bette.* Yet, perceptive as Balzac was in regard to the work of the passions, so obtuse was he in regard to political and military events, for it is a striking fact that the novels of the *Scenes from Political Life* and of the *Scenes from Military Life* include none that could be called a great novel.

Before we proceed with a more detailed analysis of *La Cousine Bette* (in *Scènes de la vie parisienne*), we may attempt to stress the distinctive characteristic of Balzac's novels. Society had two functions in them. It is the setting in which, and supplies the background against which, individual figures act out their lives, and it is simultaneously the motive power in the fate of the individual. Human existence and human behavior result from the interplay of the individual will with decadent society. To the individual, this may mean decline and deceit, creative work, or ambitious achievement. The ethically disgusting, in Balzac, implies no encouragement of immorality. It represents amoral description and is the stigma of decline.

Hugo Friedrich regards *La Cousine Bette* (1846), as "Balzac's most powerful novel" and describes it simultaneously as "the most somber creation of the myth of the nineteenth century." Since Balzac's objective was to depict the agony of society, his intent is more typically evident in this book than in many others. Yet, despite the emphasis placed on it by literary criticism, the taste of the public still assigns to it second place after the more popular *La Femme de trente ans, Eugénie Grandet,* or *Père Goriot. La Cousine Bette* forms a triunity with *Le Cousin Pons* and *Pierrette.* These three novels are stories of families described as groups in their relationship to one outstanding individual in their midst. Bette is not maltreated as is Pierrette nor expelled as is Pons. She lives within the family, and when she dies, the mourning about her is honest. There are no vicious relatives around her—she herself is the instigator of intrigue and malice. "Cousin Bette in this novel is like a spider building at once a number of webs." (M. Allem in the Garnier Edition, 1959, p. viii)

The material for the novel was derived to a minor extent from a law suit running in December, 1845, and to a major extent from Balzac's personal experiences. For, as Bette endeavors to keep her Livonian protégé financially dependent on her, so Balzac was treated by his own mother. Certain positive traits in Bette, such as the fact that she had spent her childhood years in Lorraine working hard under difficult circumstances, were taken from the biography of the poetess Marceline Desbordes-Valmore. Balzac wrote the novel from the end of June to the end of November, 1846, racing to keep up with the *Constitutionnel* which printed the work in the entertainment section—a form of first publication that had become frequent since Eugène Sue.[11] *La Cousine Bette* operates with a cast of about 150 characters. The action covers the period from 1838 to 1846.

Lisbeth Fischer, called Bette for short, is a frequent guest at the home of her married cousin Adeline, whose husband, the Baron Hector Hulot d'Ervy, is a civil-service officer working in one of the ministries. The family atmosphere is friendly, and Bette is well treated. She also has a flat of her own where a Livonian sculptor by name of Wenceslas Steinbock is her neighbor. She helps him financially. She tells Hulot's daughter Hortense about the young man, stating that he is her lover, which arouses in the girl a keen interest in the unknown man. Hortense's mother, Adeline Hulot, tries to marry her only daughter in accordance with her husband's station in society. This is the more difficult since there is no dowry. Hector Hulot's amorous adventures have consumed the entire fortune of the family. The upstart Crevel, whose daughter is married to Hulot's son, tries to lure Adeline to a tryst with financial promises, but the attempt fails because of the steadfastness of the woman. Hortense, on the other hand, does meet the Livonian when she buys at some store a sculpture which he has produced. The two young people fall in love at first sight and marry immediately. Bette hears about this from her fellow tenant Madame Valérie Marneffe, who is currently Hulot's mistress. She feels terribly deceived. Was it not she who had cared for the foreigner with maternal solicitude, holding him—to be sure—also in pressing financial dependence? Valérie Marneffe soon becomes Crevel's mistress as well and then proceeds to make Wenceslas Steinbock her lover. In back of all this is Bette. Hulot and Crevel vie with each other in making gifts to Valérie. Bette, the old maid, watches in a spirit of revenge how the ministry official goes down to total ruin. When a former admirer of Valérie Marneffe, a Brazilian, appears on the scene, plans are made to blackmail Hulot. The project does not come off, but Hulot's illegal financial maneuvers in Algeria are discovered. He has to resign his post at the ministry. The irrepressable erotomaniac escapes with the help of his former mistress Josépha to a suburb. Valérie gets a divorce and marries Crevel whereupon the Brazilian poisons her. Bette dies too, honestly mourned by the Hulots, for her monstrous machinations have never been revealed. Adeline collapses when she surprises her husband, who has left Josépha, in intimate contact with the kitchen maid. She dies, and after the funeral Baron Hulot d'Ervy leaves Paris.

The action of the novel revolves about two axes. One of these is typically represented in the following passage explaining how Bette has Steinbock financially under her thumb: "She took revenge on this young man for the fact that she was neither young nor wealthy nor beautiful. Then, after each act of vengeance and recognizing in herself her wrongs, she imposed on herself humiliations and abandoned herself to an infinite tenderness. She was incapable of offering her idol any kind of sacrifice unless and until she had incised in him with an axe the marks of her power. ... As for the wretched young man, meditative, high-flown of thought, inclined to laziness, he showed in his eyes—as the lions in their cages in the zoological garden—a reflection of the desert which his protectress had wrought in his soul. The forced labor which Lisbeth demanded of him could not defray the needs of his heart. His suffering turned into a physical illness, and he succumbed without being able to ask for, without being able to obtain the money for the pleasures which at times were essential."*

In contrast to Stendhal's style of writing, Balzac's broad narrative attitude is striking, manifest in the cumulative attributes and detailed pursuit of comparisons. The way the characters are drawn likewise differs from Stendhal's procedure. It was Stendhal's endeavor to provide his central figure with supreme integrity, and often high-flown autonomy. Wenceslas Steinbock and Hortense are doubtless the most appealing figures in Balzac's novel, but they too have been wrapped by the author in a veil of gray. Steinbock is not a true martyr nor the ideal of a young man, for he is inclined to laziness. Balzac does not operate with effects of black and white; the *Comédie humaine* presents shades of darkness. One extreme in the spectrum is Bette's monomaniac urge to care and provide which turns into an idée fixe and almost kills the young man. Bette's demeanor is morbid, perverse.

How did this state of affairs come about? The more the spinster from Lorraine falls for the plutocratic gambling rules of the metropolis, the more her natural solicitude turns into a kind of craving for power, for some official has explained to her that she could achieve absolute control over the Livonian if she were to lend him money. A comparably terrifying portrayal of monomania will not be achieved again before Mauriac, especially in his *Génitrix*.

The second mainspring of the novel is the erotomania of the two old men, Hector Hulot and Crevel. Balzac combined the central motifs by means of Bette's jealousy and her hatred of Adeline and Hortense, for her sister has always been beautiful, she herself ugly; her sister is a lady, she worked in the fields. Her niece marries a man whom she regards as her protégé. This suffices for her to wreck the future of both women by helping along Hulot's skirt-chasing propensities to the point of ruining him. There is an hypothesis by J. B. Barrère (*Mercure de France*, January, 1950) according to which Balzac meant to portray Victor Hugo in Hector Hulot and Hugo's wife, whose maiden name was Foucher, in Adeline Hulot, née Fischer. The consonance of the names is indeed striking, and the allusion would indeed fit Hugo's Don-Juanism.

Finally there is in this novel a psychological lesson. A woman ought to be many-sided, as Marivaux explained long ago in *Marianne*. Adeline ought to have in her make-up something of Josépha, and Valérie Marneffe something of Adeline. The State ought to see to it that women develop the skill to hold their husbands. These are pet ideas of Balzac's which he had previously developed in his *Physiologie du mariage*. But what determines the total picture of the novel is the mood of decline, the moral decay, and the monomaniac excesses of the characters. The relationship of Hortense and Steinbock starts out in splendor and glory, only to be submerged in the morass of universal meanness and depravity.

With *La Cousine Bette* Balzac hoped to achieve the kind of public recognition on a grand scale which the best-selling author Eugène Sue with his *Mystères de Paris* and his *Juif errant* had so far kept out of his reach. Balzac wrote this novel in order to defeat Sue on Sue's own ground: "By a double stroke, by maintaining literary standards in a grand style and by being more interesting and truer" (cf. *Lettres à l'étrangère* II, 433 and 457). This required striking contrasts in the plot, a furious display of passions, and a succession of climactic events in the development of the action.

In the pursuit of these objectives the novelist worried little about improbabilities. Is it possible for the engagement of Hortense and Steinbock to be kept secret from Bette for so long? Is it believable that Madame Marneffe can frighten four men simultaneously—Hulot, Crevel, Steinbock, and the Brazilian—with the prospect of an unwanted paternity? By means of this latter device in particular Balzac strove to make Madame Marneffe a demonic symbol of the whore which he needed in order to show to what abysmal depths a man's animal passions can sink. Balzac was out to out-Sue Sue. The reading public at large was doubtless not immediately aware of the outcome, but Balzac emerged victorious from the duel. Sue had evoked an ill-smelling gutter Paris. Balzac—whose portrayal of disconsolate hopelessness in *Père Goriot* had already shown him to be familiar with the backyard of life—surpassed him.

In *La Cousine Bette,* Balzac achieved an abundance of portrayals the like of which cannot be found in the works of any urban writer before him. A comparable flood of intimate details and gruesome character sketches will not be encountered again before Zola's *Nana.* Although the plot caters to the most vulgar public taste, the novel—if we regard it not only as a panorama of morals but beyond that as a work of literature and hence of art—reveals throughout a grandiose continuity and a prolix mastery of the word. This perfect control of the pen, maintained also in the portrayal of the monomaniac and of the vulgar, forced the respect even of Lamartine whose manner of writing was fundamentally different. He attested to Balzac's "grandeur of genius and grandeur in moral perception, his immense aristocracy of talent, his immense variety of aptitudes, and the universality of his self-awareness." If it is true that Balzac went unrealistically beyond the middle range of sober description, we may conclude that the dreamer and the visionary in him were never forced to complete silence. Seen in this light Baudelaire was correct when he said of Balzac: "He blackened the shadows and brightened the lights." To which we add, in a different vein: He mastered alike the arts of diffusion and of concentration of the age of the fable, and in *Cousine Bette* he gave free rein to his author's privilege of omniscience by providing both post-factum expositions (Chapters VIIff.) and prospective interpretation.

Thus Honoré de Balzac created in the middle of the nineteenth century a narrative form that may be called, in the most comprehensive sense of the term, the novel of disillusionment. The almost scientific principle of laying bare is essential no less to the portrayals of morals than to the stories in the *Etudes philosophiques.* It was Balzac's endeavor to fathom man's ethical demeanor both socially and individually in its ultimate deconfinement, and in doing so he strove to reduce all surface phenomena to the single idealized standard of "decadence." Stendhal's characters were at times forced to wear masks as willed by their creator. Balzac took the reality of a mask for granted and tore it away. In the process, chaotic passions come to light. If Balzac's characters are exceptional characters too, this is so in a totally different sense : In Stendhal they resist their own lack of vigor and their incommensurate ambient as they strive to rise. In Balzac they stumble, in an age of decline, along the road leading to their end. A political event initiates the process of decay; it contaminates the social domain and the realm of ethics. That is the inner coherence of the *Comédie humaine.*

When Balzac's undeniable greatness is referred to, the term rightly refers first of all to the colossal dimensions of the work and of the man behind it. This implies simultaneously the presence of shortcomings, for the kind of mass production which Balzac had to demand of himself throughout thirty years required a spontaneous and often careless composition. This explains the flaws which were at times allowed to adhere to the finished products. In those times, no one but Stendhal was a sufficiently sure-footed stylist to be able to dictate his novels "off the top of his head" in draftless finality. Balzac had to revise and polish. But the flood of novels he produced presupposes that the author possessed an inexhaustible power of imagination. This alone suffices to assure Balzac a unique place in modern world literature. His epic wealth remained unequaled throughout the century from 1850 to 1950. It was approximated, at best, by Emile Zola. "He is the creator of the modern world. For that reason every young author of today must pass through him." These words were written by Blaise Cendrars, voicing the gratitude of many of the authors of the late nineteenth and the twentieth centuries to whom Balzac was a guide and a lodestar.

The first country outside of France to recognize and cele-
brate Balzac was Russia. He visited the Czarist Empire in person
in 1843, 1847, and 1849. Dostoevski's relationship to Balzac—
regardless of the high esteem in which the Russian held
Eugène Sue—is almost comparable to that of Dante to Vergil.
As early as 1838 Dostoevski wrote to his brother that Balzac
was a great man. On the other hand, even Henry James, who
owed the Frenchman a great deal, criticized as one of Balzac's
shortcomings that he had no sense of moral edification. It was
only in 1888 that George Moore lavished high praise on Balzac
in England. Before that, Swinburne had called him the "prose
Shakespeare." In 1899, Brunetière was the first French critic
to class him unreservedly as a writer of the first rank. One of
the earliest German responses came from Goethe who had read
the mystical novel *Peau de chagrin.* In his diary, under date of
October 11, 1831, he called it "an excellent work in the most
modern vein." In a conversation with Soret on February 27,
1832, he was less enthusiastic. Gutzkow, who thought highly
of George Sand as well, considered Balzac a genius, but in
1849 numerous Germans, among them Hebbel, turned against
him. Heinrich Heine knew him personally and held him in
high esteem. In the years from 1840 to 1846, a German translation of Balzac's works appeared in 32 volumes. Karl Marx
planned to write a book on Balzac. He and Engels called him
a writer of dialecticism against his will. Marxist literary criticism, led by Lukács, has derived from this the conclusion that
Balzac must be regarded as a writer of the class struggle.
Dilthey's essay on Balzac of 1875 and Hugo von Hofmanns-
thal's introduction to the Insel Edition (1909) blazed the trail
for a large-scale Balzac revival in Germany. However, Albérès
in his history of the modern novel noted explicitly that the
appreciation of Balzac is often content with a partial aspect,
"for the realist Balzac is after all an esoteric and theosophic
author." Flaubert judged differently. His endeavor was to
supply factual documentation.

Gustave Flaubert (1821–80)—this is the essential point—did
carry the antiromantic program farther. He spoke explicitly of
his objective to "de-Rousseauize" the novel. Born at Rouen as
the son of a physician, Flaubert was decisively influenced by
his medical and scientific environment. During his school years

he already read the works of Rabelais, George Sand, Byron, Goethe (in the translation by Nerval). At the age of sixteen he edited a little periodical and wrote a great deal. As a young man he met Elisa Schlésinger the wife of an army officer in a sea-coast resort. This encounter kept him preoccupied until 1872 and was destined to determine the character of one of his novels. Flaubert went to Paris to study law. In 1843 he suffered a severe nervous crisis and did not pass his examinations. In 1844 he returned to his parents in Croisset (Seine) where most of his works were written. From 1849 to 1851 he traveled in the eastern Mediterranean. In 1858 he undertook a study tour to Tunisia and Carthage (cf. Salammbô, Chapter II). He died on May 8, 1880, in Croisset.

Flaubert created his work in isolation, living virtually the life of a hermit. His contemporaries did not always grant him recognition nor allow his work a commensurately broad effect. Yet, his rigorously maintained pessimism and the masterly polish of his language, resulting literally from a process of re-hearsing, accomplished the emancipation of the French novel from its dependence on the early nineteenth century in more than a merely chronological sense. This achievement must be valued the more highly as Flaubert was by nature inclined to abandon himself to romantic melancholy and Rousseauistic dreaming, as is apparent from his youthful works, *Rêve d'enfer*, *Mémoires d'un fou* (1838), and *Novembre* (1842), which were written under the influence of Goethe, Quinet, and Byron. In his mature years Flaubert achieved complete control and indeed a sort of hypothermia of the hectic style of these early works. In the *Mémoires d'un fou* he was still able to write: "Illusion here too. We are tied to this earth, this icy earth, where all fire dies, where all strength is extinguished. Where are the rungs on which the infinite descends to the firmness of the earth? Where is the ladder on which thought comes down without breaking? How is it possible to vanquish the giant that embraces infinity?"—

This attitude of crisis in the face of the transcendental is further potentiated in *Salammbô* and *La Tentation de Saint-Antoine* into a veritable theomania, a metaphysical nightmare. It is true, however, that the style of these works, in keeping with the subject matter, begins to reflect greater discipline.

Then too, the numerous versions of *La Tentation de Saint-Antoine* (1848 to 1849, 1856, 1869, 1874), a novel inspired by Breughel, indicate how the author advanced from the romantically picturesque, from the visionary and deconfined, to the psychology of realism. For in the end he stresses the psychophysical determination of Anthony's temptation which is shown to be a mental aberration. Thus Balzac's principle of uncovering and showing up has been carried further. *La Tentation de Saint-Antoine* appears ultimately as a critical portrayal of a religious illusion. André Gide noted in his diary on September 19, 1917, that this novel and Flaubert's late work, *Bouvard et Pécuchet*, were linked by the identity of their ultimate essence. Gide did not explain this dictum but it can only be meant to mean that the uncovery of religious delusion corresponds to the uncovery of human stupidity. We may regard Flaubert's work in its totality as a continuation of that of Balzac in terms of disillusionment, that is, in terms of the removal of illusions. A new principle and a new aesthetic procedure appear by the side of what we have called *deconfinement*, without, however, negating it, as will be clearer when we reach Zola.

From 1851 to 1856 Flaubert worked on *Madame Bovary*. In October, the *Revue de Paris* began the preliminary publication of this work in installments. Flaubert assigned himself the bourgeois theme in penance, as it were, for the early version of the Anthony novel. (There was the story of adultery in a family of his circle of acquaintances pointed out to him by two friends in the fall of 1849.) The novelist's double objective was to deromanticize himself and to apply to Emma Bovary's inner life the technique of the reductio ad absurdum.

Emma Bovary is the second wife of the country doctor Charles Bovary whose lack of ambition—coupled with the provincial life she is forced to lead—arouses in her romantic aspirations. She reads novels in keeping with her frame of mind, nursing in secret the longing for a great experience. Her social contacts are enlarged when Charles Bovary re-establishes himself at Yonville l'Abbaye. Especially the free-thinking voluble apothecary Homais and the barrister-candidate Léon Dupuis seek her company. Then she meets the estate owner Rodolphe Boulanger. He seduces the married woman. He rejects her when she insists that he must elope with her. Emma Bovary contracts a grave illness. Her husband nurses her devotedly. After her recovery she again meets Léon Dupuis in Rouen and, after some hesitation, allows herself to become his mistress. From now on she meets him once a week on Thursdays. She tells her husband that she is taking piano lessons in town. When financial maneuvers in which she has gotten herself involved wind up badly, her lovers prove unwilling to come to her rescue and she takes poison. "Emma's head was bent over toward the right shoulder. Her mouth was open giving the appearance of a black hole in the lower part of her face. Her thumbs were bent into the palms of her hands. A sort of white powder appeared sprinkled on her eyelids and her eyes were covered with a colorless glaze resembling a delicate web as though spiders had deposited it."* Charles Bovary does not survive her long. Before his death he does learn that Emma has been deceiving him. To add irony to insult, the apothecary Homais is awarded the Cross of the Legion of Honor.

There can be no doubt: Flaubert wrote this novel against his time. He assigned its central role to a middle-class woman who falls victim to her self-imposed illusions. The term "Bovarysm" has been coined to cover this complex which we define as the tendency "to think of one's self as something one is not." Flaubert described the tragedy in a style of pronounced impersonality. This cannot but impress us the more as his purpose is to portray a romantic figure and the ideological bankruptcy of romanticism.

Structurally there is a clear differentiation of three subject-matter complexes, the marriage, the false step, the downfall. The passage in which Emma Bovary becomes Rodolphe's mistress occupies the center of the novel. We mentioned before that Flaubert stated that he wanted to annoy Duranty with this novel. His hieratic dedication to language—unknown to Stendhal, to Balzac, and also to Zola, and objected to in the name of "realism" by Champfleury and Duranty—is effective on several fronts. He fights a language which "people" use in thoughtless repetition, that is, the commonplaces of a bourgeois style as well as vulgar excesses. Flaubert's style is the product of a conscious endeavor. It is to serve the function of arresting romantic exuberance and dissolution as well as the tendency of the later Hugo to make the language of literature subservient to social tendentiousness. And finally, Flaubert's style gives expression to his despair with the barrenness of his own time. This is in keeping with his frequent use of enumeration and paratactic itemization which in *Salammbô* overwhelms the reader and in *L'Education sentimentale* emphasizes the impression of hopelessness which he takes away. Through this linguistic device, the excellent loses its rank of distinction, as we shall have occasion to show in greater detail. Flaubert's interest is unrelated to Balzac's interest in encyclopedic completeness. Flaubert's inventories serve to reveal instead the greatest possible inner detachment from all things depicted. Flaubert does not pile object on object because he likes objects in cumulation but because they disgust him. This is the sadism of which Sainte-Beuve spoke. Precisely the idea that the object is an object (in the sense of the root of the term) is new in Flaubert's work, but it serves, as an idea, the principle of uncovery and of disillusionment. With verbal devices Flaubert fights the spirit of his age, its usages, and its rigid insistence on things. By the device of naming anew, Flaubert makes apparent the questionable character of what he names. This is an aspect to be traced in the French novel up to our own present. We need but think of how Sartre in *La Nausée* (1938) describes a mass.

In 1869 Flaubert's *L'Education sentimentale* (earliest version, 1843–45) was published. It is a sad tableau of the younger generation from the February Revolution of 1848 on to the year 1867. The principal figures, Frédéric Moreau and Madame Arnoux, show traits of the author and Elisa Schlésinger. It appears, then, that Flaubert's impersonal style did not make it impossible for him to choose a subject matter of autobiographical derivation, but he did not lose himself in self-descriptive indulgence, for it is not only a matter of chronology but also of inner affinity that places Flaubert nearer to Baudelaire and Mallarmé than to Chateaubrand with his exhibitionism in *René*.

In the summer of 1868 Flaubert, in a letter to George Sand, made the following comment on his endeavors as a novelist: "In fact, I do not believe that it is the writer's function to state his opinions on the things of this world. (This is part and parcel of my work and of myself.) So I restrict myself to presenting things as I see them, to expressing what appears to me as the true." Yet, how difficult this often was for him, how much self-discipline it demanded, we may infer from another letter of the same year, likewise addressed to George Sand: "But my ever-lasting novel is at times unbelievably boring to me. I find it difficult to get on with these tiny details."

On a steamer trip from Paris to Nogent-sur-Seine, Frédéric Moreau meets the art dealer Arnoux and his wife. Madame Arnoux fascinates him to an extraordinary degree and for years he goes on wooing her. When he finally achieves his goal, their happiness is short-lived, and Frédéric takes refuge in the arms of Arnoux's mistress, Rosanette. The time is that of the decline of the "Citizen King," Louis Philipe. Frédéric and Rosanette go to Fontainebleau to escape the turmoil of the Revolution. After their return, Moreau has reason to hope for a reconciliation with Madame Arnoux, but Rosanette destroys all this. Finally the Arnoux, now ruined financially as well, leave Paris. Frédéric breaks with his third mistress, the banker's wife, Madame Dambreuse, as he does with Rosanette. Years go by, and then, in March 1867, Madame Arnoux appears at Moreau's home. This leads to a definitive parting of the ways. Frédéric seeks again a closer contact with his school friend Deslauriers. Both are deeply disappointed and disillusioned with their youth which is no more, for they have achieved nothing particularly successful either in political terms or in love.

At first the novel was to bear the characteristic title *Les Ratés*, but this would have implied a value judgment not in keeping with the "impassibility" which may describe through positivistic enumeration but which may not be rash in drawing conclusions. Thibaudet and Hugo Friedrich assign to this work a very high rank both as a picture of the times and also as a work of literary art.[12] This "sentimental schooling" is important if for no other reason than that it presents the disparity between the hero's inner conceptions and the events in the external milieu, between volition and achievement, between actor and stage setting. We have here the same view that appears later as the definition of the absurd in Camus. We may illustrate this specific trait by the following lines: "Frédéric left the establishment and went to Arnoux, borne as it were by a pleasant breeze and with the extraordinary lightness which one experiences in dreams. He soon found himself on the second floor outside a door with a bell which he rang. A servant girl appeared, and a second door opened. Madame Arnoux was seated near the fire. Arnoux jumped up and kissed her. She held on her knees a little boy about three years old. Her daughter, now as tall as she was, was standing at the opposite side of the fireplace."*

What is new in this? The reality which corresponds in terms of aesthetics to Moreau's emotional disillusionment is a "leveled world," created by the author by means of parataxis and enumeration. Frédéric Moreau has just been given Arnoux's new address. "He had expected an outburst of joy." The reception, however, is quite different; it is unexpected, it is disappointing. In the domestic situation which the novelist sketches out, he actually assigns to Madame Arnoux the same level of verbal requirements as to the door, the bell, the servant girl. She simply "is" and she "has." As a figure in the novel she borders on the factual objectivity of things that are devoid of gestures of their own. By contrast, Arnoux and his daughter act and perform. They "jump," "kiss," "stand up" [*faire un bond, embrasser, se tenir debout*]. Frédéric's reaction is a mixture of disappointment and speechless wrath. "He ran off to the Café Anglais, dined there lavishly, and—while eating—said to himself : 'That *was* the place to go with my troubles! She hardly recognized me! What a bourgeois bore!' " (p. 109).

A great many things in Flaubert's world are incommensurate. In a sense they point the way to Kafka. On another occasion, Frédéric is looking for an acquaintance of his. At the café which the latter habitually frequents he is told that the gentleman in question has not as yet been seen that day but that he will surely arrive before long. Frédéric decides to wait and spends four hours waiting. He finally decides to leave. The owner of the café assures him that it is really the first time that M. Ledoux has failed to show up. " 'What? M. Ledoux?'— 'Well, yes, Monsieur!'—'I said Régimbart!' Frédéric exclaimed exasperatedly." (p. 105f.) This marks the début of the principle of misunderstanding in the modern novel. In *Bouvard et Pécuchet* (1872-80; published posthumously in 1881), this element is further accentuated. It is a novel of human stupidity, represented by the two low-echelon clerks who have come into money through an inheritance and decide to pursue higher studies. *Bouvard et Pécuchet* is a grotesque take-off on the pseudo-scientific, optimistic petit bourgeois. The work has come down to us almost exclusively in the form of a collection of slips with jottings gathered together by the author from more than a thousand books.

On only one occasion did Flaubert look at the petite bourgeoisie with more understanding and also with greater sympathy: in the novella *Un Coeur simple* (1877). Félicité, who has spent her life as a servant girl, owns a parrot by name of Lulu which becomes the center and sole purpose of the old spinster's life and of which in the end she makes a fetish in the full sense of the term. To be sure, here, too, Flaubert points up a form of religious aberration, but there is charity in the way he portrays this figure. We do know, it is true, that George Sand urged him insistently to proceed in this manner. In the end, however, there is again Flaubert's pessimism. The description of Felicité's alienation from her bourgeois environment is unmistakably the work of the same author who described the torment of Emma Bovary's death.

Balzac does not make for edifying reading; Flaubert even less so. The disgust and the contempt felt by the author are manifest in what he writes. His characters never reach the height of Stendhal's energetic and criminal individuals. The atmosphere of *La Cousine Bette*—albeit without the monomaniac exaggerations of that work—is the atmosphere of Flaubert's novels. Everywhere illusions crumble, unable to resist the first onslaught. Everywhere emptiness, asthenia, and vanity are revealed. Like Balzac, Flaubert watches a society in agony, but this society has lost the somber luster of the *Comédie humaine*. Flaubert's novels are more sober, more joyless than those of his precursor. Their morbid content contrasts strangely with the artistic perfection of their form.

The novel in the form given it by Flaubert exerted an impact on the European epic that can only be described as an impact of fascination. It did so both through its verbal artistry and by presenting a moral portrait of a bourgeois age that has passed its zenith. Upon reading *Madame Bovary*, Victor Hugo confessed to Flaubert on August 30, 1857: "You are one of the leading spirits of the generation to which you belong, preserving for it and holding up for it the torch of art." After Flaubert's death, *Le Gaulois* wrote on May 9, 1880: "None among the living, unless it be Victor Hugo, has cast upon his century a light of similar brilliance."

Among Flaubert's friends was Turgenev, with whom Russian narrative prose attained European standing. Turgenev lies buried in Bougival near Paris. In Germany Theodor Fontane took up the Bovary theme transposing it, in *Effie Briest* (1895), to a Prussian milieu, while in the Anglo-American realm the admirers and disciples of Flaubert include Henry James, George Moore, Sinclair Lewis, and William Faulkner.

There is one French novelist linked to Flaubert in a disciple-teacher relationship with the more immediate implication that he received instruction from him. This is Guy de Maupassant (1850–93). Maupassant, like Flaubert, came from the north-western part of France. Their families knew of one another. Like Flaubert, Maupassant set out studying law and subsequently held positions in the ministries for naval affairs and for education. This phase of his career lasted about a decade. Flaubert took his literary training firmly in hand. He recommended to him to sit down in a café, to count the cab horses passing by in the street, and to describe the tenth in such a way that it appeared clearly different from the preceding nine. In this way Maupassant's pen acquired elasticity and assurance. In 1880 he gave up his career in the civil service and devoted himself to writing as his main occupation. He took part in Zola's *soirées de Médan* (See Chapter IV).

We may distinguish two phases in Maupassant's work. The first, dominated by the novella and the short novel (that is, by epic forms of Italian origin), encompasses Maupassant's great achievement. The second, beginning about 1883, hardly offers anything new compared to Flaubert and Zola. This is not to imply by any means that Maupassant began by taking over compositional elements from his master Flaubert. His first great success was *Boule de suif* (1880). A postchaise leaves Rouen sometime in 1870 on a trip to the part of France not occupied by the Prussian armies. One of the passengers—the others are business men, nuns, noblemen, and a lone republican —is Little Dumpling, a prostitute known all over town. The chaise is held up by Prussian soldiers and is not to be allowed to go on unless Little Dumpling submits to one of the officers. Her companions, worried about their business affairs, urge the girl not to start just now to be prim. When she gives in so that the journey can continue, they turn up their noses at her, preferring to have nothing further to do with her. After all, she is a prostitute.

The structural symmetry in the story was taken over from *Madame Bovary*. Before the girl has agreed to submit to the officer, the ladies and gentlemen in the postchaise, knowing full well who the plump little person is, see nothing wrong in partaking of the content of her basket of provisions. Later, when all of them—except Boule de suif—have all the food they care for and travel on, no one has a good word for the girl. This short novel is a classic specimen of Maupassant's epic manner. Sex plays an essential role, but so does the irony with which bourgeois hypocrisy is unmasked. The fable with its effective climax dramatizes the point.

La Maison Tellier (1881) was written in the same vein. Here, irony and sarcasm mingle with genuine and naively human emotion. The five inmates of a brothel accompany the woman who runs the establishment on a trip to the country where Constance Rivet, the god-child of the proprietress, celebrates her first communion. Touched by the sobbing girls, whose profession is obviously not known to him, the old priest exclaims: "You are the edification of my parish. Your emotion has warmed their hearts. Without you, this great day would possibly not have been so truly divine in character." Thus great honor comes to the house of the cabinetmaker Rivet who, to be sure, attempts a few hours later—in a state of intoxication after all the celebrating—to assault one of the girls. That night the "ladies" return to Rouen. Outside their place of business the lantern is lit again, and the whole establishment goes on celebrating the beautiful day in a flood of champagne.

Maupassant had a flair for the piquant hardly equaled by any other novelist of the nineteenth century, but as he grew older and as his productivity increased—he wrote some two hundred stories—the portrayal of the laughable and the stupid gave way to a more serious description of the world as a setting for social absurdities and finally as the substratum for the workings of supernatural forces (cf. Chapter III). Maupassant's "bitter sweetness" and his grim humor turn into fear, particularly during the final years of his creative life from 1890 on. *La Maison Tellier* was dedicated to Ivan Turgenev.

One might wish Maupassant had remained the author of tales of the country of Normandy. This half rural, half urban and bourgeois society he knew well, and in describing it he was uniquely successful. In his subsequent works he attempted to gain a foothold in a narrative field of a more critical intellectuality. He strove to establish contact with and to derive inspiration from Russian literature and Zola's program. The six novels which Maupassant wrote range in theme from *Une Vie* (1883) and *Mont-Oriol* (1887), which are local novels playing in the Auvergne and in Normandy, to the analysis of the outsiders' self-awareness and of the jealousy of two unequal brothers in *Pierre et Jean* (1888), *Fort comme la mort* (1889) and *Notre coeur* (1890).

Among these novels, *Bel Ami* (1885) is the most important. The principal character, Georges Duroy, is a mixture of Balzac's Rastignac and Stendhal's will to achieve self-realization and "pursuit of happiness." We meet this handsome man, who—in contrast to let us say, Stendhal's Fabrice del Dongo—is quite insignificant in the dynamics of his inner life, as he walks down Rue Notre-Dame-de-Lorette, with just a few coins in his pocket as befits an ex-soldier discharged from service in the colonies. He winds up on the steps of the Eglise de la Madeleine, looking challengingly at the Palais Bourbon (note the variant of the conclusion of *Père Goriot*), when Baron Du Roy leads the daughter of a banker and publisher away from the nuptial altar. The man makes his way borne in his relentless ascent by his own unscrupulousness and the immorality of society.

The work is clearly a herald of Thomas Mann's *Felix Krull*. But in contrast to Mann, Maupassant does not succeed in imposing upon his frivolous subject matter a form of picaresque charm; he does not succeed in keeping it free from elements of the shilling shocker. The reason is doubtless that his bitterness about the corruptness of his age is too deep. When he describes little prostitutes and undertakes to plead their case, there is a new undertone in his voice, and the sound of it is genuine. His greatness lies in the vignette. When he tries to paint a broad epic canvass or when he attempts to be intellectually profound, it is apparent that he is lacking the power of a Balzac and of a

Zola.[13] Yet he does not deserve the comparative lack of esteem in which he is held, especially in France.

There is another author of novels of society in the late nineteenth century whose work shows restrictions in terms of subject matter and expressive scope similar to those we have noted in Maupassant. Here we are face to face with intrinsic shortcomings of the program of realism as formulated by Champfleury: To write only what one knows because one has seen it with one's own eyes.—Zola too made use of his notebook, but when some tremendous idea for a novel had caught hold of him, he designed for it a world stage. Flaubert too processed autobiographical subjects, yet he wrote no autobiography. But precisely that is what Jules Vallès (1832-85) did. He is the author of a great socialist novel, and this novel is his restless life, a life dedicated to politics, which began in the wretched setting of a family for whom the father eked out a living as a private tutor. He spent his early years in Le Puy-en-Velay, Saint-Etienne, and Nantes. At the conclusion of his school years he went to Paris and gave himself over to politics with passionate dedication. In March, 1852, after the December riots of the previous year, his father took him to a psychiatric sanitarium. Vallès was discharged and returned to Paris. Throughout the Second Empire he worked as a journalist siding so tenaciously with the opposition that Napoleon III finally had him arrested in August, 1870. He was set free under the Republic, and after September 4, he became a member of the Commune in the Fifteenth Arrondissement. After the collapse of the revolt he fled to London and was granted amnesty in 1880. His funeral was the occasion of street riots.[14]

Vallès' trilogy, *Jacques Vingtras* (1879-85)—consisting of *L'Enfant, Le Bachelier,* and *L'Insurgé*—stands under the shadow of the novels of Zola, although the third presents one of the few accounts of the Commune in French literature. *Jacques Vingtras* is a novel of the development of an individual. Thematically it is significant because it marks the beginning of the tradition of depicting life in the French provinces as life in an inferno. The same views were held subsequenly by Jouhandeau and Mauriac and also by Julien Green. By contrast, Vallès depicted the metropolis as a fertile, receptive field of political agitation. The author's biographical presence is apparent in the emotional tenor of the work. This is intentional. Vallès wanted his life and the setting of it to be taken as a representative example, and the novel—however much it rests on a foundation of individually conditioned factors—was pressed into the service of the socialist cause. Flaubert wanted to make the novel of an epoch a work of literary art; Maupassant strove to produce a piquant narrative; Zola's purpose was to present a lesson in determinism. Vallès burdened the novel with political responsibility. "My ambition has always been socialist, never literary," he wrote in 1880 to another journalist. Hugo had introduced into the French novel the theme of the socially underprivileged. Thus French narrative prose began again—before long with considerable interest in the fourth estate, as we shall see from Poulaille or Barbusse—to steer a course in the wake of Dickens. The novel began to show its commitment in terms of ethics and in terms of party politics.

But this line was not followed by the development as a whole. The nineteenth century always nursed a certain distrust of such forms of commitment, of such efforts to make of literature a helpmeet in questions of everyday life. This fact is not only apparent in the lyric poetry of Théophile Gautier. In narrative literature, too, it is manifest, particularly in the prose of fantasy. And so we shall now see that the novel of the nineteenth century flows on into the present in a trifurcate delta: in the novel of individualism; in the novel of multifarious actuality represented by the present-day human society in its dependence on factors of time and space; and in the novel of irreality which conceives of the individual's self as representing an exceptional condition. Many authors—think of Mérimée, Balzac, or Maupassant—belong simultaneously in several camps. This attitude reflects a tacit need to deconfine the here and now, to present it as one aspect, and to supplement and complete it. A viewpoint requires a perspective if all possibilities of conceiving of existence are to be tapped, even though this may still be achieved in various ways both quantitatively and qualitatively. It is thus that the novel in the nineteenth and twentieth centuries really becomes a "universe of poesy" and a "poesy of the universe."

III

STORIES OF FANTASY AND THE FANTASTIC NOVEL

Charles Nodier, Honoré de Balzac, Théophile Gautier, Prosper Mérimée, Petrus Borel, Gérard de Nerval, Lautréamont (Isidore Ducasse), Guy de Maupassant, Auguste Villiers de L'Isle-Adam

℘Toward the end of the eighteenth century German and English influences in France prepared the ground for a fantastic type of narrative prose, clearly distinct from the fable of the age of enlightenment, which had generally been didactic in its motivation and exotic in its settings. Significant precursors of the new development were Xavier de Maistre (1763–1852)[1], who wrote, under the influence of Laurence Sterne, a *Voyage autour de ma chambre* (Lausanne, 1795)—a piece of versatile first-person fiction in which the narrator, confined to his room, gives free rein to his fantasies—and Ducray-Duminil (1761-1819), who wrote, after the model of the English novels of horror coming in the wake of Horace Walpole's *Castle of Otranto*, twenty-three novels which were not particularly significant as literature but which preserved for the nineteenth century fantastic themes mediating for the novel a close contact with the realm of the miraculous. The rebirth of irrationalism in French literature as an expression of antiphilosophical tenets[2] was promoted significantly by Jacques Cazotte (1719–92) with *Le Diable amoureux* (1772). In the hero Don Alvaro, Cazotte meant to portray a latter-day Faust who withdraws to the ruins of Portici because he is tired of, and disgusted with, all things palpably empirical. There he conjures up the devil who appears to him first in the shape of a camel and then as the girl Biondetta. The two stay together for some time, but when the officer Don Alvaro insists on marrying his companion, she changes back into the devil and demands that he worship her. Alvaro does manage to tear himself away, but only his marriage to a virtuous girl can rub out the impression of his involvement with "the devil in love."

In the nineteenth century the course followed in France by the fantastic novel was set above all by the German T. A. Hoffmann and the American Edgar Allen Poe. Around 1830 and 1850, these writers became known to a wide public. Their influence, however, would have been a mere flash in the pan, had there not been a true demand and a true need for the fantastic. The prevailing mood resulted, in particular, from the political disappointment of many writers in the thirties. Fantasy became for them an escape, an *évasion*, a stronghold of refuge. Next to the prevailing aversion against the omnipotent bourgeois plutocracy and its materialistic principles, there also evolved an attitude of skepticism against the so-called exact sciences that were rooted in the Cartesian philosophy. Nodier and, half a century later, Villers de l'Isle-Adam were at one in this aversion. To be sure, in the course of the century the fantastic as an epic genre underwent considerable changes.

The picturesque receded while the philosophical pessimism and "black humor" [*humour noir*] came to the fore. There also appeared an increasingly strong preoccupation with psychology and psychological analysis intent upon fathoming ever more thoroughly the evident restiveness of man. In this way the fantastic became an essential factor in the process of deconfinement. With reference to the reception of Hoffmann in France, Nodier exclaimed: "Break these shameful chains, break the chains of the intellectual world." The best-informed student of this genre, Pierre-George Castex,[3] Professor at the Sorbonne, distinguishes three modes of the fantastic narrative. Either, mysterious events are presented by the devices of an objective technique and are explained in the end, surprisingly, through natural connections. Here we may mention, by way of example, Horace Raisson's *L'Elixir de jeunesse* (1833) and Aloysius Block's *Le Spectre* (*Revue de Paris*, August, 1831). Or the mysterious may arise from a particular state of consciousness of the hero, such as dreaming, intoxication, or somnambulism, and it vanishes as that state is resolved. This form was developed by Nodier, Borel, and Nerval as well as by Théophile Gautier in *La Cafetière* (1831), Eugène Sue in *Atar Gull* (1831), and Abel Hugo in *L'Heure de la mort* (1833). A third possibility is that the mysterious is presented as a matter of truth and that it is kept intact. This last approach was the lesson taught in particular by E. T. A. Hoffmann. Here a prerequisite sine qua non is ultimate artistic power if the reader is not to lose faith with the fiction.

Charles Nodier (1780-1844) tried, as Tieck did in Germany, to wrest from the miraculous the ultimate it can yield.[4] After Madame de Staël and before Gérard de Nerval, Nodier was the most important mediator between things German and the literature of his country. Two experiences of his early years largely determined the course of his creative life. In Besançon, where he grew up, he saw executions during the revolution, and he discovered Goethe's *Werther* which reinforced his propensities for a double inner life already encouraged by the impact on him of Senancour's novels. Finally Nodier found that he had to derive his greatest inspiration from the dreaming portion of his inner existence. The dream, to him, became the gateway to things eternal, things essential; it became the orphic idea which Nodier was to pass on to Nerval.

As early as 1800 Nodier drew poetic impulses from madness (*Moi-même*). In *L'Heure ou la vision* (1806), he used the term madman with reference to the hero who stays in touch with the woman he loved after her death. With the anti-philosophers of the late eighteenth century he shared a strong dislike of the so-called exact sciences which impressed him as manifestations of vacuous progress. In this frame of mind, which he himself felt to be a provocation and not in keeping with the age, he created the heroes of his novels, novellae, and stories—world-withdrawn and idyllic beings who cannot survive the destruction of the paradise of their childhood.

As a seer and prophet, Nodier had to endure nightmarish visions—as he described them in *Smarra ou les démons de la nuit* (1821) or, in a somewhat attenuated form, in the Scottish tale *Trilby* (1822)—until he found salvation in the dream, in novellae such as *Séraphine* or the fairy stories of *Fée aux miettes* (1832). In *Lydie* and *Neuvaine de la Chandeleur,* late products of his fantastic muse, dreams are intermingled with religious elements. The horrors of the nightmare have lost their sting.

In 1823 and 1824 Balzac was introduced to a circle of Martinists where he came to know the tenets of illuminism. This appears reflected in several passages of the *Etudes philosophiques* whose connection with the *Comédie humaine* has previously been discussed. The central motif in *L'Elixir de longue vie* is Satan's help in the conquest of the world. In *La Peau de chagrin,* elements of irrealism play an essential part.[5]

As was done later on by Baudelaire, Rimbaud, Cocteau, Antonin Artaud, and Henri Michaux, Théophile Gautier tried to gain access to an artificial paradise by means of drugs. He was not a visionary like Balzac. *La Pipe d'opium* and *Le Club des haschischins* shows how dreams are an extrapolation and a processing product of the events of the day. Gautier supplied excellent material for Sigmund Freud's theory of the interpretation of dreams.

Prosper Mérimée translated Turgenev, Gogol, and Pushkin into French. This one senses in reading the fantastic story *Lokis* (1868). As early as 1837, however, in *La Vénus d'Ille,* Mérimée proved himself a master of the fantastic. The morning of his wedding day, the son of a Catalan archeologist thoughtlessly puts the ring meant for his wife on the finger of a statue of Venus unearthed by his father. Subsequently the statue refuses to surrender the ring. The wedding takes place without the ring, but the following morning the young man is found in bed choked to death. A highly suspicious and suspected Aragonese must be released by the police for lack of evidence.

Mérimée's skill in depicting the fantastic exceeds perhaps that of any other Frenchman. His refined art of allusion which induces us to read between the lines appears replaced by black humor, frenzy, and moral provocation in Petrus Borel (1809-59), who came from an impoverished Lyonnaise family and spent many years in Algeria as a civil servant.[6] The very title, *Contes immoraux* (1833), is provocative. His Potiphar novel (1839) is a picaresque travesty utilizing all the devices of the English novel of horrors.

Gérard de Nerval (1808–55), who was known to historians of

literature in Gustave Lanson's days exclusively as the trans-
lator of German works, has been rehabilitated to a remarkable
degree in the course of the last fifty years.[7] The center of gravity
of his creative work is to be seen in his lyric poetry which places
him somewhere in the neighborhood of Baudelaire and
Mallarmé.

In general Nerval's work reflects the impact of several important facts. We note among these that throughout his life
he suffered from a spiritualist concept of love which he never
succeeded in translating felicitously into reality. He had also
discovered in German romanticism the power of the dream
which offered to him an existential surrogate of escape and
evasion. Finally, a congenial power of empathy enabled him
to fathom Oriental ideologies. In 1843, he undertook a journey
to the Far East. In the end, he evolved from Oriental elements
his personal religious syncretism which, however, was to make
him fall victim to theomaniac hallucinations. The things of this
world and visions of the beyond were fused in delusions further
promoted by Nerval's incipient mental illness. As his work progressed, so did his experiences of fear in the face of the transcendental which appeared ubiquitous and unpredictable. That
is what we mean by theomania. The Oriental tale, *L'Histoire du calife Hakem* (1847), presents exemplarily the religious
biography of the founder of a creed in the eleventh century.
The work demonstrates by means of the doubleganger motif
(derived from E. T. A. Hoffmann) the importance of drugs.
For drugs make possible anamnesis, reincarnation, and a double
existence. They open wide and wider still the gates of perception giving access to the reflection of the divine. The mentally
ill—Nodier applies to them the term of *lunatiques,* Nerval that
of *illuminés*—are praised as more than human, for their mental
deformation makes them inordinately receptive to the super-
sensual. This, to be sure, augments the risk they are running.
When Hakem becomes aware of the doublegangerdom effected
by a drug, he feels that death is near. Thus Nerval's narrative
work is of a piece with the central themes of his lyrics in verse
and prose. All he created was the expression of a spiritual and
intellectual crisis which to him became the more painful as he
kept hoping in all seriousness "to force his way through the
gates of ivory that separate us from the invisible world." The

eternal feminine, the drug, and metaphysics were to him three suitable forces, but they all deceived him. At the beginning of his creative career Nerval's lodestar was Goethe's ideal of womanhood; at the end he was dominated by the pessimistic view of Heinrich Heine as manifested in the myth of Pandora.

In the wake of Nerval's theomania, Lautréamont (1846–70) must be mentioned. His civil name was Isidore Ducasse. He had come, totally without connections, from Montevideo to France while still of school age. Under the impression of Byron, Baudelaire, the Apocalypse, and the biologist Lamarck, he became the creator of a work, the *Chants de Maldoror* (1869), in which gruesome metamorphoses[8] are to carry out a satanic cosmogony. The form of the work is predominantly that of lyric prose. The sixth canto may be considered a fragment of a novel of horrors. Lautréamont represents an extreme, especially in terms of content. As a contemporary of the Goncourts and of Zola he tears down the last taboos which the novel of realism had still respected. Deconfinement turns a somersault and what it displays is deconfinement itself. Lautréamont turns out to be the most radical of the romantics.

In comparison, Maupassant and Auguste Villiers de l'Isle-Adam (1840– 89) are more subdued in their epic mode. Lautréamont's was one of frenzy. Maupassant and Villiers were pessimists. Maupassant, who toward the end of his life passed through experiences not unlike Nerval's and who, after 1891, fell victim to insanity, imbedded his growing states of fright in the spook story *La Horla* (1887) and the totally nihilistic churchyard story *La Mort* (1887). Here the dead arise from their graves, scratch out the eulogies on their tombstones, and replace them by scornful confessions. Thus Maupassant modified the famous conversations of the dead by Lucian, Fontenelle, Fénelon, and Parini in the spirit of his personal situation.

Auguste Villiers de l'Isle-Adam, scion of one of the oldest families of France, published in 1883 under the provocative title of *Contes cruels*, short prose compositions dealing with the problems of the closing decades of the nineteenth century, in particular the moral decline, the political unreliability of the masses, the hubris of the positivistic sciences in the wake of Auguste Comte. In *L'Eve future* (1886) he heralded in a sense Aldous Huxley's *Brave New World*. He utilized for the purpose the Pygmalion motif. A scientist, bearing the pregnant name of Edison, hopes to manufacture with the help of electricity an artificial woman, the Eve of the future. His friend, Lord Ewald, falls in love with the robot and takes it along as a present on his journey back to England. During the crossing, however, fire breaks out on board ship and destroys the work. To be sure, nature and things natural prevail once again in the end, but the hubris-embued possibilities of technology are exposed at this early date—on the level of literature—to a penetrating light of warning. The *Nouveaux contes cruels* (1888) may be taken as a summation of Villiers' themes. *Les Amies de pension* depicts the vanity of women of loose morals. *Sylvabel* anticipates the "murder for free" in Gide's novel *Les Caves du Vatican*. In *L'Enjeu,* theomania and indifference of faith are presented as characteristic traits of an era of cultural decline. *Soeur Natalia* provides the Mary Magdalen theme with a mysterious convent setting. In *L'Amour du naturel,* the novelist presents a travesty of Longus's *Daphnis and Chloe*. Finally, *L'Elu des rêves* (1893) summarizes in a short novel, built around the idea of the transfer of thought, the author's protest against positivism. Villiers de l'Isle-Adam carried this spiritualism in *Axel* (1890), a play dealing with the subject of Faustus, to an extraordinary height.[9]

It may be said that the fantastic is firmly rooted in French literature, especially as an outlet for the annoyance caused by the claims of the sciences and the rule of bourgeois mediocrity. Throughout the entire nineteenth century, the novel releases energies—even in authors with the recognized claim to being realists—which give the miraculous considerable leeway. Often the delight with the fabulous turns into a pessimistic confession or into an accusation. The novel of the twentieth century, which forms with that of the nineteenth an organic continuity, develops the genre further. Through the mediation of Alfred Jarry it takes it in the direction of the surrealist novel. The episodes of wild pursuit of the novel of horrors are raised in the detective stories of Georges Simenon to an estimable literary level.

IV

THE NATURALISM OF JULES AND EDMOND DE GONCOURT AND OF ÉMILE ZOLA

❧ Naturalism raises two basic questions: What actually distinguished it from realism, and in how far do the Goncourts and Zola belong together?

The naturalist—let us not forget that the term can also stand for the student of the sciences of nature—conceives of the literary assignment as a semiscientific task, the way neither Maupassant nor Vallès ever conceived of it, though Flaubert possibly came closest to it. This premise changes the philosophical substrate, it changes the content and the appearance of the novelist's product. For naturalism follows philosophically the anti-metaphysical positivism of Auguste Comte (1798–1857) as formulated by this author from 1830 to 1842 in the six volumes of his *Cours de philosophie*. According to this approach man is content with tracing through observation and experimentation connections between the phenomena in his purview and with then proceeding to call laws whatever connections appear to recur consistently.

In keeping with this, Zola set up for each of his novels extensive card files, and Edmond de Goncourt prepared for his novel of puberty, *Chérie* (1884), a sort of Kinsey report. But Comte's disciple Hippolyte Taine (1828–93) provided a supplement approaching Darwinism. According to Taine, man must be understood in his dependence on heredity, milieu, and historical situation. The Goncourts as well as Zola accepted this concept. By way of conclusion to our first chapter we noted already that in those days Gobineau in particular thought and wrote in a different vein. To be sure, the novels of the Goncourts and of Zola evolve on different sociological levels. Zola's world is on the whole the fourth estate while the naturalism of the Goncourts concerns itself rather with the middle classes.[1] The underlying philosophy is reflected in a keener perception of details, taking in also the commonplace, the vulgar, and the things that had previously been taboo. Especially the taboo of things erotic gets removed. The language of the novel of naturalism strove to be documentary. It is enriched by technical terms, colloquialisms, and argot. Starting with Balzac, the style of the novel of factual objectivity was additionally deconfined in an encyclopedistic sense.

Due to the internationalization of literature, naturalism did not, of course, remain restricted to France, even though it is the merit of the French to have provided the initial impetus and, in particular, to have perfected the corresponding elements of the narrative form. Zola's manifesto, *Le Roman naturaliste* (1880), was followed in Germany within two years by the *Kritische Waffengänge* of the brothers Hart. In 1886, *Die Revolution der Literatur* by Karl Bleibtreu was published, and in 1891 Arno Holz' *Die Kunst, ihr Wesen und ihre Gesetze*. During the same period, the Scandinavian countries witnessed the genesis of the naturalist drama of Ibsen with its feed-back impact on the Germans Gerhart Hauptmann, Johannes Schlaf, and Arno Holz.[2]

As for French naturalism, it seems almost possible to assign to it an absolute date of birth. This is 1865, the year of the publication of *Germinie Lacerteux*, a novel which in a sense determined the course pursued by Zola's career.

Edmond and Jules de Goncourt (1822–96 and 1830–70), highly cultured sons of a high-ranking army officer, were engaged in a fraternal writing partnership which exceeded, in essence and in substance, the consanguineous harmony of the brothers Hauptmann, Mann, and Jünger. From 1860, the year of the publication of *Charles Demailly*, to the time when the younger brother died, the Goncourts wrote their great novels as common ventures. They spoke of themselves as "a single self." They were not, however, intellectual Siamese twins. Jules reached maturity faster than his brother and appears to have been more sensitive and more inspired, while Edmond turned out to be the more industrious writer. At first their interest concentrated on the eighteenth century. They wrote an *Histoire de la société pendant la Révolution,* then *Portraits intimes du 18ᵉ siècle,* and *L'Art du 18ᵉ siècle,* and also a book on the mistresses of Louis XV. They began as historians, and this is what they remained—with increasing pathological interest—also in their narrative work. The high esteem in which they held the eighteenth century led them—in contrast to Zola—to ascribe in their narrative work the greatest importance to matters of style. In their output, materialistic precision and stylistic refinement, verging on preciosity, are not at all incompatible.

With *Renée Mauperin* (1864) the name of the Goncourts achieved standing in world literature. Thomas Mann read the novel in the Reclam translation and confessed that he conceived *Die Buddenbrooks* under the impression of this upper-middle class catastrophy. A great many things in this novel are new. The very beginning is new. Renée goes bathing in the Seine with an acquaintance of hers. In the following portrayal of social mores there is something reminiscent of Choderlos de Laclos. Plans for a wedding come to be the occasion for the revelation of hidden and forbidden love relations. Renée—not unlike Madame de Merteuil in *Les Liaisons dangereuses*—instigates all sorts of conflicts until her brother Henri—the Valmont of this novel—loses his life in a duel. Renée collapses. At this point the authors abandon all literary conventions. Renée's illness up to the time of her death is described in clinical detail. —Decline and decay are recast—in the spirit of positivism—as neurological problems. In the process it becomes evident what attention the Goncourts pay to the sick. This is a point Thomas Mann learned from them. Their pathological interest differentiates the Goncourts, in terms of their basic attitudes, from the more sensualist Southerner, Zola.

Between 1864 and 1866 *Manette Salomon* was written. This is an artists' novel, with Gautier's *Mademoiselle de Maupin* as a model. As we look more closely, we recognize, to be sure, that

Manette Salomon is not so much an artists' novel in the strict sense—that of being preoccupied with depicting a creative process—but rather a meticulously documented description of the painting Bohème around the turn of the century, surpassing in its unforgettable power of impact even Murger's *Scènes*. There was no need for the Goncourts slavishly to copy Gautier in their finely wrought and polished interiors, for the literary cabinet piece was one of their own strong points. Successful highlights are the description of paintings in Chapter 48, a description of the beautiful Jewess Manette as a painter's model in Chapter 50, and the description of a studio party in Chapter 68. The novel takes a dramatic turn when Manette becomes pregnant by the painter Coriolis. The physiological processes involved in the pregnancy bring about a psychological change. Manette turns into a veritable fury (Chapters 108f.). Coriolis's friends prefer to stay away from his house which Manette fills with her own relatives. She becomes greedy; an animal mother instinct arises in her, and she forces Coriolis to give up pure art in favor of a more remunerative practical application of it. What began as a love relationship winds up as a racial conflict[3] with everything at stake. Each of the partners is insolubly committed, and a true reconcilliation is out of the question.

In 1865, *Germinie Lacerteux* was published, a novel—in Zola's words—"that cuts to the quick" [*navrant*]. Again a pregnancy is the physiological factor triggering the psychological catastrophy. This is coupled with social elements. The servant girl Germinie Lacerteux, who carefully conceals from her employers the double life she is leading, meets the son of Madame Jupillon who supplies the milk for the family. This proves her undoing, for the ruthless young man destroys her both morally and socially. Germinie sinks lower and lower, and in the depth of her misery she becomes hysterical. The description of this hysteria, which the authors based on medical documentation, occupies a broad space. In their preface, the Goncourts emphasize the genuineness of their theme. They insist that it is not a literary invention but that it is taken from life.

Germinie Lacerteux came to be important for Flaubert as a model and precurser of his *Un Coeur simple* (1877), but the fetishistic accretions shown by Flaubert on the nuclear theme of the parrot of the old spinster are vastly more spiritualistic than the medical dissection of Germinie's psycho-physiological determinism carried out by the Goncourts. With this novel Edmond and Jules de Goncourt handed Emile Zola a theme which he could henceforth consider uncontestedly as his special domain, the portrayal of the fourth estate and the proletariat.

In *Madame Gervaisais* (1869), however, the Goncourts again moved up a rung or two on the social ladder. This novel is the clinical history of a religiously exalted woman undertaking a pilgrimage to Rome. *La Fille Elisa* (1877), the earliest novel of a prostitute of literary standing to have been published in France, was written by Edmond de Goncourt alone. Francis Carco admitted subsequently that this work had shown him the way for his stories of Montmartre. The device of the flashback was used with skill in this novel. The action begins with Elisa being found guilty of murder. At this point she remembers her childhood, remembers how—as a simple peasant girl—she landed in a brothel and made there the fateful acquaintance of a soldier. This leads to a description of the discovery of the soldier's murder. Now the report shifts back to the present. Elisa's sentence is commuted to a term in prison. She begins serving her term and only now does she remember the exact details of the murder which she committed from the depth of her prostitute's hate of men. Finally she dies in prison in a state of mental incompetence. In the conclusion the author—as though citing supporting evidence—reports that he was present when Elisa died.

Here then we have the basic elements in the novels of the Goncourts. Sex—affecting in like measure the body and mind and spirit—is the great mainspring in man's behavior. Sex, pregnancy, and monomania are likewise closely interrelated. However, the exclusion of things physically erotic does not imply a turn for the better. The sick women Renée Mauperin and Madame Gervaisais perish of their fixed ideas. It was Balzac's merit to have introduced this motif in the novel. But Balzac, as subsequently Zola, depicted society in a state of agony, while the Goncourts were concerned with tracing the abnormal in individual cases.[4] Where Balzac and Zola sketched out comprehensive surveys, the Goncourts produced cabinet pieces. As Ricatte put it, "Their novels are, in a sense, a peep show." (op. cit., p. 461).

It is characteristic that the Goncourts listed Rabelais, La Bruyère, Diderot, and Saint-Simon as their favorite writers (Journal, May 21, 1862). They thought of them primarily as moralists. Yet the anti-taboo attitude of the Goncourts was kept within bounds by their aesthetic ideal. To be sure, Jules de Goncourt, in a letter to Zola of February 27, 1865, praised his own works as "morbid" and went on to state that "they partake of the passion and of the grace of the sick." Still, the description of a surgical intervention in *Germinie Lacerteux* struck the brothers as too daring. They concluded that the scene was "too true" and did not release it for publication (cf. Journal, October 23, 1864). Of course, this position cannot in any way lower their literary standing. They were at all times critical of the theories of Taine and Claude Bernard as to the respective roles of environment and heredity (cf. Journal, January 15, 1866) and relied generally on the shock produced by things seen and reported in their style of documentation. On January 14, 1861, they noted prophetically in their diary: "An outstanding trait of our novels will be seen in the fact that they are the historically most veracious novels of this age supplying the greatest number of true facts and real truths to the history of morals of his century."*

The relationship of the work of Emile Zola to that of the brothers Goncourt has previously been discussed. In addition, however, an introductory comparison of Zola with Balzac's *Comédie humaine* appears to be called for. Balzac created the French "cyclical novel," and Zola imitated it in a congenial spirit. Balzac, however, who was a partisan of the Bourbons, began his work shortly before the revolution of 1830, which put the citizen king Louis Philippe on the throne. The *Comédie humaine* was written against the bourgeois world from 1830 to 1848 and is—politically—reactionary. Zola began his novel *Les Rougon-Macquart* during the Second Empire of Napoleon III. The work encompasses in its action the two decades of the Second Empire. The completion of the cycle and the fall of Napoleon coincided to Zola's own surprise. "The catastrophy came," observed Heinrich Mann in this connection, "as though by aesthetic necessity."

While differing in political orientation, Balzac and Zola both wrote against their respective historical and social presents. In both we have portrayals of a downfall, with the difference that Balzac put the catastrophy, in the form of the French Revolution, at the beginning, while Zola put the collapse, in the form of the War of 1870/71, at the end. As we consider Zola, we are struck—in retrospect and by contrast—by the fact that the novels from Chateaubriand to Stendhal could well be grasped as works of literature without specific references to their historical etiology, for it is not rare at all that these authors wrote in total disregard of historical realities or indeed took refuge from them in unpolitical absorption. Even Flaubert placed his formative endeavor above the obligation to provide documentation characteristic of the age. It was really only with Zola that all this underwent a fundamental change.

Emile Zola was born on April 2, 1840, in Paris. He spent his childhood, however, in Aix-en-Provence where he became acquainted with the painter Paul Cézanne. On his father's side, Zola's ancestors were Dalmatian officers in the service of the Venetian republic. His father, François Zola, who came to France only in 1833, was known in his time as a construction engineer and geometer. Emile's mother was French and came from a family of the petite bourgeoisie. Emile's childhood was not happy. His father had died early. In 1857, after settling down in Paris, he came to know poverty by direct contact. Though interested in journalism, he found employment in the shipping department of the publishing firm of Hachette. In this setting he became familiar with contemporary French literature.

He tried his hand—in a highly romantic fashion—at the literature of social outcasts, coming up with the novel of prostitution, *La Confession de Claude* (1865), but the experience of reading *Germinie Lacerteux* that same year decided his allegiance to naturalism of which the first evidence in his work is *Thérèse Raquin* of 1867. The very motto of this novel identified Zola as a disciple of Taine. "Virtue and vice," he wrote challengingly, "are products as are vitriol and sugar."

At this time Zola read Claude Bernard's *Introduction à l'étude de la médecine expérimentale*, which may well be called a medical manifesto by virtue of the fact that it stressed the experimental basis of medicine and the decisive significance of physiology in all vital functions. Thus Zola came to decide to create an "experimental novel." He formulated, as a binding principle for himself, that nature had to be represented as it is manifest in a particular temperament. Things physiological and things psychological dovetail and must be described correspondingly. The writer must not judge the reactions of his characters by his own, as had been done in the novels of individualism by Stendhal and Gobineau. We note the increasing trend of objectivization. The novelist can recognize no taboo. He presents pure truth. But what is truth to the naturalist? To Zola this was, to a large extent, a social question; truth was heredity and the structural constitution to which France had been led by the Second Empire. It was only consistent, then, that Zola's work, especially with its last installments, moved progressively closer to socialism and communism. This was a development which differentiated Zola's endeavor from the totally unpolitical orientation of the Goncourts. As Hugo had done in *Les Misérables*, Zola sided militantly with the socially underprivileged.

This multi-layered structure determines Zola's main work, *Les Rougon-Macquart*, which was begun in 1869 and concluded in 1893. The war years of 1870/71 Zola spent in Marseille. In 1888 he built for himself, in the residential suburban town of Médan near Paris, a country home where he gathered around himself a circle of writers, including Maupassant and Huysmans. His marriage remained without children. His daughter Denise, to whom we owe a mass of valuable material about Zola, was the fruit of his liaison with Jeanne Rozerot.

In a preface (written in 1871) to the *Rougon-Macquart*, Zola gave expression to his inner obligation to the ideas of Auguste Comte, Hippolyte Taine, and Claude Bernard in the characteristic formulation: "Heredity has its laws. . . . It shall be my endeavor to resolve the double question of temperament and environment and thereby to find and trace the thread linking one human being with another as a matter of mathematical necessity."* What interests the author in the characters of his novels is "the slow succession of accidental events in the nervous system and in the blood which become manifest in a race . . . and which, in the individuals of that race—in dependence on the environment—manifest in turn the feelings, desires, passions, all the expressions of humanity, natural and instinctive expressions, whose effects are given the conventional names of virtues and vices."* In the vicissitudes of the families of Rougon and Macquart, which share an ancestress, the author undertook to show what multiple modifications the substance of heredity can undergo.

From 1768 to 1773, Adelaide Rougon lived at Plassans in Southern France. Her legitimate children formed the—initially—successful Rougon line, while the children borne out of wedlock followed at first in the footsteps of their progenitor. Macquart was a drinker and a smuggler. This schema seems overly simplified and may remind us of the Old-Testament problem of Abraham's unequal children from a free woman and from a handmaid. Zola needed this double genealogy, for the resulting ramification enabled him to encompass all of France.

Through Volume III of the whole work, the two blood lines run on parallel. Then, in Volume IV, the author experiments with a crossover and is able to show how far opposite environmental influences have already carried the mutual alienation. In *La Conquête de Plassans* (1874), the genetic heritage of the Rougons is fused with that of the Macquarts in the marriage of François Mouret with Marthe Rougon. The marriage follows a normal course until the influence of the priest Faujas awakens again the inner contradiction of the blood. Faujas "conquers" the family by destroying its harmony. Marthe dies in religious delusion while François, in a fit of raving madness, sets fire to his house and perishes in it. Marthe's son Sergius takes the cloth (*La Faute de l'abbé Mouret*, 1875). In him the inherited morbidity of his mother is expressed in pantheistic nature revelries until he violates his vow of celibacy.

After the coup d'état of 1851, Eugène—of the Rougons—gets the coveted seat in the cabinet of ministers (*Son Excellence Eugène Rougon*, 1881), while a branch of the Macquarts pursues, in the Parisian booze-joint atmosphere of *L'Assommoir* (1877), its decline into the social and moral gutter. It is in this world that Nana is born whose life of a prostitute fills the entire ninth volume of the cycle (1880). The theme of sexual degeneracy is further pursued by Zola in the next volume, *Pot-bouille* (1882). In *Germinal*, the geographic coverage of the *Rougon-Macquart* is extended farther north. In this miners' novel of social criticism—the subject matter of which was supplied by a revolt in the Loire district in 1869—Zola combines precise technical knowledge with socialist visions of a better future. The thematic spectrum of Balzac has been enriched by still another element.

The setting of *La Terre* (1887) is likewise outside of Paris. This is a novel of peasants in the Beauce, the crassness and brutality of which exceed by far the corresponding works of George Sand. The concluding volumes are *La Débâcle* (1892) and *Le Docteur Pascal* (1893). Here the Franco-Prussian war of 1870/71 has begun in which the Second Empire goes up in flames. While the last scion of the Macquart line, Jean, is discharged as it were as a healthy peasant, the once brilliant but decadent Rougon line goes out in mental derangement and hemophilia. Only Clothilde, a niece of the minister Eugène Rougon, carries a child whose father is the very Doctor Pascal to whom the happenings in the family had represented for a decade the source material for characterological and physiological studies. The fact that the peasant and the scientist represent the only surviving lines reflects Zola's revolutionary faith in the soil as well as his positivistic creed.[5]

The grandiose epic sweep of this family novel contrasts with the much more pronounced tendentiousness of the later trilogy *Les Trois villes* (1894–98), in which a renegade priest, with stops as it were at Rome, Lourdes, and Paris, takes the road to socialism to act as an apostle of the new positivistic-humanitarian generation, and of the tetralogy *Les Quatre évangiles* (1899–1903). In fertility, in work, in truth, and in justice, Zola sees the principles of organization of a mature and progressive world which dispenses with transcendentalism, myths, and all forms of social hierarchy in arranging its life on utilitarian lines.

By its very conception the *roman-fleuve* of the *Rougon-Macquart* had to turn out to be a work of crass brutality, if we may use that term for the present to characterize the extreme multiplicity of settings, of human emotions, and of geographical locales. We can assert today that it was lucky that the theory of the "experimental novel" and its creative exemplification in this novel of society diverged so radically that, despite Zola's strenuous attempts, the documentation of principles of science remained an aspect of secondary interest. Many of the twenty

novels in the work as a whole turned out—involuntarily perhaps—to be well-rounded works of art of epic prose.

The third volume, *Le Ventre de Paris* (1873), is a case in
point. Its central theme is the struggle of the "lean" against the
"fat," the lucky at the trough of the Second Empire against the
politically disenfranchised. Among these latter is the republican
intellectual Florent, who returns illegally from the penal colony
on the island of Cayenne near Guiana to Paris. Florent's entry
into Paris at dawn on the cart of a produce dealer and the confrontation of this emaciated member of the intelligentsia with
the full belly of Paris, the market halls, shows how Zola was
able to transcend his physiological-naturalistic program, achieving a lyrical symphony of things through a powerful poetiza-
tion of the abundant world of fact, with metaphors—which,
strictly speaking, are incompatible with the naturalist's endeavor to report—contributing essentially to this animation and
vivification of the world of the halls : "There was seafood, there
was butter, there was fowl, there was meat. The pealing of
bells passed, followed in echoing tremor by the rumbling noise
of the market being readied. Around him the sun set the produce aglow. He no longer recognized the delicate water color
of the pallor of dawn. The open lettuce hearts were burning.
The scale of greens burst out in superb vigor, the carrots bled,
the turnips were incandescent in this triumphal brazier. (. . .)
The sea continued to rise. He had felt it about his ankles, then
throughout his belly; it threatened now to rise above his head.
Blinded, drowning, his ears buzzing, his stomach crushed by
all he had seen, sensing new and ceaseless depths of food, he
begged for mercy, and a mad pain seized hold of him lest he
die of hunger in this gorged Paris, in the flaming awakening
of the halls."*

The halls and the market world, embodied in particular in
Florent's sister-in-law, the butcher's wife Lisa, turn in Florent's
eyes into a monster which he must tame. When he is accidentally offered the post of a supervisor, he accepts it. His suffering
and his leanness now acquire a meaning : Florent will take
revenge on the belly of Paris and on the city which put on fat
while he was starving. In his mind he "sets himself up as the
judge; he dreams of arising in the very market halls to smash
this rule of gluttony in food and drink." But the measures he

introduces in the halls lead to a mutiny of the yelping market women against him, and his sister-in-law Lisa finishes him off when she discovers (and reports) his renewed republican machinations. Thus Zola kept up to the very end his pseudo-sociology in terms of the contrast of fat and lean. Since the procedure lacks all scientific backing but needs some authority in support of such farfetched ideas, Zola takes the contrast back to Cain and Abel. "Cain was fat, Abel lean." (Pléiade Edition, p. 805).

What lends the novel significance is certainly not the division of mankind into types but rather the colorful portrayal of the market-hall neighborhood which turns into a reveling symphony of things physical. *Le Ventre de Paris* is the attempt of a pseudo-sociologist to present a thesis in the form of a novel. As such, it is a failure. But it is also the successful project of a sensualist possessed of the gift of bringing together in synesthetic grandeur sober products of the economy and food items in an orgy of all the senses. You may, if you wish, call naturalistic—as defined in the program—Zola's painstakingly detailed observation. Yet, Zola rises above the manner of examination of the natural scientist thanks to his power of aesthetic creation, reflected in the endeavor to reduce the multiplicity of impressions to a structural harmony. This latter aspect of Zola's has been least appreciated and has exerted the least influence. For Barbusse, for Poulaille, for Dos Passos, for Upton Sinclair, for Moravia, Zola is the novelist of the proletariat and of a socialist world reform, while the verdict of other writers in his wake—d'Annunzio, Verga, or Luigi Capuana—has been more critical, as also that of the Spaniards Clarín, Pérez Galdós, or Blasco Ibañez, because they reject his would-be scientific determinism. The two-family theme of Zola's work has been taken up in our time by Maurice Druon in *Les Grandes familles* (1948), while *La Loi* (1957) by Roger Vailland surprisingly emulates Zola as a poet of nature. The long list of these names and the multiplicity of planes on which later authors have come to grips with Zola make clear how great his posthumous influence—both positively and negatively—has been on the late nineteenth and on the twentieth centuries. His achievement is equal in stature to that of Chateaubriand and of Balzac. He put a definitive end to the influence of Chateaubriand and handed on that of Balzac in a philosophically new mutation with stylistically keener devices.[6]

A lesson exemplified for Zola by Balzac is that the colossal intent requires an expansive wealth of language. Zola's personality as a writer was intrinsically predisposed to respond to this suggestion, and we do find it possible to differentiate two components of his work. There is in his creative ego the pronounced sensualism of a native of Southern France and a determined will to be meticulously scientific in observation. The significance of this becomes clearer if we recall that Stendhal was still satisfied with reading now and again a few pages in the Civil Code in order to lower the temperature of his style and that Balzac was still concerned with progressing beyond the romantic novel of the past by establishing, on a more or less mystical basis, equations between nature and society. What is unique and new in Zola is his endeavor to achieve an at least partial depersonalization of the novel. Carried to its ultimate extreme, Zola's approach would have reduced the writer and poet to the rank of a sociological illustrator. But Zola saw even within the bounds of a rigid determinism the possibility of reserving for the creative subject a place next to the positivist. Writing— creative writing—was to him "a patch of nature seen through a temperament." This does imply, in ethical terms, a relinquishment of the classical concept of the characters in the novel, but in terms of art it implies no restraint on the imagination. The twentieth century in particular has been able to grasp how Zola's novel concedes substance and weight to the irrational and to inspiration next to the didactic and the doctrinaire. The unmistakably distinctive charm of Zola's work derives in large measure from his "myth of the locale," the garden of Reverend Mouret, the pit in *Germinal*, the booze-joint in *L'Assommoir*, and especially the market halls in *Le Ventre de Paris*. It is with a view to this feature in particular that one should read Zola's novels, for if his mastery is uncontested, it is so thanks to this point.

Thomas Mann was one of the first to understand this when he spoke of Zola and Richard Wagner as linked by an inner kinship and boldly postulated that *Les Rougon-Macquart* was a cyclical novel of mythological and symbolic significance. To be sure, to a great many of his contemporaries, Zola—revered or rejected—was the writer of human misery. The closing nine-teenth century opened up an offensive against him on at least two fronts. It was in the name of the heritage of the eighteenth century and of Voltaire that Anatole France opposed Zola's novels of the proletariat, while Joris Karl Huysmans rejected his former friend in the name of his increasingly irrational catholicism. With this we have alluded to only two of the trends in the literature for which the concept of the *fin de siècle* has come to be more than a mere label identifying an epoch.

V

NARRATIVE PROSE OF THE FIN DE SIÈCLE

Jules Barbey d'Aurevilly, Alphonse Daudet, Paul Adam,
Maurice Barrès, Eugène Fromentin, Jules Renard,
Charles-Louis Philippe, Abel Hermant, René Boylesve,
Paul Bourget, Octave Mirbeau, Elémir Bourges, Pierre Loti,
Anatole France, Joris-Karl Huysmans, Alfred Jarry, Léon Bloy

The concept of the *fin de siècle* attained slogan-like popularity after the success of the play with that title by Micard, Jouvenot, and Cohen (April 17, 1888, at the *Théâtre du Château d'Eau*), though it had been used years before to characterize, with both ethical and aesthetic implications, a certain complex of tumultuous and luxuriant trends. For a decade or so—especially since Baudelaire, through whom the concept of decadence had come to be something quite other than a purely political category—"decadent" writers were fond of applying to themselves the term *"fin de siècle,"* meaning to stress thereby their dandiesque display of modernity. Thus we can learn from the periodical *Voltaire*, on May 4, 1886, referring to such a young man: "To be *fin de siècle* is to cease being responsible; it is with virtually inescapable necessity to be subject to the impact of the times and of the environment; it is quite simply to accept one's small share of the general lassitude and corruption; it is to rot away with one's century and to perish with it."* This analysis may be partisan and one-sided, but it does suggest the essential characteristics of the *fin de siècle*: the inclination toward the abnormal (whether it be in a positive sense or neutrally) and toward the morbid hyperaesthesia with respect to crises and doom, addiction to unheard-of stimuli (including the delirious), and the predilection for the incomplete and the torso —in other words, a flashback to the literary demeanor of "romanticism."

In addition, however, this epoch derived new characteristics through being rooted in its own historical events. The defeat of 1871, the shock given the metropolis by the episode of the Commune, the Dreyfus affair, the disposal of Comte's positivism, a growing interest in psychology and depth psychology, a more thorough exposure to Schopenhauer's pessimism, and the mutual fertilization of narrative prose and lyrical poetry (as in Baudelaire, Rimbaud, and Mallarmé)—all these factors worked together to give the writers a keener awareness of decadence. Indeed, an excessively keen awareness of prevailing conditions, a mood of irritability, and the endeavor to escape— born simultaneously from disgust with the world as it was depicted in Zola's novels—into refined elegance, into excess and abandon or into religiously mystical devotion, as well as enthusiasm for Richard Wagner and political extremism came to be elements of the *fin de siècle* which thus assumes profound structural significance in addition to being a label for an epoch.

The *fin de siècle* includes Anatole France as well as Barbey d'Aurevilly, both of whom—albeit for different reasons— reverted to the eighteenth century; it includes Huysmans and Bloy who introduced, in their diverse ways, the "Catholic renewal." The continuation of the fantastic narrative is likewise a component, and exoticism—used throughout the eighteenth century primarily for didactic purposes—became, in the novel of the late nineteenth century, almost a matter of the individual's philosophy of life, for in it are subsumed late forms of the Rousseauistic criticism of enlightenment, of "Europeweariness" as a variant of decadence, and the longing of an age of highly refined civilization for the simplicity of rural and insular life and the lost paradise. From an aversion against the obvious, the palpable, the bourgeois, and the proletarian, there arose thus, at the heart of the *fin de siècle*, a new type of literature with a locus somewhere between extreme individualism and restraintless dedication to the community, between Voltairian anticlericalism and almost medieval absorption in faith. The romanticist's "ennui" was replaced by the "spleen" of the dandy of the bearing of the sectarian. And let us not overlook that in the meantime the Goncourts had drawn attention to disease and aberration in the individual and that they had been protagonists—in contrast to Zola or Jules Vallès—of a meticulously refined narrative style. These are the multi-directional channels converging in the *fin de siècle,* which—therefore and of necessity—underwent and undertook a turbulent clearing process.[1]

The student content with skimming the surface may easily be misled into leveling at this literature the reproach of formalism, for the individualistic orientation of the writers led to an unheard-of deconfinement in the style of the novel which simultaneously laid claim to (and was granted) an ever greater autonomy. Daudet alone introduced some 1800 new words into the language of the novel, and it is certain that the language of French literature from 1850 to 1900 was enriched by several thousand neologisms and new uses of archaic or forgotten terms. This occurred with the awareness that in the course of time words become worn, gray, ungenuine, so that the writer abandons them or attributes to them some special signification, probes their etymologies, and symbolizes them in a mysterious fashion. Next to the style of the Goncourts and the exotic novels of Flaubert, it was Baudelaire's *Petits poèmes en prose* which proved in particular with what expressive powers prose can be endowed.[2]

It is extremely difficult to categorize the novelists of the *fin de siècle,* for each of them was intent upon preserving his own individual profile with an intensity of determination hardly equaled in the past. But it is possible to make out that the truly essential components in this complex of forces were supplied by right-wing politics and right-wing catholicism, on the other hand by a bourgeois trend without definite orientation in terms of its underlying philosophical principles, further by a proletarian trend of left-wing affiliation, and finally by a pronounced leftist catholicism represented by a number of ivory-tower literati and aesthetes. The right-wing contribution came above all from Barbey d'Aurevilly, Daudet, Adam, and Barrès.

Jules Barbey d'Aurevilly (1808–89) was a Norman nobleman who regarded the French Revolution, as Balzac had done, as a national catastrophy. However, his Parisian contemporaries knew him not only as an amateur politician of the *ancien régime* but also as an eccentric dandy who, by 1841, when his first work, *L'Amour impossible*, was published, had managed to thoroughly undermine his health by means of alcohol and the use of drugs. His literary predilection was the eighteenth century. On May 15, 1845, he wrote to his friend Trebutien, "the most beautiful novel ever written bears the title of *Les Liaisons dangereuses*." Having reached his physical and moral nadir, he became an ardent and articulate partisan of catholicism and soon was feared as an ultramontane polemicist and literary critic who attacked, and disposed of, Cousin, Sainte-Beuve, Michelet, and Hugo and—with the same stroke of the pen—Flaubert, Scribe, Dumas fils, and young Zola to boot.

In more mature years Barbey d'Aurevilly wrote *Les Diaboliques* (1874), his principal work, which is a volume of short pieces of narrative prose. In the preface he professed a sturdy faith in the reality of the devil, revealing simultaneously his sympathies for Manichaeanism, that is, a belief in the equivalence of good and evil in the interplay of forces that make the world go round. The characters in these stories appear impelled by satanic passions. There are nymphomaniac women (*Le Rideau cramoisi*), renegade demonic priests, cynical pacemakers of the French Revolution, and protagonists of demented jealousy and the lust for murder (*A un Dîner d'athées*). This writer's somber spiritualism confronts the positivism and philosophical materialism of his age with the fires of Satan as the most evident supersensuous reality. This was not the best way to make friends. Then, too, there was the stylistic brutality which hardly lagged behind Zola in its contempt for taboos and which thus frightened the orthodox Catholics who apparently failed to understand that an author who believes in the Devil implies tacitly that God exists.[3] On the other hand, how seriously he was taken by individual contemporary writers may be inferred from this passage in a letter which Alfred de Vigny wrote on May 25, 1862, with reference to Barbey d'Aurevilly's *Du Dandysme et de G. Brummell* (1861): "The mock eulogy you present of dandyism is the most felicitous persiflage imaginable of this bloodless vanity of bearing."

Literary trial and error, novelistic experimentation in every imaginable area, with nowhere a truly great success, may be

regarded as characteristic of the work of Alphonse Daudet
(1840–97). This voluble Southerner, a native of Nîmes, tried his
hand above all in three narrative genres. The first phase of his
productive career has left us stories of the Provence. In the
autobiographical account of his youth, *Le Petit chose* (1868), in
Les Lettres de mon moulin (1869), reporting humorous events
of everyday life but containing also the animal story of *La
Chèvre de M. Seguin*, and finally in *Tartarin de Tarascon*
(1872), a caricature and parody of the heroic novel, Daudet
impresses many of his readers, and some critics of today, as a
witty and lovable raconteur. His own time, however, thought
otherwise. In his efforts to gain recognition he moved closer to
the Zola school but found it impossible to identify himself with
Zola's social tendencies. It seemed to Daudet that the north-
south tension in France might yield subjects congenial to him.
This led to the composition of *Numa Roumestan* (1881), but
dyed-in-the-wool natives of the Provence see in this work rather
a persiflage than an *apologia* of their ethnic idiosyncrasies.
Finally, Daudet's novels of morals, with their Parisian setting,
suffered from the fact that they were overshadowed by Balzac
and Zola. Subsequently Daudet moved into the camp of the
political and social opposition and produced in *Les Rois en exil*
a work avowedly advocating a royalist restoration.[4]

The same evolution from the political left to the political
right, the same multiplicity of stylistic and thematic experiments may be noted in Paul Adam (1862–1920), who began as
a naturalist, proceeded to write the novel of social criticism,
Le Mystère des foules (1895), and then reverted to a superficial exoticism. His tetralogy, *Le Temps et la vie* (1899–1903),
represents a hardly successful attempt to reconcile these various
tendencies in harmonious unity. Finally, in *La Ville inconnue*
(1911), Adam glorified French colonialism.

Thus it remained for Maurice Barrès (1862–1923) to carry
these hints at restoration to doctrinaire heights but also to a
doctrinaire rigidity, obliterating in a sense the specific characteristics of the *fin de siècle*, that is, the unrest and indecision
of the characters depicted, their self-denigration and self-pity,
their receptiveness for everything new, and their foundering
from excess and versatility.

In a sense Barrès may be said to have overcome the *fin de*

siècle. He was born in the east of France, in Charmes-sur-Moselle. Here—according to the generally accepted account—the war and the Prussian invasion of 1870 surprised and shocked him most deeply. But, as a boy of eight, he was doubtless too young for such a reaction, and his later chauvinism must rather be seen as the product of the education typical of his time and environment. A second decisive experience was his stay at a boarding school in Nancy. Gradually Barrès learned to understand the value of the individual. And gradually—in addition—he became a "national rallier."

From 1883 on Barrès lived in Paris where he attracted, as a disciple of Stendhal, a certain degree of attention with his confessions in the vein of a "cult of selfhood." This philosophy of life found its first significant literary expression in his novel *Un Homme libre* (1889). At that same time—in 1889—he also became representative of Nancy in the Chamber of Deputies. As an individualist, who for a while had been sympathizing with socialism, he learned to despise thoroughly the parlimentarian system as it was exemplified by the Chamber and by the "barbarians," to use the term he applied to the republican majority. In 1906, Barrès became deputy from Paris and was known as a consistent right-wing politician. In terms of his personal philosophy he now came to be interested in an extended variant of determinism which accepts and stipulates the dynamics of the nation's history and of blood and soil as obligatory factors conditioning the role and the demeanor of the individual within his people. The east of France, a region "on outpost duty," as it were, came to be the symbolic setting for his nationalistic novels. In *Les Déracinés* (1897), with Nancy in 1879 as the setting, a racially emancipated humanism and liberalism, represented by the secondary-school professor Bouteillier, intellectually uproots seven young men and has them stagger on into a *fin-de-siècle* life.

Ultimately the chauvinist and missionary of revenge evolved into a political Catholic swearing by the common cause of discipline in state and church, rigidly eradicating all religious illuminism of the kind attempted in those days by Huysmans and Léon Bloy. That is the message of the novel *La Colline inspirée* (1913). The total work of Barrès was written simultaneously against the hated Prussia and for the ideal—a truly mythical ideal—of a rational, Latin humanity. It seems possible that he sensed himself how exacting and also how boundless his demands were when he wrote, for his own relaxation, the Oriental story *Un Jardin sur l'Oronte* (1922). At that time the educated public in France had already turned away from him, giving preference to Proust and especially to Gide. Nonetheless, the impact of Barrès cannot be overlooked in the works of Mauriac in his younger years, of Montherlant, Malraux, Drieu La Rochelle, and Camus.[5]

Far less politically committed is the bourgeois, at times petit-bourgeois realism of Fromentin, Hermant, Boylesve, and Bourget. Especially the painter and writer Eugène Fromentin (1820–76), chronologically at the beginning of the *fin de siècle*, effected in his novel *Dominique* (1862) his emancipation from late romanticism and from positivism. *Dominique*, written in the wake of Goethe's *Wilhelm Meister,* is the confession of a youthful experience and represents a rejection of the romantic gospel of the unqualified rights of passion (so consistently upheld by George Sand) and simultaneously of the doctrines of Auguste Comte. Dominique de Bray does not have the courage to marry a girl he loves but he also finds it impossible to relinquish and forget her when she belongs to another. Because of this reaction, a melancholy aura of imagined guilt and penance envelops his entire life.[6] A plethora of pale-color epithets projects the inner state of the protagonist into his environment. Two decades before the *fin de siècle* proper, this author supplied already a subtly differentiated picture of human contact deficiencies, climaxing in the description of the dark realms of an elementary coming-to-grips with existence. This little-known novel should be counted among the precursors of modern existentialist literature. By its amazing analyses in depth it contrasts sharply with the numberless French novels of playfully flirtatious love.

In terms of their subject matter, the novels of Jules Renard (1864–1910)—with their frequently rural setting—do not appear to fit in with the atmosphere of the *fin de siècle*. We mention *Crime de village* (1888), *Sourires pincés* (1890), *Poil de Carotte* (1894), and *Bucoliques* (1905). We should also note that Renard's stylistic sobriety, distinguishing his works strikingly from George Sand's or Zola's, makes his prose seem undistinguished, a fact which would seem to have contributed, together with the author's personal eccentricities, to fostering oblivion rather than fame. Yet, there is nobility in the stylistic ideal as visualized by Renard. "To write in the manner in which Rodin sculpts" (Diary, March 9, 1891). In *L'Écornifleur* (1892), in which the bohemian world of writers and the philistine world of the bourgeoisie are made to clash, the picture of an emotional and social crisis is drawn on the basis of the illustrative example of a trivial love story. It seems possible that Renard for so long received so little attention because Gide, making use of the same style of pregnant sobriety, was engaged at just that time in taking up and overcoming the mood of crisis of the closing nineteenth century.[7]

Likewise in the shadow of Gide, who spoke with praise of his pithy prose, stood Charles-Louis Philippe (1874-1909), who took as his subjects his own childhood and youth in the Bourbonnais (*Quatre histoires de pauvre amour*, 1897; *La Mère et l'enfant*, 1898) and the bohemian experiences of his brief Parisian years (*Bubu de Montparnasse*, 1901). These works reflect the author's self-imposed limitation to things trivial with the supreme requirement of authenticity.

The same reticence in delineation characterizes the work of Abel Hermant (1862–1950) and of René Boylesve (1872–1926) with their ever alert interest in the psychological penetration of life. Hermant's bourgeois realism belongs clearly in the Goncourt tradition. His pictures of society, with their mixture of righteousness and degeneracy, assign to him the role of a mediator between Balzac and Maurice Druon. Boylesve, on the other hand, who was a master of the short novel and of the sensitive description of the heartache of lonely men and women in the provinces (*Médecin des dames de Néans*, 1896; *Mon amour*, 1908), attempted to combine the stylistic freshness of Stendhal with his own realistic subject matter of petit bourgeois provenance.

No one of these novelists contributed as much to the history of the *fin de siècle* in psychological terms as did the mathematician's son Paul Bourget (1852–1935), who began his career by studying literature in Paris under the influence of Taine and Sainte-Beuve. He made a name for himself in 1883 through his *Essais de psychologie contemporaine* in which he rediscovered

Balzac and Stendhal. In his own novels he emulated Benjamin Constant and Stendhal with the avowed objective of confronting the physiological novel of the school of Zola with a psychological novel of intellectual orientation. His first themes were taken from the world of society (*Cruelle énigme*, 1885; *André Cornelis*, 1887). But subsequently, with *Le Disciple*, he transcended all models and in fact his own education, for through this novel of responsibility, both Stendhal's egotism and Zola's determinism appear to be challenged and found questionable. A respresentative of scientific determinism, Adrien Sixte, is informed that his disciple Greslou has killed a girl. The pretrial investigation establishes the fact that while Greslou did not commit the deed, he did allow himself—in his zeal of psychological experimentation—to drive the girl to kill herself. Greslou is acquitted by the jury, but the brother of the dead girl takes justice into his own hands and shoots him to death in the street. The scientist collapses. In a preface, the author explained that modern youth is confronted with the need of finding and testing a way of its own, skirting three dangerous heresies. These are cynical enjoyment of life, brutal pursuit of success, and intellectual epicureanism. Instead, Bourget recommends the cultivation of love and will power and the recognition that man's nobility emanates from beyond nature in something that cannot be grasped in material terms. From these ideas derives the demand that the individual assume responsibility for his fellow. The end of the novel is characteristic. When Adrien Sixte collapses by the side of Greslou's body, he attempts to recite the Lord's prayer. At that moment a word of Pascal flashes through his mind: "You would not seek me if you had not found me."

Thus one segment of the French novel of the *fin de siècle* returns under God's tutelage. The collapse of positivism is necessarily followed by greater religious depth. Here we have the beginnings of the "Catholic renewal" in French literature that was destined to achieve, in its development via Bloy and Huysmans, a significant literary climax in Bernanos, Mauriac, and Green. As for Paul Bourget himself, he spent himself in this *roman à clé* of the late nineteenth century, for in his subsequent products we find routine in lieu of vital urgency.[8]

The stock themes and forms of the picaresque novel—shrewd

servant morals and episodic abundance—were enriched by Octave Mirbeau (1848–1917), the author of *Le Calvaire* (1886) and *Le Jardin des supplices* (1898), in *Le Journal d'une femme de chambre* (1900) by the coldly detached portrayal of erotic aberrations. The political lies of the antisemite and rapist murderer Joseph, the fellow worker, lover, and husband of the heroine of this first person novel are to be taken as a critical accounting with the opponents of Dreyfus and, generally, the entire *belle époque.*

Bourget—no less than Barrès and France—marked the endpoint of one of the continuities in the *fin de siècle* which may suitably be identified by the catchword of "evasion." Bourget completed and transcended the beginnings of Bourges and Loti. The first of these two, Elémir Bourges (1852–1925), a native of southern France, friend of Barbey d'Aurevilly, Mallarmé, and Bourget, continued the tradition of the fantastic narrative. As Nodier had done a half century ago and as his contemporary Villiers de l'Isle-Adam was doing, he rejected the idea that it is possible to see in life a fixed continuity of measurable concatenations of functions. He wrote as a novelist visionary, with an almost religious dedication to language reminiscent of Flaubert. His novels, in which he dealt with the leading themes of the *fin de siècle* (*Le Crépuscule des dieux,* 1884; *Sous la hache,* 1885; or *Les Oiseaux s'envolent et les fleurs tombent,* 1893), were written against the then prevailing predilection for naturalism and yellow journalism. The very title *Le Crépuscule des dieux* reflects symptomatically Bourges's admiration for Wagner.[9] By comparison, Pierre Loti (1850–1923) seems considerably more superficial. His novels, it is true, are embued with a pessimism of honest intellectual depth, but time and again this is masked by individual episodes clearly designed to cater to the taste of the public.[10] Loti's exoticism was in fact the precipitate of a grave crisis. On December 10, 1898, he wrote in his diary: "I should be far away and still I am here, for I do not know where to turn, where to go or to throw myself, surrounded as I am on all sides by threats, uncertainties, anxieties."[11]

Intellectually, then, Loti represents exemplarily the *fin de siècle,* for his work reflects as symptoms of an age of decline— in functional interdependence but incapable of mutual resolution—fear of death and hunger for life, a sense of the permanent and the consciousness of the transient ephemerality of things.

Pierre Loti was born in Rochefort and attended the École Navale from which he graduated with an officer's commission. He plied the seven seas and came to know, by direct experience, how much the world can be a paradise but also how unpredictable our destinies are. His pessimism and his cosmopolitanism were thus closely interlinked. His literary fame began with his novel of Tahiti *Le Mariage de Loti* (1880). What he began in this work—dreamy nostalgia, melancholy reveries of nature, elegiac plaints, and exalted praise of the primitive —carried the subsequent publications as well. Among these the artistically most significant are not the exotic *Madame Chrysanthème* (1887) or the old-Turkish novel *Les Désenchantés* (1906) but the Breton fisherman's tragedy *Pêcheurs d'Islande* (1886) and the Basque novel *Ramuntcho* (1897). Although Loti's portrayal of the exotic remained superficial, it did release a wave of novels with an exotic subject matter, such as those by Louis Bertrand (1886–1941), Claude Farrère (1876–1957), or Gilbert de Voisins (1877–1939). Of these the last-named—with *Le Bar de la Fourche* (1909)—initiated the long series of wild-west stories which are to be regarded as a special variant of the exotic novel. Strictly speaking, nothing of lasting value was produced in this area before Malraux.

The literary orientation of the young Anatole France (1844–1924) was as varied as his literary education. *Le Crime de Sylvestre Bonnard* (1881) was still clearly in the wake of Dickens. When he broke with the naturalistic principle that one must write only what one knows by one's own experience, he moved closer to Rabelais and Voltaire. *Thaïs* (1890), a novel of religious relativism, evoked Alexandria and Egypt in the third century after Christ. As a disciple of Voltaire, the "religious comparativist" France could not see an ideal occurrence in the replacement of Antiquity by rising Christianity. Beginning with *Lys rouge* (1894), a "Florentine Baedeker" (Kurt Wais), the scene of France's novels moved closer to his European homeland, the setting of the four volumes of the humanitarian *Histoire contemporaine* (1897–1901) in which France appears as a defender of Dreyfus. Yet, despite all its commitment in the politics of the day, France's work retains somehow, in a graceful way, the feel of paper, a fragrance of letters and bookishness. This applies strikingly to the satirical novel of growth and education, *La Rôtisserie de la Reine Pédauque* (1893) which follows the progress of a kitchen boy on his way to becoming a book dealer, paying due attention to a number of piquant intermezzi, and extoling the preoccupation with wise and graceful books over and beyond the vital urges of hunger and of love. The ridicule to which he exposed priest and presbytery in *L'Île des pingouins* (1908) was perhaps a little excessive. This utopian satire reports how a Christian missionary christens penguins—by mistake, for he mistook them for humans—whereupon God changes them into humans since the sacrament of baptism cannot be rescinded. In the subsequent, all too human, demeanor of these creatures, France castigates inquisition, blind faith, and political clericalism.

In *Les Dieux ont soif* (1912), the action of which is set during the era of Robespierre, we witness the corruption of the individual through the lure of power. A painter turns into a bloodhound of the Terror until the fall of Robespierre takes him to the guillotine. *La Révolte des anges* (1914) is, in terms of the underlying philosophy of life, a statement of France's creed. In Promethean colors the now old and elderly Anatole France describes the fallen angels that teach men humanity, art, and ethical greatness, while God as a demon, in his cosmic aloofness, merely deceives them. Thus, the novelist succeeds in the most important of his later works, in the course of the composition of which he moved close to communism, in combining the major strands of his narrative procedures: the pleasure of telling a story, the delight with the exotic, and the humane sense of obligation to enlighten men in an anticlerical vein and to save and improve them. France's work bears certain traits of the orientalizing didactic narratives of Voltaire. New is the author's socialist engagement which heralds André Gide's attempts of leading men, in a spirit of contempt for the gods, to a courageous self-realization. The unfairly neglected *Contes merveilleux* (*Les Sept femmes de Barbe-Bleue; Le Miracle du grand Saint-Nicolas; La Chemise*) and also *La Vie de Jeanne d'Arc* are enlightening prose in the best sense of the term. When legends form, and especially when it is their function to provide religious edification, denial and opposition are called for.

Jeanne is no celestial being; Bishop Nicholas is not the creator of a better world; Barbe-Bleue is not a depraved monster. In all of them the skeptic France recognizes men of everyday life.[12]

Most of the traits that might be culled from the four-teen sketches of novelists presented so far in this chapter in order to draw a composite picture of the *fin de siècle* as a time of change and upheaval in thought and literature appear concentrated exemplarily in the work of Joris-Karl Huysmans (1848–1907). In it we find the time's hectic pursuit of the idio-syncratic, of the thrill of the unique. We find reflected in it decadence endured and decadence sought after. Joris-Karl Huysmans was born in Paris and died there. On his father's side he was of Flemish descent. He was employed in the minis-try of the interior and held his position there until 1898. As a writer he first became known to a small circle of connoisseurs and friends—including a number of impressionist painters—with his *Le Drageoir à épices* (1874) which made him appear as a latter-day romanticist. The printing costs for this work the author still had to bear himself. His second book, *Marthe, histoire d'une fille*, was first published in Brussels in 1876. When a Paris edition appeared in 1879, Zola praised the naturalistic theme and deplored simultaneously the exuberant style. The same criticism was repeated by Flaubert on reading the novel *Sœurs Vatard* (1879). We thus note at the very start of Huys-mans' creative career the latent tension existing between his work and parts of the literary conception of Flaubert and Zola. Huysmans' short-lived inclusion in the circle of Médan did not alter these facts. But there is more: The structure of Zola's work as a whole differs from that of Huysmans' work in ulti-mate essentials.

Zola's immense cyclical novel reveals, despite all the late-romantic inserts, an inspired integration in conception and execution, while we note in Huysmans a tragic disruption affecting his life as well as his work. With illumninistic ardor he felt attracted by the monastic ideal, while it seemed impossible for him to forget the world and its vices. It is no accident that the action of *Marthe* is set in a world of prostitution. Heaven and Hell, gutter and Church play roles in Huysmans which are related by functional interdependence rather than through mere alternation. In most instances the mood of the hero shuttles restively to and fro between these realms. This is attested to in particular by *À Rebours* (1884) of which an imitation was supplied in 1891 by the Englishman Oscar Wilde with his *Picture of Dorian Gray.* Huysmans' *À Rebours* was written "against the grain" in two ways: The novel is a settling of accounts with Zola's world and with the American "way of life." The first of these objectives is hardly surprising, for the struggle to come to terms with Zola is unbiquitously a major characteristic of the *fin de siècle.* The second objective is the more surprising as it is presented with extreme vehemence. Americanism was to Huysmans anti-occidentalism; it was standardization and plutocracy; it was "chants of impurity before the impious tabernacle of banks." (Chapter XVI).

In the introductory paragraphs of this chapter we alluded to the explosive deconfinement of the novel in the latter part of the nineteenth century. What was meant there is reflected in the fact that it is difficult to summarize the fable of *À Rebours.* The novel consists essentially of inner monologues, lyrical descriptions of moods, reflective and delineatory scenes. One has the impression that it was precisely by dispensing with a clearly continuous action and by dissolving systematically the boundaries of the genres that Huysmans recognized his best chance of writing against the epic principles of Zolaism. In the beginning we merely hear of the aestheticism of the hero Des Esseintes whose name covers the author himself but also contemporaries of his, such as the dandy Robert de Montesquiou. Des Esseintes is the last scion of an old noble family who nursed in utter inactivity his hyperesthesia and his neuroses and who lives in an artificial cocoon world of his own spinning with the intent of destroying everything vulgar within himself and in his environment. At first he attempts to achieve his goal through eccentricities and costly vices. Somehow he does not succeed. He then proceeds to establish in the province a home for himself in accordance with his own taste. He finds for it exquisite furniture, tapestries, books, pictures, and plants, and he makes of it an imaginative museum of the *fin de siècle.* Sculptures play no role to speak of, for they tend to remain rooted in the world of realities. By the use of narcotics and through a dilettantic communion with music, books, and pictures, Des

Esseintes creates for himself an unnaturally oppressive atmosphere which he claims to be commensurate with the unique role he demands for himself. One passage in the book shows extremely well what aesthetic realms attract him in particular and, in addition, what *fin de siècle* in its most genuine form really is:

"In the perverse fragrance of perfumes, in the overheated atmosphere of this church, Salome—her left arm extended in a gesture of command, her right arm bent back to hold at the height of her face a large lotus—advances slowly on tiptoes to the chords of a guitar of which a crouching woman plucks the strings. Her face collected, solemn, almost august, she begins the lewd dance which is to awaken the dormant senses of her ruler Herod. Her breasts undulate and—with the rubbing of her necklaces which swirl—their points stand up. On the moisture of her skin the diamonds, attached, scintillate. Her bracelets, her girdles, her rings spit sparks. On her triumphal robe, embroidered with pearls, bedecked with silver, spangled with gold, the armor of jewelry, of which each mesh is a stone, rises in flames, flashed serpents of fire, seethes on the mat flesh, on the tea-rose skin, like resplendent insects with dazzling elytrons, crimson mottled, dotted with dawn yellow, speckled with steel blue, spotted with peacock green."*

It is apparent that to Huysmans only a choice language of ceremonial pomp befits an unusual event. In order to emphasize the point, he presents next to his own description the Biblical account, the language of which is that of a straightforward report. Des Esseintes has before him a picture by Gustave Moreau which this painter had exhibited in 1876. It is *L'Apparition* and shows Salome beginning her veil dance before Herodias and the tetrarch. The head of John appears transfigured under the cupola of the palace which Des Esseintes (or Huysmans) mistakes for a church. The interest the author and his hero take in this particular picture is not coincidental, as little as Moreau had chosen the subject because he could think of nothing else. For Herodias and Salome meant to the *fin de siècle* roughly what Satan, Cain, and Prometheus had meant to the Storm and Stress and to the romanticists, that is, lodestars—"leading images"—in which the epoch hoped in secret to recognize itself. So all the representations of Herodias or of

Salome of the nineteenth century differ in essence from all earlier ones, for instance from that by Titian. The new element was introduced in European literature by Heinrich Heine with *Atta Troll.* Flaubert took it up under the impact of Moreau's painting in his story of Herodias (*Trois contes*), and Mallarmé began his *Hérodiade.* These are events to which Huysmans could hark back. As he described Moreau's painting, he did so with the vocabulary of Mallarmé and Flaubert of whom we know that they strove to emancipate their style from all dependence on everyday life and preferred the choice term, the unusual epithet, the refined metaphor, and the far-fetched comparison.

Huysmans took over this stylistic ideal and carried it to an exaggerated extreme of luxuriance and artifice as, for instance, when he described the skin of the dancing Salome as being of the color of a tea rose and—not satisfied yet—proceeded in the description of Salome's ornate appearance with the creation of a long chain of comparisons the factual referents of which it is no longer possible to translate with reliable exactitude. Once this language had caught fire on an aesthetically appealing subject, it assumed a separate existence of its own and attained the highest individuality. The style is fulsome and baroque while its message potential is low. But the point is precisely that it was not meant to report flatly but to reveal, to allude, to surprise. A striking detail is further the use of two originally negative attributes in this cascade of description, both in positions of a clearly positive charge: "The perverse fragrance of perfumes, in the overheated atmosphere." They contain a profession of allegiance to a decadent philosophy of life, as Baudelaire had proclaimed it, in which the unusual is given its pedestal apart, through extreme exaggeration and indeed through excess and eccentricity. Overheating and perverseness impressed the writer of the *fin de siècle* as points of refuge from the trivial, the narrow, the standardized, and the positivistic. The fantastic alone was no longer enough. That is the new element of which we spoke. And all of it appeared embodied in Salome. She is the virgin monster, narcissistically absorbed in her own physical beauty, indulging her satanic lusts, and thus combining in her person the commonly uncombinable opposites of innocence, eros, luxurious refinement, magic, and death.

At the end of *À Rebours,* however, Huysmans did take a step beyond. Des Esseintes, who has discovered the poetry of Mallarmé and has come to value it as the highest expression of decadence because in it he finds depths of thought and magic of style to be interrelated and on a par with one another (Chapter 14), falls ill in the atmosphere he has created for himself. He falls victim to neuroses until there is for his overwrought spiritualism no way but the unconditional surrender to faith. His end coincides with that of Adrien Sixte, in Bourges's *Le Disciple.* Positivism and decadent aestheticism can be resolved only in the divine. As his hero Des Esseintes had done, so Huysmans too now moved closer to catholicism via the aesthetic experience of the Catholic cult. This latter point represents a heritage handed down by Chateaubriand's *Le Génie du christianisme,* but the dualism of Huysmans's nature could not be immediately resolved in its entirety. In 1891 *Là-bas* appeared, a novel of an almost medieval faith in the Devil as Barbey d'Aurevilly had described it, while *En route* (1895) glorified a blissful mysticism. After Huysmans had in fact and form returned to the Christian faith, his creative powers began to dry up. *En route* is in its structure already a mere survey of the churches of Paris, and in *La Cathédrale* (1898), a song of songs of Chartres, Huysmans continued to be essentially a religious reporter. The same holds true for *Les Foules de Lourdes* (1906)[13] which was intended to be an answer to Zola's novel of Lourdes.

The principle of "against the grain" runs as a common thread through all of Huysmans's works. It was in the name of aesthetic or religious aristocracy that he attacked Zola and (in *Les Foules de Lourdes*) the catholicism of the vulgar crowd. But beyond this rejection he was unable to rise to a creative level of his own. It is not surprising, then, that the reaction of Huysmans's contemporaries[14] was extremely varied. Maupassant called *À Rebours* the "story of a neurosis," while Barbey d'Aurevilly felt that after this publication there was nothing left for Huysmans but suicide or unconditional catholicism. Paul Valéry, who had read *À Rebours* five times before 1890, still spoke of it in 1895 as his "bible and bedside book." What he valued in it was in

particular its stylistic refinement, certainly not its religious concern. Such verdicts illuminate and emphasize once again the
many-layered structure of the *fin de siècle* in which we see
converge, as in a flickering focus, all the literary achievements
but also the entire problematic heritage of the eighteenth and
nineteenth centuries and from which they radiate again, in a
milder or sharper form, to be handed on to the twentieth.

We understand now, too, that the era of the *fin de siècle* was
prone to indulge in exaggeration and excess. The cathartic function of this trait has been stressed. The two authors who moved
farthest in that direction substituted, for the world of refined
living of Des Esseintes and for the bourgeois atmosphere of
Fromentin and Bourget, the cry from the gutter. They took
Rimbaud and Verlaine into the novel. Their names are Alfred
Jarry (1873–1907) and Léon Bloy (1846–1917). Jarry is better
known as a playwright and as the creator of the farcical figure
of Ubu. As a novelist (*Messaline,* 1901; *La Papesse Jeanne,*
1908; *Gestes et opinions du Docteur Faustroll, pataphysicien,*
published posthumously in 1911), he sought themes that
could be expected to prove shocking. His extravagant language
of the Bohème reflects a revival of the *"gauloiserie"* with its
mixture of turbulence, grotesquery, and frivolity. Jarry's manifest "shock literature" did help prepare the way for the
surrealists.

While Jarry was known to only a small circle, Léon Bloy
attracted a larger audience. His life as an author doubtless remained unique and unequaled throughout the entire *fin de
siècle.* It was a life of bitter need and care. Under the influence
of Barbey d'Aurevilly's polemic style, Bloy started out as a journalist, acquiring before long—thanks to his proletarian gall—a
feared and hated notoriety. In 1875 there was nothing left for
him but to start work in the employ of the railroad, just in order
to be able to go on living. He founded a periodical whose motto
indicated that it was meant "to be unbearable." As time went
on, Bloy moved more and more into the camp of left-wing
catholicism and assumed the role of the admonishing evangelist
who appeared on the scene "when it was opportune and when
it was not." In 1886 his autobiographical novel *Le Désespéré*
appeared with its utterly un-French abandon and lack of moderation. It is replete with uncompromising militancy against

"the children of this world" and their works. A somewhat stricter coherence characterizes *La Femme pauvre* (1897), a novel which likewise reflects the author's personal philosophy and in which the human vale of tears appears confronted with the bliss to which the poor find access only through faith. The style of Bloy's novels was firmly established with the publications mentioned so far. The action is slight, but there is an abundance of reflections and simultaneously the inclination to speak out and on with expressionist intent. This is the style of *À Rebours*, only with a vulgar accent.

A short sojourn in the homeland of his Danish wife, enforced by material hardship and lasting only from 1898 to 1899, had for Bloy all the characteristics of a hard-to-endure religious and national exile. After his return to Paris he carried on his lone struggle on all fronts. In *Je m'accuse* (1900) he attacked Zola, while the eighteen volumes of his *Journal* (1898–1929) attacked and strove to pillory conservatism in politics and religion, the economic transactions of the Church, and technical progress in all forms. Thus Léon Bloy made himself the apocalyptic of the *fin de siècle*. His uncompromising posture deserves more recognition (as Karl Muth and Ernst Jünger have explicitly agreed) than does his literary achievement. It was in his time and not only thereafter that French literature began to take a critical look at itself in the renewed awareness that the equilibrium of idea and form, of content and vessel distinguishes the work of art in its ultimate essence. In Proust, Martin du Gard, Rolland and above all in Gide, the French novel reacted against the *fin de siècle*. Despite the continuing presence of crucial structural problems, the novel regained its broad strength and in fact began again to recognize confines and definitions of genres.[15] To be sure, we need not wait for future generations to demonstrate that the novel from 1900 to 1960 did not find its way back to the inspired greatness of Balzac, Stendhal, Flaubert, and Zola. This may be attributable to political and social upheavals. Still, the literary work of art is in its essence something other than a reflection and an expression of its time. The time may be chaotic. The work lives through the form imposed on it. And the novel of the twentieth century in particular is more deeply involved in the problems posed in these premises than might be assumed at first blush.

VI

THE NOVEL OF REALIZATION

*Marcel Proust, André Gide, Pierre Drieu La Rochelle,
Henry de Montherlant, Raymond Radiguet, Maurice Toesca
Alfred Kern, Françoise Sagan*

℞ "Proust and Freud have initiated a new way of asking questions of their consciousness." This statement by Jacques Rivière needs to be explained more fully if Proust and Gide and Radiguet are to be grouped together with five other writers of the twentieth century[1] under the concept of "the novel of realization." Rivière's bracketing of Proust with Freud signifies first of all that the psychological novel progresses in its process of deconfinement as Freud, transcending the limits of classical psychology, penetrates into the preconscious depths of the human mind. The real literary disciples of Freud, however, are the surrealists (typically represented by André Breton) who utilize Freud's methodology of psychiatric therapy to record the dynamic events in the subconscious and to present the resulting record as literature. But from this Proust differs in very essential points.[2]

Marcel Proust was born in Paris in 1871. He was a delicate and high-strung child, though after a near-fatal attack of dyspnea in 1880 he became still more sensitive, and his state of health made it impossible for him to prepare for a practical career. Instead he soon came to be the spoiled darling of aristocratic social gatherings in Paris. In 1896 he published his first book, *Les Plaisirs et les jours,* for which Anatole France wrote the introduction. In this work late romantic self-alienation and inner disharmony, introversion and an awareness of the abyss between the worlds of imagination and reality prepare the transition from the climate of the *fin de siècle* to the genesis of Proust's mature works. Gide in particular has the merit of having pointed out that the later Proust, with all his characteristics, can be traced in this work of the nineties, though perhaps with the qualification that the syntactic devices of his style grew progressively more expansive.

Even before Proust came under the influence of Ruskin, he sketched out in *Les Plaisirs et les jours* his ideal in art (See, especially, *Mort de Baldassare Silvande,* 1894) as well as the artistic theory of knowledge that was to become the distinguishing mark of *À la Recherche du temps perdu.* In *Mélancolique villégiature de Madame de Breyves* (1893), the problem of "realization"—that is, of making real and present—was conceived as the problem of the graded continuity of "hallucination-dream-recollection-memory" [*hallucination-rêve-souvenir-mémoire*].

La Confession d'une jeune fille, in which the color motifs of the decadent literature around 1900 play a striking role (mauve, black, violet, rose), reveals Proust's struggle with the more and more deified mother figure, from whom all moral aberrations—especially those of the deviate—are to remain concealed.

From 1895 to 1904 Proust was at work on a broadly conceived novel which was published only in 1952 under the title of *Jean Santeuil.* Here Proust achieved mastery of the comprehensive epic sweep. Although *Jean Santeuil* is presented as the posthumous work of a fictitious narrator, autobiographical parallels cannot be overlooked. These include the mental and spiritual lability and the weak health of the hero, and his strong attachment to his mother. The motif of remembrance does appear in numerous variations but not as yet with the pregnant functions it assumed subsequently in Proust's great cycle. As a work of literature and art, this prose is somewhat disappointing, but it is significant in that it represents a preparatory phase leading on to *À la Recherche du temps perdu.* Proust's subsequent development was decisively influenced by his contact with the work of John Ruskin, for this Englishman made him aware of the problems involved in the relationship of morals and art, of reality and art, as well as logical truth and art. To Ruskin the exclusive criterion of genuineness in art was beauty.

Before Proust got ready to write his magnum opus, he laid, as it were, its theoretical foundation in *Contre Sainte-Beuve* (1909), attacking Sainte-Beuve as a critic of literature and rejecting his method of deriving literary and poetic results from autobiographical premises, for in Proust's opinion biographical details, no matter how rich, can never explain the core of a literary creation. Proust's voluminous correspondence, which comprises thousands of letters, gives us an insight into his way of life. A striking observation is his close dependence on his mother, though this is to be explained not only from factors inherent in his character but also by starkly material causes (Cf. the letter to Jeanne Proust of October 22, 1896). The fact that Proust took pride in his correspondence and social contact with noblemen (Robert de Montesquiou, Anna de Noailles, Prince Antoine Bibesco, and others) cannot make us overlook that he was painfully aware of the fact that the circle of these men and women embodied a dying world. From the nineties to the fall of 1922, Proust hardly wrote a letter in which he did not complain about his declining health, also about the stages of his imagined literary failure, and especially about the humiliating necessity of negotiating with the publishers Fasquelle, Ollendorff, Gallimard, and Grasset. The letters reflect most distinctly Proust's hypersensitive response to criticism and praise, especially in his exchanges with André Gide, Gaston Gallimard, and the critic Paul Souday. From 1902 on, Proust was bedridden for long periods of time. After 1909 he left his house more and more rarely and generally only at night.

"I understood that Noah had never been able to see the world as well as he did from the ark, although it was closed in and although it was night on earth." This paradox, which will require further clarification, was meant to refer in particular to his existence as a writer and poet faced with the task of mastering in the twilight of his room the gigantic subject of *À la Recherche du temps perdu*. From 1910 on this work grew up as the intimately dovetailed jointure of two worlds: the one on the side of the upper bourgeoisie of the Swanns and the other on the side of the high aristocracy of the Guermantes, portrayed during the years before the outbreak of the First World War. Through the power of his memory, the narrator Marcel assumes in the novel the role of a dream wanderer between those two hemispheres. As a result the task of the reader is not an easy one, especially since Marcel seems less concerned with distinguishing the past from the present than with interweaving the past and the present. The work is to him—the narrator or the author—a race with time. A metaphor running through it as a leitmotif is that of the "traveler" [*voyageur*]. Quite generally, metaphors assume increased significance in this procedure of conjury. Marcel learns to be a "traveler" in time as in the spheres of society, for his aging ego must reassure itself of its childhood as of its present, and in addition there is the to and fro and back and forth between the domains of the Swanns and Guermantes. A striking point—in contrast to Balzac and Zola—is the fact that social problems owe their interest above all to their being societal fields of force in which psychological contrasts are released.

At the beginning of the cycle, the Swann side and the Guermantes side, to be sure, are kept painstakingly apart; one might say, they are kept hierarchically apart; but throughout the novel we witness an undermining of the confines of the social classes, and in the end the bourgeoisie and the aristocracy are united in marriage. As the work opens with a recollective flash-back to Swann's childhood, no such eventuality can possibly come to mind, and—in particular—there is nothing in the early portions of the novel to suggest the significance which is in fact to be ascribed to such a union. To Marcel the Guermantes, whom he sees only from afar, moving about in their world of high aristocracy, appear as inaccessible figures in a setting of incomprehensible names and concepts. Gradually, this fabled realm of names and concepts assumes reality through an actual acquaintance with the side of the Guermantes, with the result of a progressive disillusionment. Now Marcel grows consciously aware of how far idea and reality can fall apart and how little either one by itself can be relied upon. This lesson in the social realm is repeated in love when Swann marries a seemingly ideal woman, Odette, who is in reality a frivolous person. In the mind of the narrator this realization assumes the proportions of a horrifying suspicion that perhaps there cannot really be a true "you" since every idea we form of someone else appears to be necessarily false. Two human beings—even though they be in love with one another—are never, it appears, "communicating vessels." In the extreme formulation it no longer matters to whom love as a physical act is given. Love and perversion are no longer distinct. This is shown particularly in the unit, *Sodome et Gomorrhe.* The impenetrability which Marcel was at first inclined to account for through the class differences between the Guermantes and the Swanns has much deeper roots. The individual, regardless of its social quality, is "a sealed vessel" [*vase clos*]. The question arises whether this might not put an end to the search, whether life does not lack in fact a force imparting a meaning to it. But such a force— a force that is qualified to impart meaning to life—does exist. The epic "I" persists for so long in the remembered past while simultaneously it lives out its life in the present that finally the aspects of the narration become identified in the first person. This is salvation and discovery, for now permanence is guaranteed.

Art is the force which imparts meaning in so far as it overcomes what dissociates. Art is simultaneously the basis of communication between and among men. Viewed in terms of this exacting answer, which implies that language is a medium giving its user the dignity of a priest and which Proust had taken over from Baudelaire, Flaubert, and Huysmans, the possibility of interpreting Proust's novel cycle as a social *roman à clé* loses greatly in importance and turns out to be a matter of at best secondary interest. *À la Recherche du temps perdu* holds in the history of the French novel, especially by virtue of its final volume, *Le Temps retrouvé,* a position apart, because here we have more than merely a description of the refined circles of the Faubourg Saint-Germain, because here an author lets a new sensitivity become an aesthetic reality in which association, dissolution, and reconquest begin a seemingly hopeless struggle to achieve an understanding of the world. This will be clearly appreciated on the basis of the following passage quoted from the exposition: "It happened at times that—as Eve arose from a rib of Adam—a woman arose in my sleep from an awkward position of my thigh. While the pleasure I had been about to enjoy had formed her, I imagined that it was she who had been about to offer it to me. My body feeling in hers my own warmth, strove to be united with her body, and I awoke. The rest of mankind seemed far removed next to this woman whom I had left but a few moments ago. My cheek was still warm from her kisses, my body crushed by the weight of hers. When—as it happened at times—she bore the traits of a woman I had known in life, I vowed to devote myself wholly to the objective of finding her, not unlike those who undertake a voyage in order to see with their own eyes a longed-for city imagining that one can savor in a real thing the delight of a dream. Gradually my recollection of her waned; the girl of my dream was again forgotten."*

Nietzsche always praised in French literature that it visualized things psychological in connection with things physical. Of that, the foregoing Proust passage is an illuminating example, for it defines the concept of the psychological novel in a way that is particularly valid for France. Proust visualized the physiological, the psychological, and the mythological in a causal chain. That is a surprising concatenation. But quite apart from Proust, this idea was of burning interest to the *fin de siècle* and the early twentieth century, in particular when, even before Freud and Jung, the work of the psychologist John Mourly Vould (above all *On the Dream*) became known in France. For Vould studied dreams which occur after the application of stimuli to the lower extremities. This is precisely the situation in the Proust passage.

In explaining the duality of being, Proust used the mythological theme of the father and the mother of the human race from Genesis. As a narrator he started out by reporting to the reader an experience in its full immediacy. He described in particular the inherent tactile stimuli ("warmth," "my cheeks were still warm from her kisses," "my body crushed by the weight of hers"). Then there is the visual impression of a possible recollection, with the consequent release of new sensations and the decision "to find her, not unlike those who set out on a voyage to see with their own eyes a longed-for city imagining that one can savor in a real thing the delight of a dream." There is in this a peculiar contradiction. The metaphor of the "longed-for city," which is to impart to the occurrence such high merits and the concomitant skepticism with respect to the possibility of realizing this dream manifest a dilemma which is the basic problem of the entire Proust cycle. For À *la Recherche du temps perdu* annihilates unobtrusively in the course of the inner action of the novel the longing of man that the desires of his dreams might be fulfilled in life. In quite this sense Proust had written in 1913 to Anna de Noailles: "It is quite apparent that reality does not stand up and is unable to equal our dreams." (*Correspondance générale* II, 197)—But how then are we to understand the value of recollection? "Gradually my recollection of her waned; the girl of my dream was again forgotten." Is recollection but a chimera or is it the gift of a moment of grace? The latter holds true, particularly when Proust uses the word *souvenir* which he distinguishes from the intelligible *mémoire*. The search cannot be forced. The narrator can only—patiently and hopefully—listen within himself or wait until some external happening triggers the mechanism of recollection. This is new in Proust that spiritualism and materialism as philosophical principles are balanced, that the ideological heritage of Taine is kept at bay by Bergson's philosophy, especially as it appears in *Matière et mémoire* (1896). When Proust wrote, "Memory . . . came to me like a helping hand from on high to rescue me from the void from which I would not have been able to escape by myself; in one second I traversed centuries of civilization," (op. cit., p. 5) he referred to something preliminary, one might almost say to a sort of raw material. "Memory"—the word Proust used is *souvenir*—is the power prepared to gather up an entire world. It initiates in a sense the collection of materials, but it never imparts permanence. That is something art alone can do, though, in À *la Recherche du temps perdu*, it appears in total cogency only at the end of the cycle where it achieves a definitive form of world vanquishment. The search began in the realm of men and society and winds up in the world of aesthetics.

One thing Proust learned from Ruskin is this: A work of art derives its inner coherence from the fact that it can be unraveled, that it can be understood, starting at its end. *Le Temps retrouvé* resolves all the tensions of the cycle of novels as a whole. The psychological scale, "perception," "sensation," "knowledge," "recollection," and "memory" (the last two representing *mémoire* and *souvenir* and not prepared for

Proust in Bergson), has—if it is viewed as a pyramid—its top in the world of art: "But was this discovery, which art could enable us to make, was it not ultimately the discovery of ... what otherwise would forever remain unknown to us, our true lives, reality as we have sensed it to be but which differs in such measure from what we believed it was like that we are filled with happiness when chance affords us the memory of it?"*

The labile state of what Curtius has called the "seasons in the year of the soul," the forever porous fable of Proust's novel, expressing—through its deconfinement—a universal totality (with the result that the fable escapes every effort at summarization) while simultaneously accounting for the dissolution of the classical character of the hero into catenations of portrayals of situations and descriptions of reactions, and finally the propensity of individual figures of the novel to a kind of morbidezza may well represent in some fashion poetic re-interpretations of Proust's own experiences.

It was not given to Proust to care himself for the publication of more than part of his work. In November, 1913, *Du Côté de chez Swann* was the first volume to appear. In 1919, *À l'Ombre des jeunes filles en fleurs* followed. The award of the Prix Goncourt established Proust forthwith as a famous author, by virtue of a work the manuscript of which Gallimard, acting on the advice of André Gide, had first rejected. When Proust died on November 18, 1922, the publication of the cycle had reached the volumes *Du Côté de Guermantes* and *Sodome et Gomorrhe,* and the contemporary reader had indeed reason to believe that Proust was essentially a novelist of decadence. He had to wait another five years before the last volume appeared, making clear the real achievement of the author: to stipulate the impenetrability of what modern man can hardly be thought able to penetrate, and to do so—unlike the surrealists in 1924 —without declaring art's bankruptcy.

Mauriac's verdict on Proust seems harsh. "Consider," he wrote, "this single individual, fighting inch by inch unto death against the rising flood of memories, this weakling Hercules who is grasping at the flow of time or abandoning himself knowledgeably to its reflow. He has died of the insane venture." It might almost seem that Mauriac failed to understand Proust's concern. But as we listen again, his words take on the sound of words of distinction. Then too, it should not be forgotten that it was Mauriac who (in an article in the *Revue hebdomadaire* of February 26, 1921) took a stand in defense of Proust by declaring that the question of morality or immorality appeared irrelevant and ill-formulated in the face of Proust's work (Cf. also Proust's letter to Mauriac of September 24, 1919). For what is it that Proust proclaims if not the dignity and the power of creative men who, emancipated from the fetters of caste and pondersome moods can become masters of the world? Here we see a point of contact of Proust's work with that of André Gide. The great admiration Thomas Mann had for Proust is reflected in this passage from a letter to René Schickele of April 15, 1932: "I cannot share in any way," he wrote, "the current belief in the decline of the European West which still so recently brought forth a phenomenon of the artistic and literary format of Marcel Proust."

Beyond Proust, Gide established himself as an epic master in the tradition of the psychologists and moralists and as a seismograph of European cultural life throughout the entire first half of the twentieth century. His work demands of man —as does *À la Recherche du temps perdu*—that he come to terms with existence and with the world without outside help and become an imparter of meaning "on this side," without the help of a beyond. To be sure, we cannot but conclude that Proust, through the sociological as well as the aesthetic orientation of his work—especially when he is to be gauged by Gide's career—remains more intimately connected with the nineteenth century than with the twentieth. He completed the novel of crises of the *fin de siècle* while Gide was striving—for himself and for his age—to withstand and to resolve everything there was by way of crises.

André Gide was born in 1869 in Paris as the son of a Catholic mother from the north and a Protestant father from the Languedoc. When the boy was only eleven years old, his father died. So he grew up in the care of his mother and of female relatives. An almost morbidly exaggerated bent appeared in him to stand apart in narcissistic preoccupation with himself. He took part in Mallarmé's Tuesdays through which he was introduced at an early age to an extreme degree of the stylistic tradition of symbolism. In 1891, Gide made his first public appearance with the *Cahiers d'André Walter*. These are philiso-phico-lyrical excerpts from a fictitious posthumous diary in which a young soul portrayed itself artistically in its inner struggles. The book, *Poésies d'André Walter* (1892), is likewise a product of Gide's narcissicism. This was followed by a *Traité du Narcisse,* dedicated to Paul Valéry. This treatise is concerned with the myths of paradise and of Narcissus through a con-ceptual definition of the key words *visage* and *vision,* that is, "appearance of the world." The work culminates in the lesson, "not to prefer one's self to truth." No such thing was ever de-manded by Proust. It was only several years later that Gide succeeded in effecting a breakthrough from self-mirroring to active realization as a result of his having learned—during a journey through North Africa in 1893 and 1894—to take his life into his own hands. *Paludes* (1895) was a satire in a double sense. In the central character of the herdsman Tityre, a figure taken from the eclogues of Vergil, the reader meets an indi-vidual who drifts aimlessly through life. He lives in swamps from which he cannot bring himself to break away. He finally writes a novel with the title *Swamps.* This motif of a novel within a novel occurs elsewhere in Gide, for instance in *Les Faux-monnayeurs.*

A crucial aspect of *Paludes* is Gide's purpose of castigating the bourgeois salon culture of the *fin de siècle* which holds the spirit captive and bogged down, and simultaneously to ridicule his own inactivity and narcissism. The work is Gide's self-portrait before the African journey, but it was written after-wards in the Jura Mountains of Switzerland. Yet—although he explained in his preface to the second edition that it was the mission of this book to clarify the contrast, manifest to him since his African experience, between his spun-in and (in terms of religion) timid existence in the circle of the symbolists and the subsequent emancipation of his existence—Gide did not dare ridicule Mallarmé, Valéry, and Henri de Régnier. In *Paludes* Gide was already cultivating the open form which came to be so characteristic of his entire work. It is a form which suits per-fectly the idea of liberation and deconfinement. The praise of inner restlessness—"being enamored with one's own anxiety"— begins to assume the extreme form of a concept utilized by Gide later on in *Les Caves du Vatican* as the very theme of the novel, that is, the concept of the "free act" [*acte libre*] which in the other work is referred to as the "gratuitous act" [*acte gratuit*]. Thus the direction appears identified in which, more or less consistently, Gide was to keep moving throughout all the phases of his creative life up to *Thésée*, his final work, written when he was almost seventy-five years old.

The call for a break with the anemic tradition and the determination to achieve self-realization through a turnabout to pulsating life are still most strongly the theme of *Nourritures terrestres* (1897). Here Gide's African experience found expression in enthusiastic exclamations, such as "fervor, voluptuousness, desire, intoxication, ardor" [*ferveur, volupté, désir, ivresse, ardeur*]. It was through his critical encounter with Barrès' novel *Les Déracinés*—through "self-criticism in the guise of criticism of others," as von Stackelberg put it—through the rejection of the principles of "home and soil and rootedness" and the emphatic priority assigned to mobility as a principle of both life and thought (a visiting card which Gide had printed at the time bore under his name the specification "in transit" [*en voyage*]) that he finally, some time before the turn of the century, found his way to his true self.

Still, the content of the *Immoraliste* (1902) remains problematic. The title must not be taken to suggest the advocacy of a life without morality but only of a life set off from the morality of the masses. Utilizing autobiographical elements and not without traces of the influence of Oscar Wilde's life and work, Gide presented in this first-person account the description of a young scholar's progress to the fulness of life in rigorous nonconformism, characterized by an enthusiastic preference of the non-culture of the Goths over the refinements of civilization. To be sure, the hero's quest for self-realization appears coupled with a total lack of consideration for those around him. Of this his ailing wife must bear the brunt until she finally dies. So the work comes to a close without fulfillment and without resolution. The influence of Nietzsche (which Gide, to be sure, could never bring himself to admit to its full extent) is quite evident in the implications of this conclusion.[3]

We get an inkling of the epic greatness of Gide, manifest in particular in the multiplicity of his themes and formal approaches, when we note that it was in 1891 that he began work on *La Porte étroite* (1909), a narrative in which there is hardly a trace of either Wilde or Nietzsche. The student Jérôme is in love with Alissa who is a profoundly religious and withdrawn girl. Since her sister Juliette shows clearly her interest in Jérôme, Alissa takes this as the pretext for renouncing her friend. This renunciation would seem to lose its basis when Juliette marries another man, but Alissa remains steadfast, for she does not wish to prefer a human being to God. After her early death, her diary falls into Jérôme's hands. It is to him a profoundly moving revelation. Among the last entries there is for instance one, dated October 13, which reads in part: "Have read over my diary before destroying it. It is unworthy of a great heart to pour out its troubles. I think it was Clothilde de Vaux who spoke these beautiful words.

"As I was about to throw this diary into the fire something seemed to hold me back. It was as though the diary no longer belonged to me, and that I did not have the right to take it away from Jérôme, that I had never written anything not for him. . . . My God, grant that he may sense in it at times the awkward tones of a heart madly desirous of pushing him to the pinnacle of virtue which I myself despaired of attaining.

"My God, lead me to the rock which I have not the strength to reach."

This shows clearly the technical function which the diary passages have at the end of *La Porte étroite* in the economy of the novel. They are to tell Jérôme how Alissa, between God and a man she loves, achieves renunciation. That is for Alissa the "narrow gate" of which the Gospel speaks. On October 10, she notes: "Oh joy, joy all too human, that my rash heart hoped for . . . was it to hear this outcry from me, O Lord, that you let me despair?" In the end, Alissa's sacrifice appears all too clearly as a torment, for her turning away from Jérôme leads her less to genuine bliss than to despair. Terms like "sad, tired, hopeless" [*triste, fatiguée, désespérée*] abound in the descriptions of her state of mind. The closing sentence in the diary reads: "I wish I would die now, fast, before I understand once again that I am alone."[4]

What then—for this is the problem in *La Porte étroite*—is man's destiny and mission? Is he to look for happiness in this world or in the world beyond? In *Nouveaux prétextes,* Gide himself called Alissa, in whom we can discern traits of his wife Madeleine (cf. *Et nunc manet in te*), a "gratuitous heroine" [*heroïne gratuite*] whose Calvinistic ethos could lead nowhere and was hence meaningless. It is true, Alissa's renunciation impresses us as unnatural even though it may be tragic. And thus we reach a point where we are able to see clearly in what sense *La Porte étroite* occupies a focal point in Gide's work as a whole, for it replaces God as the ultimate objective of life by man himself. Claudel saw in *La Porte étroite* a critique of Protestantism, but this does not touch the core of the matter. *La Porte étroite* is a humanistic narration in the fullest sense of the term, and the Protestant setting represents little more than autobiographical reminiscences.

From now on Gide called in his works for man's self-realization through his own powers. His future epic and dramatic work was to become a manifestation of this faith in the here and now, it was to represent a fight for happiness here on earth. This change in Gide's philosophy can be observed in his diary. To be sure, phases of a more religious motivation continued for a while to alternate with entirely non-religious phases, but when on March 8, 1932, Gide referred to the "dedication to a noble cause," this reflected already a turn toward world Communism. At times, the social complex of questions replaced problems of ethics and religion. The development follows a direction diametrically opposed to that found in Proust.

The dimension in which this change took shape and in terms of which the real Gide can be understood over and beyond all matters involving party politics is the *sincérité* which, in his case, represents the final outcome of a religious search of conscience. Thus it is that Kurt Wais could call Gide "the most unprejudiced and most open-minded Frenchman of his age." Gide's "openness," his receptivity for the things of this world is simultaneously reflected in his determination to remove the mask of illusion from everything vacuously traditional in order to free man for the realities that really matter. The fact that we can trace this development in Gide's diaries imparts to them their great value. From 1889 on, he consistently kept a diary, and it is invariably in this source that we first encounter the themes that interested him. The aspect of his character with which we are here concerned manifested itself in a special form in the satirical novel of rogues, *Les Caves du Vatican* (1914), which Gide himself called a *"sotie"*—the term used in literary history for a late medieval genre of short farcical plays with allegorical figures. The classical paucity of factual events, which permitted us to think of *La Porte étroite* as belonging in the tradition of the *Princesse de Clèves*, is replaced in *Les Caves du Vatican* by a virtually inextricable tissue of action. In the central figure of the amateur criminal Lafcadio, who commits a "murder for murder's sake" [*meurtre gratuit*], Gide undertook to create in mythical terms an embodiment of absolute freedom. In this sense the novel goes even beyond the ethical program of the *Immoraliste*. The explicit reference to the genre of the *sotie* suggests, to be sure, that the turbulent abundance of action must not be taken seriously in all its elements. The novelist wanted to write a book "against the banal rhetoric which argues the case of what must be done and against the cheap aroma of efficiency." However, the absence of responsibility and obligation in the central figure and its nonconformism exerted a strong influence on the younger generation of the time.

It may be of interest in this connection that Gide maintained a relation of close personal friendship with Pierre Louÿs (1870–1925) whom the discovery of a Greek antiquity exempt from the doctrine of the Fall and of man's sinfulness inspired to novels and narratives of sensuous frenzy (*Sanguines*, 1903, a.o.) whose exaggerated sweep, to be sure, was skeptically interrupted in one highly significant instance, that of *La Femme et le pantin* (1898), by the myth of Pandora.

In terms of form, Gide returned once again to *La Porte étroite* in *La Symphonie pastorale* (1919). This is a narrative in diary form evolving around the enlightenment-oriented motif of blindness. When Gertrud, who has been blind from birth, asks her foster father, a protestant clergyman, whether everything in the world is as beautiful as the pastoral symphony to which she is listening, he does not have the courage to answer in the negative. Shortly thereafter, when thanks to a bold surgical operation, the girl is made to see, she takes her own life. The world of ideals in which she has been living has been replaced by a shattering reality which she is unable to endure. Religious conflicts—the son of the clergyman had aroused Catholic sympathies in her—and the tension between gratitude and affection (for both the father and the son endeavour to win her love) make her choose voluntary death as a solution.

Gide's most powerful manifesto against the false and the phony, against contrivance and distortion, the most powerful manifesto the older generation dared offer the young, appeared in 1926 under the title of *Les Faux-monnayeurs*. This, by the way, is the only narrative product of Gide's that he himself called a novel. Despite the insertion of letters and excerpts from diaries and countless reflections, the composition of this work is as clear and transparent as its guiding idea. Edouard is busy gathering material for a novel, and being allowed to witness the genesis of it arouses the enthusiasm of two young men, Olivier Molinier and Bernard Profitendieu. This applies in particular to Bernard who becomes Edouard's secretary, motivated by a profound disappointment with his family. The title is doubly symbolic, for the term "counterfeiters" applies to both the members of the adult generation and to a group of criminal juveniles of the postwar generation. The initial conceit of this work Gide took from press reports of the years 1906 and 1907 which he reworked and reinterpreted in his own way. The intellectual and moral counterfeiting of the parents causes the children to go wrong. The novel ends on a problematic note. Only Olivier persists in siding with Edouard. Bernard returns to his family, while a member of the gang of counterfeiters, seeing no way out of the situation, takes his own life.

The narrative works which were published during Gide's communist intermezzo (1930–36)—the trilogy *L'École des femmes*, *Robert*, and *Geneviève*—lag far behind the artistic significance of Gide's last epic work, *Thésée* (1946). Here Theseus is shown as a successor to Prometheus and as a leader of mankind, in a way that makes it easy to recognize in the title figure the author himself. For Theseus and Gide have in common their non-conformism and their struggle against the gods and against vacuous tradition. Both are representatives of sincerity and readiness [*sincérité* and *disponibilité*]. Both face grave dangers early on their way. There is, for Theseus, the labyrinth of the Minotaur; there is, for Gide, narcissistic self-mirroring and fantastic excess. And finally, the two are linked through their secret love for a being in polar opposition to themselves. For Theseus this is, in the narrative, his partner in dialogue,

Oedipus; for Gide it is his wife Madeleine whose image he was to conjure up once again the following year in *Et nunc manet in te* (1947). The idea of *Thésée* had occupied Gide as early as sometime in the thirties, but the actual writing was done only in 1944 in North Africa. It was accomplished within a few weeks.

In this work, Theseus attempts to build up his existence on the principle of "going beyond," though not in the sense of either a "free act" or a "gratuitous act" but (and this makes clear the humanitarian progress since *Paludes* and *Caves du Vatican*) as an effort to achieve self-realization by working simultaneously "for the good of mankind." Aegeus, the father of Theseus, commends to his son, as the objective in life: "Be aware that you must show men what one among them is able to be and what he proposes to become. There are great things to be done. Find yourself."* And Theseus, "going beyond and determined not to be delayed," does attain his objective, that of setting the example of a balanced and fulfilled life and of founding the city state of Athens as an exemplary community of men.

When André Gide died on February 19, 1951, his last words were: "And ever the struggle goes on between what is reasonable and what is not." They are as difficult to interpret as Gide's literary life's work, which cannot possibly be reduced to one simplifying formula. Vaguely we seem to discern a spiraling course—a turning away from Christianity, a phase of sympathy with world communism, followed by disappointment with the Soviet Union after the trip of 1936, a freer humanism—but the closing figure of Theseus, in which we see Gide perhaps at his greatest (not before 1947 was Gide awarded the Nobel Prize for literature), is only one aspect, and if it harks back to the figures of Lafcadio and Alissa, it does so exclusively by virtue of the intervening mutation of the idea of freedom. Proust's self-realization was ultimately purely aesthetic, Gide's was humanistic: Everything man is able to do and to achieve he must put in the service of life here and now in order to bring joy and happiness to his fellows.

How great the power of radiation of this program was will become clear from the work of Albert Camus.[5] It is true that Gide learned from Nietzsche how essential it is for the age we call modern that a critical mind should question and even doubt its ultimate bases, but pity and care appear in his work to the same striking extent, witness the fact of Gide's deep interest in the Russian novel of the nineteenth century, in particular in Dostoevski. It is in this duality, in this reunion of seemingly irreconcilable spheres that Gide's greatness should be seen, and it is the more impressive as we observe how the French novel of realization moved away after Gide from his humanitarian objectives toward a posture of egotism.

Pierre Drieu la Rochelle (1893–1945) was able to speak only with despair of the future of mankind and in particular of the French nation. In an epilogue to *Gilles* (1939), he called decadence the directive theme of his work and characterized the inner form of his narrative prose by calling it an accounting. He thought of himself as occupying a position somewhere between Céline, Montherlant, and Malraux. Drieu La Rochelle formulated his political commitment in essays which aroused great interest and much controversy. His place in French narrative prose appeared clearly defined—after *L'Homme couvert de femmes* (1925) and *Le Feu follet* (1931)—with the publication of *Gilles*. This extensive work, which Picon lists among the great novels of the century, was written after 1934. When it appeared, none of the critics had the courage to praise it without qualification. The subject was too ticklish late in 1939. The career of the hero Gilles Gambier in this "new *Éducation sentimentale*" (as Paul Géraldy called it) began, like that of Rousseau's *Émile*, without the protective warmth of a family setting. It progresses toward an existentialist kind of isolation in which this Norman irrationalist hungers for life while the world about him is that of an enlightened party democracy. Gilles's connection with a rich Jewess at the time of the First World War lays the foundation of his lifelong antisemitism. "Never would Gilles have thought it possible that anyone believed in equality and progress." He feels persecuted by the trauma of ubiquitous sterility spread by the egalitarian principle. Sterile is the politics of socialism; sterile the formalism of Marxism; sterile and flabby appears, to Gilles, the literary revolt of surrealism (here the work is clearly a *roman à clé*); sterile finally is his young wife Pauline. Boldness, that is, the will to power and to self-realization, the hero finds only among the

Fascists. In the falangists of the Spanish Civil War he celebrates positive symbolic figures, for they are able to face death without material backing. We know that Drieu La Rochelle originally intended to give his novel the title of *La Mort et l'argent*, in order to name and label the ultimate horror. The dreadful confusion of the hearts, caused by the monied bourgeoisie and by bolshevism, implies ultimately also a pervasion of the relationships of love which become interchangeable. In his description of the ephemerality of things erotic, the author comes close to equaling the mastery of Aragon.

It is from Stendhal, Gobineau, and Barrès that Henri de Montherlant (born 1896 in Paris) took over the mythological concept of the Mediterranean overman, but he was no longer able to shape from it truly fascinating novelistic figures. Especially his male representatives of the aristocracy are all too often little more than frozen monuments. In tauromachy Montherlant saw a pre-eminent possibility of testing a man's being a man and of self-realization. Having taken part for the first time in 1909 in a corrida and having killed his first young bull in Burgos in 1910, he collected in Spain in 1925 material for *Les Bestiaires* (1926). In this epic exaltation of tauromachy we make the acquaintance of Alban de Bricoule and his friend Soledad. The girl encourages Alban's manly ambition to prove his courage in the arena, but the closing situation is reminiscent of Schiller's ballad, "The Glove." When the torero leaves the ring victorious, the girl has ceased to mean anything to him.

What distinguishes Montherlant's novel of realization in particular is his endeavor to show a pure world of men as an aristocratic form of life (*Les Célibataires*, 1934; *Les Jeunes filles*, 1936–39). His assertion that in order to be perfect a man must be in succession Vincent de Paul, Kant, and Casanova is more indicative of the writer's arrogance than of his actual creative powers in the portrayal of character. As a faithful disciple of Barrès, Montherland fought—in particular in the trilogy *Les Jeunes filles*—the feminine, the soft, and the sensitive and dolorous as manifestations of decadence in man.

After years of silence as a novelist Montherlant came out in 1963 with *Le Chaos et la nuit*. This novel—obviously conceived under the impression of Pío Baroja's novel of exile *La Ciudad de la niebla,* with which it shares the motif of the unequal pair of father and daughter—is strangely unreal and simultaneously time-dependent. Celestino Marcilla, a Spanish anarchist, has left his country during the Civil War choosing Paris as his place of exile. Except for his daughter Pascualita and a small number of Spanish friends he has no human contacts. After an absence of thirty years he is called back to Madrid to settle a matter of inheritance. He suspects a trap of the régime but goes anyway. What Montherlant now presents is a picture of Spain which thoroughly does away with the postal-card romanticism of the conventional idea. Thus Don Celestino's growing uneasiness about his homeland is made credible in minute detail. In a disappointingly unsuccessful *corrida de toros* held in bad weather in early spring, Celestino's world-weary annoyance reaches its climax. To what extent this implies a personal confession of Montherlant must remain an open question. Celestino identifies himself with the hunted, tormented bull. He returns to his hotel and dies there all alone. The author intentionally fails to explain whether Don Celestino has been murdered, has been hunted down and shot by the Secrete Police, or has fallen victim to an accident. In any event, this conclusion marks a reorientation of Montherlant's work as a whole.

It might seem that we have here a trend that started in *Les Bestiairies* to go on to Camus' *Malentendu*. But a more appealing interpretation is possibly that Montherlant in his later years has discovered in things Spanish, which had fascinated him from youth and stimulated him as a dramatist, the tragic grotesquery of Don Quixote as it is manifest, for instance, in Unamuno's commentary on Cervantes. The virile austerity of the individual prepared the downfall of the lone outsider. Thus seen, Montherlant does not abandon his consciously untimely basic tenets. He does look through them, and the one who plays the part becomes a moving and stirring figure.[6]

Raymond Radiguet (1903–23) is at least Montherlant's equal, even though his circle of readers has remained surprisingly small. Radiguet lived his short life in the suburbs of Paris. He was a friend of Max Jacob and of Cocteau and was a great admirer of *Les Pléiades* by Gobineau. He left us two novels which he had written on the side while working as a journalist. They are *Le Bal du comte d'Orgel* and his main work, *Le Diable au corps* (1923). The latter work is in its outer appearance a novel of love written in the manner of Choderlos de Laclos or Benjamin Constant, but beyond this it shows a love delivered into the hands of the times. The subject matter is auto-biographical. The setting is that in which Radiguet himself lived, that is, the bourgeois world on the outskirts of Paris during the First World War. The action is a simple triangle. Prompted initially more by the cruelty of youthful curiosity than by true passion, a sixteen-year-old high-school student courts his childhood friend Marthe who is married to a soldier at the front. The young woman, who lives a life without fulfillment, quickly falls for him. But, having seduced her, the boy does not succeed in shaping the relationship in accordance with his ideas. He is not even able to give his growing dissatisfaction a firm and determined expression. When it becomes apparent that Marthe is pregnant he tries to dissolve the relationship by deceiving her with a Swedish woman, but he does not succeed. So the novel ends in the mood of *tristesse* which three decades later Françoise Sagan was to try to revive. Three years before Gide's *Les Faux-monnayeurs* Radiguet presented in this novel the portrayal of a war generation which does react to its disorientation by conceiving grandly soaring plans, only to prove unable to translate them into fact. Radiguet's performance must be valued the more highly since he was able, at the age of twenty, to build from a personal experience a mature portrayal in which the inner discord of the hero becomes clearly palpable.[7]

Another author, likewise concerned with behavioral studies of human relationships, albeit of slighter weight, is Maurice Toesca (born 1905) who is possibly better known as the biographer of George Sand. In *L'Expérience amoureuse* (1954) and *Simone ou le bonheur conjugal,* Toesca shows how partners in marriage often try to maintain themselves in opposition to one another. But Toesca was as little concerned as Sainte-Beuve had been in the related novel *Volupté* with the realistic details one might expect from the titles, for his primary interest was the psychological, that is, intellectual as well as spiritual, dynamics. A typical example is the notation: "The gold of silence is not as pure as it might seem, and moderation in love often conceals coldness." In such nicely sensualist formulations we recognize the former student of the philosopher Alain.

A similar echo of educational influences can be discerned in the books of Alfred Kern (born 1919 in the Ruhr). Before the late war, Kern had studied theology but in 1945 he switched to philosophy. Reading Proust must have been of decisive importance to him, for in his fourth publication, *Le Clown* (1957)—preceded by *Le Jardin perdu, Les Voleurs de cendre,* and *Le Mystère de Sainte Dorothée*—he discovered the discrepancy between outer appearance and inner experience which is most tragically manifest but perhaps also potentially resolvable in the grimace of the clown. In Kern's novels, the individual is presented with challenging situations whose mastery demands almost superhuman spiritual achievements. In *Le Clown*, life appears metaphorically represented by the circus. The clown is consumed with the ambition to do justice in his work at the circus less to the run of-the-mill demands of the balcony than to those of his inner person. In *L'Amour profane* (1959), a priest fails in life because a Mother Superior, in whom he sees a woman, confronts him as a representative of things transcendental. It seems possible that we have here a turning point in the development of this gifted author.

In comparison with the novels of Alfred Kern, those of Françoise Sagan (born 1935) reflect the problem of self-realization in vastly more profane terms. In all the Sagan novels that have so far appeared, the central figures take a particular stand in the face of particular situations in order, at least momentarily, to live down the vicissitudes or sweet surprises of everyday life. This is something Françoise Sagan learned from Stendhal and from Radiguet. There is no denying that this author has not been able to repeat so far the lucky jack-pot hit of *Bonjour tristesse* (1954). Her later productions are *Un Certain sourire* (1956), *Dans un mois, dans un an* (1957), *Aimez-vous Brahms* (1959), and *Les Merveilleux nuages* (1960). An essential feature of the integrated autonomy of these novels is the interplay of a banal subject matter, banal characters, and a banal language.

In *Bonjour tristesse,* Cécile cunningly fights her father's plan to marry a Parisian fashion designer. After the death of her "rival"—presumably a suicide—the girl (in whom many contemporaries have seen a faithful portrayal of the author herself) gives up her position, and nothing remains but stale sadness.

The *"ennui"* which shows up in Françoise Sagan is not the world-weariness of the romanticists nor the spleen of Baudelaire but a log-jam of energy evoking listlessness and boredom. It is for this reason that there are no pairs of real lovers in the works of Françoise Sagan. Love, in her interpretation, is a partnership of accomplices meticulously concerned lest they be caught off their guard one by the other. Thus it is that Paula in *Aimez-vous Brahms* cannot fully bind her older friend to herself even by marriage.

In reading these books one senses how Françoise Sagan has learned in particular from Stendhal how two human beings fear in almost morbid self-scrutiny to be duped or fooled by one another.[8] What the French novel of realization in the first half of the twentieth century did in fact manage to achieve could not become fully clear until the *"nouveau roman"* radically questioned man's self-realization in the world. (This is the theme of our Chapter XIV.)

VII

THE NOVEL OF DEVELOPMENT

Romain Rolland, Marcel Arland, Jacques Chardonne,
Jacques de Lacretelle, Gabrielle Sidonie Colette,
Henri Alain-Fournier, Valery Larbaud, Franz Hellens

❦ The modern French novel presents—when it emulates
Stendhal—existence as a chain of "attitudes" in the face of abruptly arising situations; it attempts—in the wake of Balzac—
to conceive of society as a superior community of beings; or,
finally, it proclaims—harking back to Fromentin and Proust—
the enigmatic as a principle of life. In none of these trends is
the modern French novel intrinsically akin to the novel of
development and education.

The novel of development and education of modern times
—though harking back to the novel-like epic of *Parzival*, to
Grimmelshausen's *Simplizissimus*, or to Wieland's *Agathon*—is
essentially the tribute and contribution to European letters of
German Romanticism and of Goethe, and it is characteristic
that it was outside of Germany precisely the great admirers of
Goethe—such as Thomas Carlyle in *Sartor Resartus* (1833) or
Romain Rolland in *Jean-Christophe*—who tried their hands at
works in this genre. This is not meant to imply, of course, that
no French writers other than Rolland were inspired by the
novel of development. In fact, the list of representative cases
is not altogether short, especially if we let it include names
which belong elsewhere, too, and others for which the connec-

tion is somehow indirect. A point to remember is that these writers did not benefit in their work from the fructifying climate of pietism favoring their German peers. Furthermore, they lacked the characteristically nineteenth-century faith in the ultimate values of culture through which young people were led to set up for themselves the high objective of self-training. But Rolland and Chardonne, Alain-Fournier and Hellens did portray things growing rather than things grown.

Romain Rolland (1866–1944)—born in Clamecy (Département Nièvre), from 1886 on a student of Brunetière's at the École Normale—received his first decisive influence from the work of Tolstoy. Here he saw exemplified epic breadth as well as the idea of compassion. The basis of the Germanism in his work was laid first by his admiration for Goethe and then also by his acquaintance with Malvida von Meysenbug in Rome where he taught at the French School from 1889 on. Rolland once called this woman "a last reflection of the old idealistic Germany of 1848." She took him to Bayreuth when Wagner had become an experience for him adding depth to his musical enthusiasm. In 1897 he was called upon to teach history of art at the École Normale where Charles Péguy was among his pupils. From 1903 to 1912 Rolland taught history of music at the Sorbonne.

His literary production began with dramas and historical portraits. Yet, his biographies of Beethoven, Michelangelo, and Tolstoy have somehow the appearance of preparatory studies for his ten-volume novel *Jean-Christophe* which was published by Péguy from 1904 to 1912 in the *Cahiers de la quinzaine*. In terms of national French literature and in terms of world literature, this *roman-fleuve* differs from its forerunners in that the author attempted to fuse the romantic tradition of the novel of education with the novel of artists and the novel of reconciliation of nations. The figure of the hero, Jean-Christophe Krafft, reminds us both of Beethoven and of Rolland himself. Having grown up as the son of a ruined family in the Rhineland, Krafft must go through all the phases of the school of life and of artistdom: friendships, love of woman, *liaisons dangereuses*, envy and persecution in his own fatherland. When he flees to Paris, he misses in French art the accent of morality and ethics until his friend Olivier Jeannin helps him discover under the frivolous mask of epicureanism and intellectual flirtation "the other France" of heroism and sacrifice. When he dies in Switzerland after years of restlessness and wandering and of searching and questing for organization and structure—with music coming to be for him ever more powerfully the mediatrix of a Goethean serenity as his hold on life—we hear for the last time the leitmotif of the novel: Father Rhine, the river of Fate, destined to become the bond of Europe's reunion, and simultaneously the embodiment of a metaphysical symbol of flux. For, in Rolland's philosophy of life, the individual is a point of transition for the one all-inclusive stream of life. Every individual must decide for his own person whether he can conceive and confirm the fact of his belonging and the implied experience of sympathy with the whole or whether he wants to overlook that fact and deny it.

Jean-Christophe was meant by its author to become a novel that would "embrace millions." In keeping with this, the British writer Galsworthy regarded *Jean-Christophe* as a major contribution toward the liquidation of pure aestheticism as the heritage of the *fin de siècle*. Here the work of literature appeared restored in its moral functions. The years immediately after 1945, during which *Jean-Christophe* was discovered as a novel of reconciliation, have witnessed—in Germany in particular—a notable up-grading of Rolland, though in almost all cases it was overlooked that Rolland could not instill into his portrait of a genius, that is, his portrait of the composer Krafft, more of the genius than he himself had. Unfortunately the author himself was hardly aware of this. So the errors, uncertainties, and lengths in the conduct of the action and the portrayal of character weigh only the more heavily.

The pendant to this cycle is Rolland's *L'Âme enchantée* (1922–33), another *roman-fleuve*. The progressive disenchantment of the soul of the French woman Annette, her development from girlhood into a mother who loses her son in the struggle against Italian fascism, represents for Rolland the symbol of a new spiritual posture. In his optimism he keeps faith in the salvation of the soul through the female principle, the principle of a *natura naturans*, of total love.

In order to do Rolland justice and to assign to him his real rank one must have read his *Colas Breugnon* (1919), for here his astonishingly rich, though not always firmly attuned keyboard of multiple epic possibilities becomes evident. This book is the chronicle of a craftsman in Clamecy, written in 1614. It is a book full of well-fed *esprit gaulois*, like Balzac's *Contes drôlatiques* or some of the works of Anatole France and of Marcel Aymé. This juicy early seventeenth-century panorama of Burgunday is a pleasantly relaxing compensation after *Jean-Christophe.*[1]

Discontinuity and mixture are likewise qualifying characteristics of the novel of development as represented by Marcel Arland (born 1899). Arland, currently editor of the *Nouvelle revue française*, showed in his first stories—such as those in the volume *Terres étrangères* (1922)—his affiliation with the American story and short novel of the later nineteenth century. The guiding theme of his entire production up to this time, consisting in large part of novellae, stories, and essays, is the human endeavor to work out a *modus vivendi* both with the ego and with the world outside. It seems a simple matter, but in Arland's narratives it proves to be an infinitely difficult assignment. Arland's couples, for instance in *L'Eau et le feu* or *À Perdre haleine,* wear themselves the more down the longer they stay together. The most mature work of this author is doubtless the novel, *L'Ordre* (1929) which was distinguished with the Prix Goncourt. Here Arland combines the continuity of a novel of development with the portrayal of character of a Radiguet, whose *Diable au corps* had appeared six years previously, or of a Stendhal.

The work opens in 1919 with Gilbert Villars having reached the conclusion of his scholastic education. He sets himself a high-flown program of life: "to be master of one's nerves . . . not to show one's sensitivity . . .—I look upon life as a drama. And in this drama I am determined to play my part grandly and unmistakably." (p. 44). Gilbert moves from Clermont to Paris where he becomes a journalist working for the leftist press. From this position he fights his half-brother Justin who is a conservative member of the Chamber of Deputies. He succeeds in winning over Justin's wife Renée, the daughter of his guardian. Their love relationship, however, degenerates rapidly into a progressively more unconcealed hate and profound aversion which are further fanned by Gilbert's unfaithfulness. His temporary removal to Indochina brings the marriage partners together again. His sudden return, however, draws all the seeming order and safety into question again. From an aspiring student, Gilbert has grown to be an outlaw and a diabolic meddler. When he dies, this is confirmed by Justin: "As though everything were not of necessity to fall back in line." (p. 541). *L'Ordre* is the novel of the development of an individual intent upon using his arrogant Stendalesque drives to secure for himself a place outside of tradition, mores, and decency. Fate destroys Gilbert's amoral escapades. The proximity to *Le Rouge et le noir* is striking, but Arland does not regard his hero, as did Stendhal, with pride and love. The motif of the unequal brothers likewise marks a notable difference. In this novel of development, which is simultaneously a novel of fate, we have —to boot—a novel of bourgeois morality. Gilbert Villars violates the rules, he becomes a foreign body in the bourgeois organism and is rejected. Hardly another author of the twentieth century has understood Stendhal and has simultaneously overcome Stendhal as did Arland. That establishes the significance of *L'Ordre*.[2]

Jacques Chardonne (born 1884) hails from a family of Protestants in South-western France. In his novels he followed primarily the development of the reciprocal formative influence of the two individuals in married life. He first took up this motif in *L'Épithalame* (1922). Bertha and Albert met early in life and later on married. But now their love faces real dangers until they discover that their living together in intimate simplicity provides a more solid foundation for their happiness than stormy passion. With *Les Destinées sentimentales,* a family trilogy covering the period from 1905 to 1935, Chardonne left temporarily his most personal preserve to which he returned, however, with *Romanesques* (1937). This is the novel of two lovers of whose development in married life the reader learns through their common confidant. The final accounting of Chardonne's psychology of married life as given in this novel appears to state that partners in marriage—though they may have been together for as long as seven years, though they may have done their best to grow ever more alike—preserve an impenetrably intimate personal recess. For Chardonne it is a valid principle that "it is really life that man loves in a woman." Through this endeavor, which is both humanistic and idealistic, and worldly withall, man approaches maturation. The mission of woman is meanwhile, as Chardonne puts it in *Romanesques*, to air the secret of life.[3] Such ideas will again appear in Giraudoux.

In 1964 Chardonne finally published under the title of *Catherine* a short novel written much earlier, at about the time of Gide's *La Porte étroite*. This love story has its setting at the beginning of the century on the Riviera in the world of sanitariums for lung ailments. François, who obviously has read Nietzsche and Bourget, tries systematically to demoralize his partner Catherine until she does break through the wall of conventions cemented by her upbringing. When she appears to have changed sufficiently and is ready to give in to François, he withdraws with cool reserve, for his objective was to enlighten rather than to conquer. The tragedy of love which is the theme of Chardonne's later works appears to be prepared in germ in *Catherine*.

As little known outside of France as Chardonne is is also Jacques de Lacretelle (born 1888). He is the son of a diplomat from the Mâconnais. His most important contribution to the French novel of development of the twentieth century is *Silbermann* (1922), a student novel with the problem of how a Jew can fully become a Frenchman. This development proceeds in *Silbermann* in two parallel continuities. The reader is first introduced to the Jewish boy Silbermann as he is ragged by his classmates in school; we then see him evolve an outstanding analytical intelligence which he devotes to his dream of a messianic socialism; and finally we learn of Silbermann's resigned decision to become rather a rich man in the United States than an intellectual servant of France. In parallel to this development there is that of the narrator, a Protestant, whom a confusedly fanatic Catholic classmate first misleads to embrace anti-Semitism but who then becomes Silbermann's champion, giving himself the assignment of making Silbermann feel more closely bound to France, until—after the latter's departure— he falls back to his former position. This conclusion seems at first surprising. Is it possibly an expression of Lacretelle's pessimism with respect to the spirit of the times? Possibly. But it is certain that it illustrates the psychological thesis that youth implies developmental potentialities, with rectilineal consistency rather an accident than a principle. The revolutionary nonconformism, which places the Protestant next to the Jew—possibly also motivated by a latent sympathy for any religious minority—subsides and is forgotten as soon as Silbermann disappears from the student's view. This signifies with respect to Lacretelle's literary situation that he is intent upon showing as radically as possible the principle of change in youth. In the sobriety of this approach no one can be compared to Lacretelle but possibly Valery Larbaud.

The strength of Gabrielle Sidonie Colette (1873–1954) lies elsewhere. The complete bibliography of Colette's novels comprises the titles of more than forty works written in part by her alone and in part in collaboration with her husband Henri Gauthier-Villars ("Willy"). They form a single great novel of development divided only seemingly in two halves, the novels of love and the novels of animals, for the focus of interest is always the person of the author herself. It is her way through life from the provinces to the Parisian stage of entertainment and finally to literary fame that form the theme of these books. Thus we have *Claudine à l'école, Claudine à Paris, Claudine en ménage, Claudine s'en va,* and *La Vagabonde.*

Colette's contemporaries were lavish with friendly praise for her. Paul Valéry called her the only author who understood "that writing is an art." Montherlant put her above Gide. In all this, it is not quite clear whether such compliments were addressed to the author or to the fascinating woman. It is undeniable that the femininity of Colette's heroines is always distinguished by a vein of authenticity. Colette obviously wrote only—in keeping with the naturalist program—of what she knew from her own experience. Herein lies the charm of her novels but also their incontestable limitation. Thus we may want to accept as the most fitting verdict the formula contributed by Jean Paulhan: "She was our best journalist who got side-tracked into the novel."[4]

It is rare that the author of a single novel arouses as much attention as did Henri Alain-Fournier (1886–1914), whose creative career was abruptly terminated when he died on the battle field. In the idyllic novel, *Le Grand Meaulnes* (1913)—next to Franz Hellen's poetic prose the most delicate lyrical narrative since 1900—he spread out in pastel-like pictures of moods the story of a childhood companionship and love, held together by the title hero's refusal to grow up. The novel, which is a concealed portrait of the first-person narrator, is set in the Departments Cher and Yonne. One day the tall Augustin Meaulnes shows up as a boarder in the family of the teacher Seurel. He embodies the tragic figure of youth sensing that the loss of childhood is a loss of paradise. Roaming through the woods, he finds at a castle a group of young people, including Yvonne de Galais with whom he expects to preserve youth intact. But their wedding terminates their happiness. Meaulnes leaves his wife. When he returns from his aimless wanderings she is dead. But his child lives. So there is for Alain-Fournier in the quest for a lost paradise only the double possibility of death or again a child. The resonance of Charles Nodier and structural links to the work of the Russian Chekhov cannot be overlooked. Like Nodier, Alain-Fournier sees in the growth of the individual no positive development of young life to something higher but an increasing loss of vital substance. As maturity is achieved, an intact world breaks down. This mythical and fairyish theme is placed by the author in a concrete frame of regional reference. The aftereffects of this process are of significance: They are to be found in Giraudoux, Hellens, and the American Truman Capote in *Other Voices, Other Rooms* (1948).[5]

The picture of the world of children, as Valery Larbaud (1881–1957) saw it, is more complex, more cruel, more disillusioning. Larbaud was born in Vichy where he also spent the last decades of his life, unable to leave for reasons of health. Like Gide he enjoyed at all times absolute financial independence. He was among the founders of the *Nouvelle revue française*. A citizen of the world in the best literary sense, he undertook to foster among his countrymen a fuller appreciation of Whitman, Samuel Butler, James Joyce, and William Faulkner. His most original creation was the figure of the globe-trotter Barnabooth whom he introduced as the author of *Poésies* (1908) and of a *Journal* (1913). In addition, there are three volumes of narrative prose in a stricter sense, *Fermina Marquez* (1911), *Enfantines* (1918), and *Amants, heureux amants* (1924).

The setting of *Fermina Marquez*—the novel of a restive generation—is an international boarding school. From the motley student population, the narrator picks a random number of life stories, quickly destroying the initial exotic hue through devices of disillusioning child psychology. The complex of bitterness and sweetness in the development of children and youths is further accentuated in *Enfantines*, a collection of miniatures of children, while in *Amants, heureux amants* the novelist returns to the cruel principle of disclosure which was characteristic of *Fermina Marquez*. He holds up to us his portrait of a lost generation, climaxing in the philosophy: "The important thing is to learn to stand alone in life as one day I shall stand alone in death." In this way Larbaud introduced elements of stoicism into the novel of development. The individual's development consists in his learning to take into consideration, and to cope with, the contingencies and unreliabilities of existence.[6]

In Franz Hellens (born 1881), finally, we meet a Belgian author whose importance is as yet hardly appreciated outside of French-speaking lands. After his university years in Geneva, Hellens became a librarian in Brussels. Here he established the important periodical *Disque vert* (1922ff.). He made friends with Jessenin, whose poems he translated, with Maxim Gorky, with Ehrenburg, and with Stefan Zweig. In his writings he progressed from surrealism "by anticipation" in *Mélusine* or *Réalités fantastiques* to become a psychologist, reflecting in the poetic prose of his novels the experience of childhood and youth as an intellectual and emotional ripening in the moldy atmosphere of forgotten Belgian towns among which Bruges plays a special role.

Childhood and youth appear more than once as a paradise lost. Thus Hellens wrote in *Les Saisons de Pontoise* (1956): "In adulthood we write the lines but the thinking we did when we were children." The novel of development became with Hellens a vehicle of longing and memory, of conjuring up into reality things that no longer are. What childhood means to him he summarized in his deepest novel of development, *Mémoires d'Elseneur* (1954)—in which autobiographical elements intermingle with the themes of Parzival and Hamlet—in a passage marking the end of the hero's years as an apprentice and journeyman: "I have reached the age of snow eternal, I am alone. No, solitude is not this glacier devoid of vegetation nor this sky devoid of stars. The sky and the earth have merged; there remains but one dimension which I would call the spirit if I had not lost on my way the little I had left of human memory."[7] (p. 365).

VIII

THE WAR NOVEL

*Henri Barbusse, Roland Dorgelès, Joseph Delteil, Ernest Psichari,
André Malraux, Jean Lartéguy, Christian Murciaux, Antoine de
Saint-Exupéry, Manès Sperber, Vercors (Jean Bruller), Jules Roy,
Robert Merle, Roger Nimier, Louis-Ferdinand Céline, Julien Gracq,
Noël Devaulx, Armand Lanoux*

❦ This chapter and the one following it form an organic
whole. The tragic events of world politics in the twentieth century have precipitated out of the novel of adventure the broadly
founded subgenre of the war novel which has attracted the
most qualified literary talents, for it seems hardly possible for
an author to describe an existence of adventure without grant-
ing war a decisive role somewhere along the road.

With *Le Feu* (1916) the war novel of the twentieth century[1]
took up the thread of Émile Zola's *Débâcle*. This in itself suf-
ficed to assure its author, Henri Barbusse (1873–1935), his rank
and role in the history of literature. Barbusse was passionately
committed to the pacifism of the Communist International and
stood with his very person for a program of reconciliation
among peoples. His father was a Frenchman, his mother an
Englishwoman. He himself died in 1935 in Moscow, having lectured repeatedly in Berlin as a friend of Carl von Ossietzky
and Kurt Tucholsky of the *Weltbühne*. Under the influence of
Catulle Mendès, whose daughter he married in 1898, Barbusse began as a lyrical poet representing a tardy symbolism.
He knew Heredia and Samain. In his first novels, *Les
Suppliants* (1903) and *L'Enfer* (1908), he represented the idea

that the individual is always alone and that patriotic enthusiasm misleads man to suicidal devotion to things devoid of genuine value.

His experiences during the first two years of the First World War supplied Barbusse with the subject matter for the challenging accusation of his trench and dugout novel *Le Feu*. Here Zola's pacifist rhetoric and Dostoevski's and Tolstoy's compassionate sense of brotherhood appear combined with the bitterness of one betrayed and deceived, resulting in a violent polemic against the governments whose machination lead to wars which the peoples must wage. In contrast to Zola, whose language remained restrained, no matter how vulgar the objects it described, Barbusse broke this last taboo deconfining his narrative style by argot, poilu slang, and reckless allusions. "Barbusse is not writing a *chanson de geste* but the psychology of life in the line of fire; he does not sing *arma virumque* but reports sad happenings and their reflections in suffering man" (Leo Spitzer). Through the award of the Prix Goncourt the militant pacifist was assured that at least some of France's men of letters had made his cause theirs. They included Anatole France and Jules Romains but also the Spaniard Blasco Ibañez (who, like Barbusse, was a disciple of Zola) and the Germans Stefan Zweig and Erich Maria Remarque with *Im Westen nichts Neues* (1929). It is in keeping with the tragic vein in Barbusse's life that his last work bore the title of *Staline* (1935).[2]

It was under the impression of *Le Feu* that Roland Dorgelès (born 1886)—who belonged to the Montmartre group of the painters and writers Utrillo, Picasso, Carco, and MacOrlan—wrote in 1919 his *Les Croix de bois*. Like Barbusse, he dispensed with the clear continuity of a central action and presented instead sketches from life at the front. The anonymous mass of the *poilus*, and their forms of speech give the work its substance. How in Dorgelès's work things would go on after *Les Croix de bois*, may be inferred from a passage in the book itself: "People will forget. The veils of mourning will fall like dead leaves. The picture of the soldier who is no more will be no more in the consoled hearts of those whom he so loved. And all the dead shall die for a second time." In lieu of Barbusse's optimism there is skepticism, and indeed, *Réveil des morts*

(1923) is an accounting on a world-stage scale, of revenant war victims with the war profiteers. It is unfortunately a fact that the novelist Dorgelès' attempt to cope creatively with the Second World War in *Carte d'identité* (1945) is no longer on a par with his earlier works.[3]

From among the accounts of the war of 1914–18, the prose epic *Les Poilus* (1926) by Joseph Delteil (born 1894) must be mentioned. Its germanophobic tenor follows the lead of Maurice Barrès. There are political passages taking the reader to the theaters of war as seen in particular through the eyes of the simple enlisted man in the trenches, alternating with comments on human nature in the grueling test of mortar-barrage nights, all seen—in the spirit of the naturalists—as involving no more than mechanisms of bodily urges and drives.

Aside from the work of these three writers, there is, in the literature of war, the entirely different orientation of Ernest Psichari (1883–1914), who went harvesting in the area of bellicose adventure in foreign lands. Psichari was a grandson of Ernest Renan and received an early education of a wholly secular kind. His encounter with the work of Charles Péguy prepared a change. In the fall of 1903, at the time of the great inner crisis in his life, Psichari volunteered for military service and was sent, in 1906, to the Congo. The hard years of apprenticeship in the army he described in *L'Appel des armes* which was published in 1913. His years in Mauretania from 1909 to 1912 affected his future outlook on life in a fashion similar to Gide's African experience. Psichari broke with his as yet idle idealism and also found his way back from the positivistic philosophy of his grandfather to the Catholic faith. The account of these new experiences was *Le Voyage du centurion* which appeared posthumously in 1916. The outbreak of war in 1914 prevented Psichari's entry into a monastery. He fell in the course of the first warlike actions in Belgium. In his work we find the figure of the soldier as a crusader. His approach to his subject matter appears to be conditioned to a large extent by his own experiences. His peculiar soldierly ethos is reflected in the phrase formulated in 1908: "All done for war and longing for it as a painter longs to paint." This meant in his case that he was ready to apply the principle of commitment primarily to himself, that he was ready to sacrifice himself. Péguy as well as the extremist of the right, Henri Massis, implored him, in his own words, "to redeem France with his blood." We must not overlook, however, that Psichari's idea of crusaderdom belongs, in terms of the history of ideas, in a broader context,[4] for his work coincided in time with the beginning of a—in part —anti-intellectual and anti-rationalist century and of a development equally manifest in Gide's *Nourritures terrestres* as in traditionalism and mythical love of country, in the action ethos of Malraux as in the principle of realization in Sartre's existentialism.[5]

The very person of André Malraux (born 1901) has the fascination of the hero of a novel, and all his works are fragments of one great confession. Malraux's literary production in its present form covers two domains. It includes the war novel (1928–45) and the psychology of art (from 1947). As holds true for other "commuters between meditation and deed"[6]—such as Hemingway or Jünger—Malraux's work can hardly be appreciated or even understood without reference to the figure of the author himself.

His early, not entirely legal excavations of temple reliefs in Cambodia Malraux described in *La Voie royale* (1930). In Indo-China he became a cofounder of anticolonial fighting units. In 1925 he became affiliated with the Chinese Comintern organization at Canton. This led to *Les Conquérants* (1928). After the split of the Chinese revolution into the Communist group and the group around Chiang Kai-shek, Malraux returned to Europe. As a sort of apologia, the novel *La Condition humaine* appeared in 1933. In the same year, Malraux accompanied Gide on a trip to Berlin for the purpose of bringing about the release of the Communist leader Thälmann. See *Le Temps du mépris* (1935). In 1936 Malraux flew sixty-three missions in Spain as a pilot on the side of the Republic. Like Hemingway, Stephen Spender, Stefan Andres or José Maria Gironella, Malraux made a literary contribution to the Spanish Civil War in the form of his novel *L'Espoir* (1938). After the Hitler-Stalin pact in 1939 he finally broke with Communism. In 1940 he became a German prisoner of war. See *Les Noyers de l'Altenburg* (1945). After his escape he joined the resistance movement. In 1945 Charles de Gaulle made him a member of his cabinet of ministers and did so again in 1958.

After *Les Conquérants* (1928), which was a "documentary" novel written in the sober style of the reporter, *La Condition humaine* (1933) appeared as the novel of the solitary existence of the hero whose monadic isolation stands out in times of war in particularly striking relief. It is the *conditio humana* to stand alone. This potentiates the function of dialogue in the novel, for through it the individual attempts to break out from his isolation, to establish meanings, to communicate or to learn about the meaning of existence. To achieve full self-realization signifies that the individual—in the face of no matter what sociopolitical situation and especially in the face of war—takes a stand for a better future for all. In this way decisions reached in solitude bear on values which concern mankind as a whole. This is all too easily overlooked in the case of Malraux.[7]

La Condition humaine was distinguished with the Prix Goncourt in recognition of this new mythos of the hero. The time of the action is 1927, the place Shanghai. The heroes, fighters in the Revolution, live, struggle, and die to impart to their insignificant personal existence a meaning qualified to stand up before the whole people. "How could he, as death looked upon him, fail to hear the echo of human sacrifice making him understand that the stout heart of a man is to the dead a refuge well worth the spirit?" (p. 363). These are reflections of the patriot Kyo in the face of death. He goes down against the Stalinist measures and against the social misery of his country. "To die is to endure, but to kill oneself is to do." (p. 361). Thus Kyo chooses to die by his own hands. That is the gravest problem in the novels of Malraux. The author himself spoke of it as a "tragic humanism." Toward the end of the work, one of the survivors says: "I never really loved people. It was through Kyo that I was linked to them; it was through him that they existed for me." (p. 397). In this way the suicide of the revolutionary exerts on those around him the impact of the death of a redeemer, devoid—to be sure—of any metaphysical hue.

This is further confirmed by a glance at *L'Espoir*, the swan song of Malraux's Communist illusions. During an encounter in Madrid, Malraux and Hemingway agreed almost facetiously to divide between them the Civil War for their literary purposes. The American wrote *For Whom the Bell Tolls* (1937), while Malraux took over the period from the summer of 1936 to March, 1937. The main characters of *L'Espoir* are again intellectuals. The problems are whether the Communist regards war as a means to an ulterior end or as a means of liberating a people and what must be the mutual relationship between politics and ethics, between the revolutionary individual and the revolutionary group, and between the idea of the revolution and the revolutionary deed. Malraux's tragic humanism once again looms up behind innumerable human and political absurdities and "crevassed situations" to which he applied the term "Manichean" (Part III, Chapter 12) in his endeavor to give socio-political tensions a philosophical interpretation. At best the "stout brotherliness" [*fraternité virile*]—in *La Condition humaine* it was the "stout heart" [*coeur viril*]—can bridge the abyss. The figure of the French air-force officer who strives to cope in human terms and by means of this principle with the seemingly irredeemable situation shows more autobiographical traits than any other character in the work, while the Spanish engineer Manuel, introduced explicitly as a "born Manichean," suffers most from the incompatability of things.

The strength of Malraux's novels should be looked for outside the area of the narrative efforts of the chronicler. *L'Espoir*, in any event, is concerned only with the beginnings of the war which—as reflected in the title of the work—promised victory for the republican forces. Beyond this—and this is decisive—these novels present individuals under the stress of the supreme test as human beings. Yet these individuals lack the crusading spirit of Psichari's characters. They do not fall head over heels for war brides; their girls are neither chauvanistic nor vainglorious. Their struggle is a struggle with their own lives, not one with proclamations addressed to others for a better world of social justice. This is not always easy to understand in Malraux, especially when the reader is still short of intellectual maturity and experience of life. In all instances, however, the honesty and the virility of these works are profoundly moving.[8]

The same cannot always be said of the books of Jean Lartéguy (born 1920) who fought at Dien Bien Phu in Indo-China and also in Algiers and whose *Les Centurions* was the best seller of the year 1960. In 1939 Lartéguy volunteered for wartime military service and subsequently belonged to de Gaulle's army of liberation. Later he fought in Palestine, Korea,

Indo-China, and North Africa. For two whole decades of his life he was a soldier. His work, written in the captivating style of the novel of factual reporting, does make us sense, for instance, how and why there came to be a Secret Army Organization (OAS) in Algiers, but over and beyond the portrayal of the times it presents no human program.

A book on the Spanish Civil War (*Notre-Dame des Désespérés*), written in the style of the novels of Sir Walter Scott by Christian Murciaux (born in 1914 in Constantine), transcends the mere description of warlike actions and has us witness the development of little Juanito—a boy from Seville—to adult manhood. Manuel in *L'Espoir* was also shown in his development, but in terms of psychological depth the two figures stand worlds apart.

We now turn to the novelists who were concerned almost exclusively with the Second World War in Europe. Among them Antoine de Saint-Exupéry (1900–44)—like Henry de Montherlant and Romain Rolland—meant much to the younger generation after 1945. This applies to all of Europe and to Germany in particular. An uncritical enthusiasm—comparable to that which placed Gerd Gaiser's work *Die sterbende Jagd* above all the other writings of this author—was responsible for the fact that Saint Exupéry's philosophical fairytale, *Le Petit prince,* a symbolic outline of the author's creed, was often misunderstood as a juvenile book of entertainment. The figure of the little prince was created as a symbol of the noble quest for beauty and poetry in the content of life. In various allegorical figures the author criticized simultaneously our mechanized world with all its absurdities of routine and specialization. The presentation in the guise of a fantastic fairy tale may account for the fact that the ideological content was often overlooked. The same, after all, held true also for the *Roman du lièvre* of Francis Jammes.

It is significant that Saint-Exupéry did not use this same poetic form in any of his other writings. It was at odds with his avowed moralist's mission to grasp and to hold up for admiration the greatness of man. In this the ethos of the war novel met him halfway, and his posthumous success seemed for a while to bear out his philosophy of life as well as the principles of style in his works. But here again history of literature has the function of adjusting the time-dependent verdict. It seems possible that the success of this author resulted from his attempt to lead mankind from the distress of war to a humanism of the kind the nineteenth century could honestly uphold and thus to spare the reader the gruesome pictures of the novels of Malraux. Saint-Exupéry's works are above all aviator novels, such as *Vol de nuit* (1932), *Terre des hommes* (1939), and *Pilote de guerre* (1940). The last-named in particular shows that the man in the cockpit of his lonely reconnaisance plane—who in the case of Saint-Exupéry may be identified in every instance with the author himself—owes the emptiness of space about him the possibility of clinging to and coping with his faith in human culture and his reliance on the ultimate victory of what is good in man, while thousands of feet below the sacred brotherhood of men appears contorted in the most dreadful agony. The preponderance of reflection accounts simultaneously for the remarkable paucity of action in the novel. His engagement as a soldier and as his brother's keeper, lived out exemplarily by Saint-Exupéry—"what I have done no animal would have done"—exceeds his verbal powers as a creative novelist.

Between 1935 and 1944—up to the day when the author, flying a mission over the Mediterranean, went down (or was shot down)—he accumulated an ever-growing number of jottings, of unprocessed and unprocessable flashes, of sketches recalcitrant to narrative polish (recorded in part on magnetic tape), which were published posthumously (in 1948) under the title of *Citadelle*. Perhaps these fragments were meant to become and could have become a summa of Saint-Exupéry's philosophy of life. On one occasion he noted, "What is forever needed is to keep alive in man what is great in him and to convert him to his own greatness." No other war novel of the twentieth century shows again so simple and simultaneously so aristocratic an optimism. Nothing like it can be found anywhere, not even in Julien Gracq. Other writers remain confined to the conviction that war and war-like killing are demoniac, evil, and bestial.[9]

One of these is the Polish Jew Manès Sperber who was born (in 1905) in the Austro-Hungarian monarchy and who grew up with German as his first language. Under the patronage of Malraux, of whom he may be regarded as the most important disciple, he found his way into the French novel. He belongs to the generation of 1917 which hoped that the revolution that had begun in Russia would create a better world and which turned away from it in disappointment when the movement of liberation adopted a totalitarian course. After 1937 Sperber left the Party. His trilogy, *Et le buisson en cendre, Plus profond que l'abîme,* and *La Baie perdue* (1949-53), starts out in 1931 in Berlin with a meeting of the leaders of the Yugoslav Communist Party. The development of this group is regarded by the author as typical of the relationship between world Bolshevism and national communism.

The hero, Dojno Faber, lives through the Stalinist terror of "weeding out" in the Balkans, the capitulation of the German Communist Party to Hitler, the Spanish Civil War, Stalin's pact with Hitler, the German triumphs on the battlefield, the anti-semitic crimes, the military defeats, the resistance, and the collapse in 1945. In this way Sperber continued Malraux's work in terms of time. Yet the unconquerable of the *Condition humaine* appear now as men in dispersion and despair as the revolution releases its children. Sperber may be regarded, in inner terms, as having completed what Malraux had begun. He described what his master no longer had the courage to utter.

In comparison, both the human content and the epic powers in Jean Bruller's work fall off. Bruller (born 1902) wrote under the name of Vercors. *Le Silence de la mer* (written in 1941 and published in 1942 by the underground *Editions de minuit*) is probably the best-known novel of resistance and collaboration. It relates how the German officer Werner von Ebrennac of Prussian Hugenot descent, is quartered in Southwestern France. After the fall of Briand, his father had made him promise "never to go to France unless it be in army boots and helmet." Now the son, a soldier in the army of occupation, dreams of uniting his fatherland and France under German hegemony in a new Europe. Then, during a short leave in Paris, he learns that the military government has decided that France shall be anihilated. He thereupon requests to be transferred to the Eastern front. For the first time his host's daughter now speaks to him whispering the one word, *adieu*. To be sure, Vercors managed to take over from Rolland's *Jean-Christophe* the theme of reconciliation, but his melodramatic bent makes him thoroughly spoil his book by the conclusion.[10]

In addition a number of attempts deserve mention, such as the aviator Jules Roy's (born 1907) *Vallée heureuse* (1946) with its descriptions of air attacks on the Ruhr territory or Robert Merle's (born 1918) Dunkirk novel, *Weekend à Zuydcoote* (1949), which describes what was from the allied point of view the most critical moment of the war in a style purporting to be soberly documentary as befits wartime reporting. In lieu of the meditation, which both Barbusse and Malraux built functionally into the novel, we now have detached, almost stenographic accounts of what happened. The same style, though combined with the personality cult of Stendhal and Radiguet, was also used by Roger Nimier (1925-62)—who joined de Gaulle's army of liberation at the age of nineteen—in the portrait of a young follower of Pétain in *Les Epées* (1949). Nimier's second publication, *Le Hussard bleu* (1950), is clearly autobiographical and appears to have been conceived after the model of Norman Mailer's now famous book, *The Naked and the Dead* (1948). Parallel to Mailer's theme of the conquest of an island in the Far East in the fight against the Japanese, we have in Nimier the allied advance into the Rhineland. As in the American model, several strands of action run on in parallel, mostly handled in monologues and designed, apparently, to reflect the various strata in French society and their counterparts in the army. This interpretation of Nimier's intent is further borne out by his detailed descriptions of acts of cruelty and of erotic excesses which make of the book a portrayal of morals in the ambient of the military. Nimier's language is pronouncedly veristic as it strives to express realities as realistically as possible. To be sure, the work is dangerously reminiscent of the mass-produced assembly-line type of novel which utilizes the events of the war for the purpose of telling piquant stories, such as Cécil Saint-Laurent's *Prénom Clotilde* (1957). Nimier's cloak and dagger novel *D'Artagnan amoureux ou cinq ans avant* (1963), was published posthumously.

The breadth of which the war novel is potentially capable both in meaning and in form may finally be illustrated by two basically different authors with the discussion of whose work this chapter is to be rounded out.

The first is Louis-Ferdinand Céline (1894–1961). This physician of the poor of Meudon near Paris underwent a change of attitude through which he moved from the extreme political left—in particular after a disillusioning trip to Russia—to the extreme political right where he polemicized as a Fascist and anti-Semite in precisely the tone of voice that he had learned from the socialists of populism, such as Thérive, Lemonnier, Dabit, and Poulaille. His first novel, *Voyage au bout de la nuit* (1932), which made of the vulgar a principle of style, was surpassed in its plebeian revolt—if this is at all possible—by Céline's anti-Semitic pamphlet *Bagatelles pour un massacre* (1938). What Céline asked for in a tone of blasphemy in *Voyage au bout de la nuit* was before long to come to pass : "If you ask me, let the Germans come; let them kill and destroy and burn everything, the hotel, the crullers, Lola, the Tuileries, the ministers and their friends, the Coupole, the Louvre, the big department stores; let them break into the city to pour God's thunder and Hell's fire over this rotten amusement park of vanity . . ." In 1940 the time was ripe. When, four years later, Paris was liberated by the Allies, Céline went with the government of collaboration to Sigmaringen castle. In 1945 he fled to Denmark where he remained interned until the Fourth Republic allowed him to come home. In *D'un Château l'autre* (1957), the stages of his blind high treason and of his penitence appear displayed in the same unchanged and unmistakable style of panting chaos.[11]

Julien Gracq (born in 1909) teaches at a lycée and is a disciple of the philosopher Alain. His published work is slim in terms of quantity. In the course of 25 years he has produced just about ten titles, but he has established himself as a novelist with whom stylistic care matters more than a subject of popular appeal. In this he may be compared to Noël Devaulx (born in 1905) who has demonstrated in three volumes of stories— *L'Auberge Papillon; Le Pressoir mystique;* and *Bal chez Alféoni*—and in two novels—*Compère, vous mentez* and *Sainte Barbegrise*—that he wields an amazingly steady pen as a mythical narrator. Gracq's contribution to the war novel— especially *Le Rivage des Syrtes* (1951) and *Un Balcon en forêt* (1958)—is rather the contribution of one who holds himself politically aloof than of an author intent upon being heard in questions of the day. Gracq is a personal friend of Ernst Jünger, and his *Le Rivage des Syrtes* appears to have taken many a cue from *Auf den Marmorklippen* (1939).

The book was primarily meant to become a poetic novel, and its elevated style appears to have the function of subliminal evocation. One might dub the procedure magic realism. On another plane, however, the book is a novel with a political structure. The fictituous Mediterranean State of Orsenna vegetates in the haughty jadedness of political lethargy with which young Aldo suffers more than any of his peers. He has himself transferred as "observer of the forces in the sea of the Syrtans." Here mythical forces of the landscape arouse him to increased political activity. In addition, there is his encounter with Vanessa, who appears as the embodiment of the forces of danger and of the forces instigating to war—the age-old role of woman, the incitress from the time of the Icelandic epics on. Ultimately war flares up again on the shores of the Syrtan Sea after three centuries of seeming calm. What is it that Aldo has triggered? And how are we to understand this novel, anyway? This work, as well as the later *Un Balcon en forêt*, must be taken as a structural representation—i.e., a representation not concerned with being historically documented—of the "phony war" of 1940. Both works reflect an attitude of waiting which impresses us as negative in the case of Orsenna and as positive in that of Vanessa, while it triggers in Aldo an "obsession with the possible."

It seems highly unlikely that Gracq meant to describe here the relationship between Germany and France in the form of an allegorical novel. What is certain is that the experience of the Second World War made him ask the question as to how wars are really caused and as to how the young soldier sees the State and the adventure lying beyond the borders. But the work also contains an unromantic component in the form of Fate, for super-personal powers—embodied essentially, it is true, in Vanessa—as well as mythical emanations of the landscape lead Aldo in his will and in his wishing. But do they relieve him of his responsibility? The question remains open.[12]

A generation of writers would certainly be guilty of betrayal in terms of its mission if it were to withdraw completely to ethical fabulation and mythical interpretation in the face of a dreadful war. But we may see evidence of the unbroken power of French narrative prose when the subgenre of the war novel copes in such breadth of style with such an abundance of content, reaching from battlefield reporting to the analysis of the etiology of war in the abstract.

In 1963, Armand Lanoux (born in 1913) operated in *Quand la mer se retire* on three narrative planes, that of war-time reporting of the Allied invasion in Normandy, that of a love story in the sixties, and finally that of a detective novel. A Canadian girl goes to France in the company of a friend of her fallen fiancé in order to look for the latter's grave (which actually does not exist) and to learn the details of his imagined death as a hero (which no eyewitness has the courage to tell her). Equally many-layered is the style of the work. There is straight reporting, inner monologue, and the flash-back device. First-person novel and chronicle are to supplement each other. The undeniable weakening of the theme calls for greater art in terms of the narrative form.

IX

THE NOVEL OF ADVENTURE

Francis Carco, Georges Simenon, Paul Morand, Blaise Cendrars,
Romain Gary, Roger Vailland, Pierre Benoît, Jean Giraudoux

After having treated in the preceding chapter the war
novel as representing a specifically contemporary variant of the
novel of adventure, we still have to deal with four types of
"adventurous" subject matter and the corresponding groups of
authors. Carco and Simenon are concerned with Paris as the
setting for adventurous events. Morand and Cendrars deal with
cosmopolitan globe-trotting. Gary and Vailland are closer than
the others to the war novel. Benoît and Giraudoux, finally, enrich and deconfine the genre by introducing highly romantic
and metaphysical factors.

Francis Carco (1886–1958) was born in New Caledonia as
the son of a prison official but spent his childhood in Southern
France where his sense of landscape was provided the enrich-
ing dimensions of the imagery of a turgescent nature. He began
his writing career as a lyrical poet in the wake of Verlaine and
Francis Jammes. As a novelist he produced a number of books
in the tradition of Paul Bourget's psychological novel. These
include *L'Homme traqué* (1922) and *Rien qu'une femme*
(1923). Carco achieved creative originality when he depicted
the world of Montmartre where—after the artist epoch of Montparnasse had passed—the crooked little streets between Place

150

Blanche, Place Pigalle, and Sacré-Coeur were the setting for a peculiar mixture of lively Bohemianism and tourist traffic, an atmosphere in which genius and crime fused in a distinctive kind of local color. In the novel *Jésus-la-Caille* (1914), later on in *Les Innocents* (1916), *Scènes de la vie de Montmartre* (1919), and *Rue Pigalle* (1928), we have a lasting monument to an epoch and a style of life. *Scènes de la vie de Montmartre,* in particular, evokes the artistic endeavors of the Cubist painters and of the lyrical poets who—like Carco himself—recognized their masters in Baudelaire, Rimbaud, and still more in Verlaine, living an adventurous life among crooks and women. All this Carco managed to describe with such charm that his style almost manages to excuse, and to make us forget, the wretched and often criminal elements of this world apart. Carco's autobiographical books after 1934—*Mémoires d'une autre vie, De Montmartre au Quartier Latin: Nostalgie de Paris*—are a significant contribution to the study of the artist groups of the École de Paris.[1]

While Carco after 1945 failed to recover and to maintain the reputation he had acquired in the thirties, the Belgian Georges Simenon (born in 1913 in Liège), with an output—so far—of roughly 170 novels, has consistently maintained himself both in the favor of the reader and the good will of the critic. Gide, in particular, was among his admirers. A portion of Simenon's novels are descriptions of society in the perfect style of entertainment of Eugène Sue. One such, of recent date, is *Le Président* (1958). Then there are stories of social criticism in the style of Dabit and Lemonnier, while the Galapagos novel, *Ceux de la soif* (1951), takes up the myth of the lost paradise.

Best known, however, and at his best, is Simenon as a writer of detective novels, among which the Maigret series occupies a special place. In contrast to his British counterpart, Edgar Wallace, who strives to captivate his readers by a turbulent torrent of hair-raising action in the manner of Horace Walpole's *The Castle of Otranto,* Simenon is less interested in the course of a criminal adventure than in the adventures of criminological detection, with psychological deduction coming in for the largest share. The undeniable freshness of Simenon's works may have to do with the author's habit of writing them down, virtually in one sitting, withdrawn for a few days to his room, often in a hotel. In terms of artistic achievement, there are always outstanding descriptions of the rainy sky over Paris, the atmosphere around the Quai des Orfèvres (the seat of the criminal police), and of Montmartre.[2]

Paul Morand (born in 1888) may be regarded as a master of the cosmopolitan exotic shocker. Morand's father was a painter. Like many other French authors, he began his career in the foreign service. As far-flung as was his career is also the subject matter of his novels, among which we mention *Paris-Timbouctou* (1928) and *Air indien* (1932). The style is characterized by syncopation and by the same surprises as the content. "It has all the qualities one expects from the ideal travel companion: It is civilized, lacks conformity, and has sincerity, freshness, the gift of sympathy, and a love of color."[3] The fact that Morand sided with the Vichy government is responsible for the recriminatory silence meted out to him from 1945 on.

All the more lively has been the interest which Blaise Cendrars (1887–1961) was able to arouse throughout his career. Through his father and his Scottish mother his cosmopolitanism was predetermined. As a traveler in the jewelry business he visited Asia early in life and later on America as well. During the First World War he served in the Foreign Legion in North Africa. His importance in terms of the history of literature relates more specifically to his lyrical output, for Cendrars —who discovered Negro poetry at an early time—was in a sense a surrealist before surrealism. The jazz-like rhythm of the expansive flow of his poetry is also characteristic of his narrative work of which *L'Or* (1925), *Moravagine* (1926), and *Les Confessions de Dan Yack* (1929) deserve mention. The style is commensurate with the likewise anarchic material. Cendrars' hatred of (to his mind) worn-out and used-up traditions—for which he was admired by the Americans Henry Miller and John Dos Passos—did not, it is true, derive from experience alone. When, for instance, he presents in *Moravagine* the figure of a moloch fanning the Russian revolution and then being chased all over Europe in a rush of action which finally spreads to America, the autobiographical elements are clearly intermingled with literary emulation reflecting indebtedness to Lautréamont and the Marquis de Sade. In Cendrars, the adventurer shows up as a great criminal, not in the glorifying sense of the Renaissance, of Stendhal, or of Nietzsche but as a terrorist and gory scourge. As though meant as a literary last will and testament, *Emmène-moi au bout du monde* (1956) once again summarizes shockingly Cendrars' preoccupation with an adventurous subject matter in autobiographical form.

The heroism of Romain Gary (born in 1914) follows diametrically opposed lines. It is regrettable that Gary has not been able to provide his views and attitudes with the required creative emphasis. He was born in Kiev as the son of a diplomat and spent the first fourteen years of his life outside of France in Russia, Poland, and Italy. In Aix-en-Provence he later acquired a doctorate in law. During the Second World War he served as a fighter pilot and managed to make his way to join the French movement of liberation in England. After the war, André Malraux encouraged him to write. In 1945 he published his *L'Education européenne,* a Polish resistance novel with such low-order claims to artistic merit that even the blindest kind of Communist propaganda-mongering would hardly be able to underbid them. *Les Racines du ciel* (1956; Prix Goncourt) was written by Gary against Hemingway's African short stories. The subject matter is the same: adventurous big-game hunts, but totally different in terms of description and implied value judgments. Gary's love of animals derived creative impulses from Kipling's *The Jungle Book* (1894). In *Les Racines du ciel* it is the author's hope that in a world of massacre the motif of the animal sanctuary might assume the magnitude of a message of love for all, both human and animal. Gary's most recent work, *Promesse de l'aube* (1960), is a moral self-portrait which reveals how the novelist, in all his adventures as a cosmopolite and soldier, derived from the thought of his mother the courage required in the assumption of responsibility for others.

On October 4, 1957, the periodical *Arts* labeled Roger Vailland (1907–65) as "a petit bourgeois intellectual in search of adventures." The occasion was the award of the Prix Goncourt to Vailland for *La Loi.* This was Vailland's seventh novel. Among his early attempts, *Drôle de jeu* (1944) is the most significant. Outwardly an autobiographically based resistance novel with the way stations of Paris and Bourg-en-Bresse, the book places the heroic outsiderdom of Marat and Annie, two intellectuals in the service of patriotism and resistance, in the center of the plot. Decisively significant are the dialogues concerned with the problem of a "virile humanism" and the controversial concessions to socialist-communist party demands. Marat says of himself: "I shall walk about in the Party as I have been walking about in the bourgeois world, pleased with the countryside rather than disliking it, but just the same, no more than walking about, all by myself." The book winds up with a comparison of the French resistance to the March of the Ten Thousand successfully eluding the Persian king. Through this reference, Vailland proclaimed the victory of the full-blooded individual over slaver and mercenaries. Reflected in this free manipulation of history is less Vailland's hate of the Germans than his effort to show that there still are in our modern world ample possibilities for a man to prove himself as a man. Malraux's conception of the adventure of war bears fruit.

The novel *La Loi* (1957), which André Billy called "a novel which would have delighted Stendhal," was written between November, 1956, and spring, 1957, in southern Italy on the peninsula of Monte Gargano which is also the scene of the action. Indeed, Stendhal would have been enthusiastic about this work, not only because its setting is Italy, the land of Stendhal's dreams, but also because it denies nowhere the author's Stendhal discipleship. In particular, *La Loi* is a novel of the most extreme lack of compassion, for the "law" is the right of the mighty, and in this late feudal world there is little to interfere with its sway. The course of the intrigue is set when a Swiss tourist couple is robbed of a considerable sum of money. Now the lines of power come into play. Matteo Brigante, who controls everything and everybody in Porto Manacore, who guides and represents both crime and law, learns that the girl Mariette, the daughter of the *uomo universale*, Don Cesare, has committed the theft without letting him in on the project. The whole novel is in a sense concerned with nothing more than Marietta's attempt to get to the top of the pyramid of powers. All the adventures implied in this for her and the minor personages in the novel—pagan love feasts, bloody settlings of accounts, flights, and acts of violence—are premises or effects of this unqualified determination of a single individual to go it alone. In comparison, even the threat of malaria in this murderous land and the social repercussions of the prevailing feudalism have no more than secondary significance. Vailland was as little concerned with writing a novel of society as Stendhal would have been.

Vailland's next novel, *La Fête*, reflects possibly a further development along the lines from *Drôle de jeu* via *La Loi*. If in the first novel the concrete situation was provided by the resistance and in the second by an idealized picture of Italy, the third presents adventure exclusively in the form of conquest in love, with a further regression in the delineation of character. The hero goes out to win a mistress, and what he means by love is less lasting fulfillment than a feast, a conquest, and a departure for new adventures. The ethos of the work has, not surprisingly. met with divided opinions. It seems certain that *La Fête* did not come up to the level of Vailland's earlier novels. Critics have pointed out that the novelist, in trying to write a novel of adventure which simultaneously would be a novel of artists and a pastoral novel, did not succeed in fusing these elements without visible seams.

The world of the novels of Pierre Benoît (1886-1962), a native of Albi in southern France, is history—*Koenigsmarck* (1918)—and, when history seemed to be too narrow and not brilliant enough, utopia. In 1919 Benoît became world-famous with his novel of utopian adventure *L'Atlantide*. The action is projected in the African desert, where a Circe-like woman causes the death of everyone coming from civilization into her mysterious realm. Immediately after the publication of the book, the author had to defend himself against the massive accusation of plagiarism from Henry Rider Haggard's novel *She*, but he did receive the prize of the Academy for the book. With the Mormon novel *Le Lac salé* (1921), with *Le Puits de Jacob* (1925) and *Les Environs d'Aden* (1940), Benoît continued in the vein of his thriller art of colorful descriptions of lively adventure, generally in romantically remote areas. Considering the level of his work, his admission into the Académie Française was a hardly merited confirmation and distinction.[4]

In Jean Giraudoux (1882–1944) we meet, finally, a writer who doubtless gave his best as a playwright. His novels were written during the early and intermediate phases of his productive career (before 1938). The guiding themes of Giraudoux's work as a whole are hostility against the gods—in which he agrees with André Gide and Albert Camus—and the idea that woman appears in the world as the mediatrix of the absolute to which man hardly has access. This is often reflected in Giraudoux's narrative works. His early book, *Suzanne et le Pacifique* (1921), already showed the all-pervading impact of this ideological orientation. On a voyage from France to Australia, Suzanne's ship goes down. All alone she lands in a island paradise. Here, far from the world of men and the routine of life, she recreates in her mind the Europe that is lost. Recalling Robinson Crusoe in a comparable plight is of little avail to her: "I was amazed by the scantiness of the lessons which my male precursor could teach me."

Juliette aux pays des hommes (1924) is built up on the motif of the ill-matched pair, of a truly Giraudouxesque stamp: "A young man of the old age of twenty years, by the side of a young woman of the young age of twenty thousand years." Juliette, disillusioned about her fiancé, goes out to find the ideal partner. When, after meeting important scientists and artists, she makes the acquaintance of a Russian in exile who impresses her like a demigod, she kills him because he is too perfect. Then she drowns herself.

Bella, together with *Siegfried et le Limousin,* and *Églantine* (1922-27), form a political trilogy. Giraudoux's hatred against the Poincaré group in French politics proved stronger in certain passages than his powers of literary creation. *Siegfried et le Limousin,* being a novel of reconciliation, does maintain a certain level of significance. Here Giraudoux described the adventures of a man on both sides of the frontier between two hostile nations. Jacques Forestier, gravely wounded and abandoned between the lines in 1915, recovers under German care and turns into a German. Brought back to his native Limousin, he finds his way back to himself. In a later stage arrangement of the same theme, Giraudoux made of it a drama of Fate of Greek dimensions revolving about the figure of a man who does not know in his deeds what he is and what he is doing.

Combat avec l'ange (1934) describes how a young Argentinian woman, representing a young race without the wear and tear of civilization, goes to pieces in her encounter with the over-refinement of Europe. *Choix des élues* (1938), finally, presents once again the adventure of a perfect individual in the day-to-day routine of an imperfect marriage. The pair Pierre and Edmée must separate because the woman is an overwoman. The run-of-the-mill and the unique destroy one another outside the realm of guilt and accusation. Just once Giraudoux waivered in his portrayal of woman, trying to assign roles of prominence to the man and to the child. But *Jérôme Bardini* (1930), seen as a work of literature, is not really finished. Bardini breaks out from the routine of his marriage and goes off roaming through America. There a boy saves him in a mystic way from his increasing loneliness. With this work Giraudoux thus moved very close to Christian ideas of salvation, a fact further emphasized by the detail that Bardini's redemption through the child occurs in wintertime. Subsequently Bardini returns to France, but, it seems, not to rejoin his wife. It is not only this lack of clarity in the conclusion but also the numerous contradictions in Bardini's character that must be carried on the debit side as one tries to evaluate this novel.

What then remains as the distinctive quality of Giraudoux's novels? The most striking point is the frequency with which the author dispenses with a clear-cut plan of action and sharply delineated characters. In addition, Giraudoux's style in the novel is poetic rather than epic, and metaphor has a major role. Not only is the external form poetic, so too is the behavior of many characters who prefer what is extraordinary to what is practical or conventional, who prefer escapades to the accepted norms of social intercourse. The only adventure that seems worthwhile to them is the quest for the lost paradise or the effort to defend such an intact condition against a fallen world of trivialities. All this came to Giraudoux most strikingly through reading Jean Paul. But the state of paradise is never anything other than an exceptional state. Suzanne on her island is rescued; Juliette kills herself after meeting her Russian; Edmée as a woman is too close to the ideal for Pierre. The unusual, precious style cultivated by Giraudoux is meant to be a palpable reflection of his novelistic ethos. Above the trivial world it established a refuge for the beautiful, for the intact, even though it be only transiently. Thus Giraudoux marks the spot where adventure touches the realm of metaphysics. In terms of world literature his procedure signifies that the French novel has established contact with Tieck, Novalis, and Jean Paul also in the area of the epic narrative.[5]

X

THE RELIGIOUS NOVEL

Emile Baumann, Georges Bernanos, Luc Estang, Marcel Jouhandeau,
François Mauriac, Julien Green, Gilbert Cesbron

Pierre-Henri Simon, in his monograph *La Littérature du péché et de la grâce* (Paris, 1957), distinguishes three phases in the religious literature of the time following the "Catholic renewal" toward the end of the nineteenth century. The decades from 1880 to 1900 are characterized by an attitude toward Catholicism exemplified by Verlaine, Huysmans, and Bloy. Then, from 1900 to 1920, there are Maurras, Péguy, and Claudel with their ideas and major works. Claudel's writings in particular are replete with nostalgia for a religiously intact pre-reformation age. After 1920, we finally have the dawn of a "theological age" in French literature. For this latter, literary criticism has indeed chosen the period designation "Catholic novel."[1]

It is true—if we disregard Gide's *La Porte étroite* and *Symphonie pastorale* with their different orientation—the world of Catholicism does represent the determining basis of the religious novel of the twentieth century. But to proceed from here to identify the religious novel with the Catholic novel would imply that it is apologetic in nature, that it is intended to serve the Church, or that it is aimed restrictively at the Catholic reader. It seems more commensurate to call it the novel of grace. In its purest form, it strives to attain a level above con-

fessional differences.[2] In *La Grâce* (1959) by Renauld-Krantz
we find indeed a mixture of the metaphysical principle with
the individual's endeavor to achieve self-realization. As a genre,
the religious novel belongs in the continuity of naturalism,
though—it is true—a naturalism additionally deconfined by
poets of lyrical prose such as Rimbaud and Lautréamont and
by the narrative literature of the *fin de siècle* as represented by
Huysmans with his "thirst for the absolute," for while the world
of realities is embraced in full precision and crassness of portrayal, also included is an attitude of openness to receive things
not seen and things supernatural. The doctrine of salvation reflected in this novel derives its essential orientation from the
dualism of Blaise Pascal: "Man's misery without God—man's
grandeur with God." That this does not result in a curtailment
of the individual author's idiosyncrasies is sufficiently guaranteed through differences in geographic locale. The world of
Bernanos is the Artois and the northwest of France; Mauriac's
novels take us to the region around Bordeaux and to Paris;
Jouhandeau built for himself, after the model of his central
French homeland of Guéret, the fictitious city of Chaminadour;
while the cosmopolite Green can use Virginia, Wales, and northern France as the settings for the action in his novels. There
is, in addition, the characteristic affiliation of Bernanos with
Bloy, of Jouhandeau with the French moralists, and of Green
and Jean Cayrol (in *Je vivrai l'amour des autres* and *Le
Déménagement*) with Poe, Hawthorne, and Kafka. Finally,
within the genre itself, there occurred an evolution to ever
greater complexities.

The religious novels of Emile Baumann (1868 to 1941), a professor of strictly Catholic descent, do know the guiding theme
of guilt and conversion—*La Fosse aux lions* (1911); *Job le
prédestiné* (1922)—but in the portrayal of character they
remain reminiscent of woodcuts. It marks the greatness of
Georges Bernanos (1888 to 1948) and his importance in the development of the genre that he operated in his psychomachous
creations with eruptive and indeed hallucinatory movement
reflecting genuine struggles of the soul. The antagonism of good
and evil in man's soul, and with man's soul as the prize, is the
basic motif in the action of these novels which provide a palpable embodiment of such inner processes, and the interests

of such concrete sensuousness are served as well by the appearances of the devil as by heavenly visions.

Bernanos—like Mauriac and like Julien Green—took his orientation from the *Pensées* of Blaise Pascal. Man, without God's grace, is a nothing abandoned to ultimate evil. At the same time it is true that man is closest to mediation through grace when the satanic carries on its wildest antics. This provides the works of Bernanos with their "tension." Man is driven to the edge of despair in order to be saved. (If objections against the genre of the religious novel are in order, then at this point.)

Bernanos spent his early years in the Artois. With some qualms he completed part of his scholastic training with the Jesuits. After the First World War, in the course of which he was wounded three times, he worked as an insurance agent. Always traveling, Bernanos began to write on the train. This was the origin of *Dialogues d'ombre* (published posthumously in 1955) and of *Sous le soleil de Satan* (1926), a book presented to the French public by Léon Daudet in April, 1926, with the following prophetic words: "Tomorrow, the first book, the first novel of a young writer, Mr. Georges Bernanos, will be in everybody's hands . . . I say—referring to him, as I once said referring to Marcel Proust—that a great intellectual and imaginative light has appeared in the literary sky. Let us not make a mistake in this."

From now on Bernanos devoted himself entirely to his literary pursuits. From 1934 to 1937 he lived on Majorca. Here he worked on *La Paroisse morte*, a book completed only in 1943 in Brazil and published there under the title of *Monsieur Ouine*. On Majorca, Bernanos likewise wrote *Journal d'un curé de campagne* (1936). After his return to France he composed *Les Grands cimetières sous la lune,* which is an indictment of Spanish fascism. The readiness of the western powers to play into the hands of Hitler at Munich in 1938 induced Bernanos to emigrate to South America—first to Paraguay, then Brazil. Gravely ill he returned to his homeland in 1945 to devote most of his energies to the political questions of the day.[3] The newspaper articles which he published at this time showed again the old polemicist. He enriched his literary work by one more title, the play *Dialogues des carmélites*. He died after an operation on July 5, 1948, at Neuilly.[4]

The central figure of the novels of Bernanos is the Catholic priest—not Stendhal's cleric in the conflicts of Red and Black nor Balzac's nor Barbey d'Aurevilly's priest as a figure in the social hierarchy and, finally, the precise opposite of Zola's clergyman in *Trois villes*, who comes to accept a positivistic form of enlightenment.[5] "He is concerned, above all, with making clear —both existentially and through faith—the reality of eternal damnation through the experience of the doom and perdition that are possible in the world of time and space... Bernanos does not—as so many Christians are doing—reason about damnation; he takes us close to sensing it."[6]

In *Sous le soleil de Satan* (1926), Germaine Malorthy, called Mouchette by most, gives in to the impulse of killing the father of her illegitimate child. This happens in the parish of the priest Menou-Segrais, who is old and ailing and who has just been accorded the help of a young vicar. The young priest, whose name is Donissan and whom Menou-Segrais regards initially as a dolt, discovers with the sixth sense of the great pastor Mouchette's depravity and begins to wrestle for her soul. Above all, he takes away her pride with what she has done. His efforts immediately earn him the ill will and the criticism of the "righteous." But Abbé Donissan becomes more and more like Christ himself, most strikingly so as he arouses the accusation that he associates with sinners. His purpose, however, is not to be a smooth drawing-room cleric but a pastor ready at all times to accept the fighting challenge of what is evil in the world. To what extent Bernanos accorded the same reality to ultimate evil as to ultimate good is apparent from a scene in *Sous le soleil de Satan*. The devil is tempting Donissan, trying to cast him in deep despair. "A man tied with both hands to the top of the mast, losing of a sudden his gravitational equilibrium and seeing below in yawning depths no longer the ocean but the world's abyss and—boiling over endless miles—the foam of nebulae in gestation to the ends of an emptiness which nothing can measure but which his own eternal fall must cross, would not experience within his breast a more absolute sensation of whirling giddiness. His heart beat with redoubled fury against his ribs and then stopped. Nausea gripped his entrails. His fingers—clutching desperately, alive while the rest of his body was frozen with horror—dug into the ground like claws. Perspiration trickled down his back between his shoulders. For once, in his boldness, buckling now and torn from the earth by the enormous call of nothingness, the man knew himself lost beyond recovery. And still, at this very moment, his all-pervading thought was vague defiance."*

The abyss which temptation opens up in Donissan is the same *gouffre* or *abîme* which Pascal explained from the misery of the individual living far from God. Bernanos described Donissan's condition by the metaphoric expression *abîme sidéral*— the world's abyss—suggesting the sensation of a total lack of anything to hold on to, of being tossed about without any possibility of resistence. Sin and temptation signify isolation and removal from the community of saints; they signify a repetition of the fallen cherubim being hurled into Hell. It is specifically by means of such devices of space symbolism—first developed in terms of language in the Biblical account of genesis—that the element of psychomachy in the creative work of Bernanos reaches impressive heights. Sanctity and struggle belong together through their very being. This is not the same as sanctity and theological ratiocination trying to ward off or indeed to deny temptation by means of intellectual arguments. Donissan is no brilliant Father of the Church. His figure rather resembles early Christian Egyptian monks, such as Anthony, or the saints of the Eastern Church, that is to say, figures of no brilliant external appeal.

While discussing the work of Psichari, we noted an anti-intellectual vein in the novel of the twentieth century. Bernanos deconfined the anti-intellectual—by his unqualified recognition of the supernatural in life—with the description of how temptation turns a holy man almost into an animal. Not only reason fails; it is also in vain to look for the solution in a sentimental kind of humanism. Before man is ready for service, as a member of the community and in its interest, he must weather the encounter with the all-evil, and in this he would have no chance without the grace of God.

This concept of sanctity was further developed in the double novel, *L'Imposture* (1928) and *La Joie* (1929). Cénabre uses deceit to have himself admitted to a theological seminary and is ordained. His growing self-righteousness makes him lose faith and charity. When he opens his heart to an old priest, even this man's simplicity is no longer able to resolve his hardened state. The heroine of *La Joie* is the girl Chantal, who passes on to the world the blessed strength of the old priest from *L'Imposture*. As a child already, Chantal appears as the antagonist of her grandmother, who is presented as a person "full of hatred and of sin." For the Abbé Cénabre she becomes a simple mirror of sanctity. To be sure, in his arrogance he understands all this only when the girl has been murdered by a servant of the house. Her death must not be taken as an ordinary crime that might interest the police but as a sacrifice of atonement for Cénabre's sinful ways. In this fashion, the continuity of the novel absorbs liturgic elements.

Measured by such standards, *Un Crime* (1935)—the tragedy of a woman who commits murder wearing the robe of a priest —is only an unsuccessful detective story. The following year, Bernanos recovered his old strength in *Journal d'un curé de campagne* (1936). Ambricourt is the new village priest, reminiscent of Abbé Donissan and of the simple priest in *L'Imposture*. When taking over his work, he decides to keep a diary to which he can entrust his pastoral cares as well as his personal suffering. "My congregation has fallen prey to indifference. That is the word! Like so many other congregations! Indifference takes hold of them under our very eyes, and we can do nothing about it. . . . What chance do we have, we who have accepted once and for all the terrifying presence of the Divine at every instance of our poor lives. . . . What good is it to try to determine what chance there is? One cannot stand up against God."* This priest breaks down within a short period of time, both in his health and in his inner life, in his struggle for the souls of his congregation, in which the family of the Count causes him the greatest worry. He dies like a saint. He fulfills the conditions which Léon Bloy once formulated for such a verdict: It is necessary to be poor, to be simple, to be without significance in the world, if one is to be granted grace in the fullest.

The hallmark of the pneumatological novel of Bernanos is apparent, by way of summary and completion, in his last and most difficult work, *Monsieur Ouine* (1943). There is in this work no clear character portrayal and no clear continuity of action. The style seems somehow cumulative; the threads of the action seem tufted at random. But that is precisely a reflection of the ethos of the work. The world—which has to be ready for everything, even the appearance of the devil—cannot be represented in smooth continuities. Any single-track psychological motivation of the behavior of the acting persons would be out of place. Ouine—the name is derived from *oui* and *non* and might be translated as Noyes—lives as a long-time tutor at the Castle of Fenouille in northern France. There he is, in the midst of a dead parish—originally the novel was to bear the title of *La Paroisse morte*—impressing us as an endangered figure, if for no other reason but that, as he admits, there has never been in him any kind of moral conflict. He is not aware of having a soul which ever again must decide for good or for evil. The indifferent intelligence of Ouine has often been the basis on which this character was taken to be a scathing portrayal of Gide, and this idea can certainly not be rejected offhand. For "availability," "curiosity," and "sincerity"—by virtue of their involving no commitment—are characteristic of Ouine. He represents a threat to his environment because he knows everything, because he attracts the inexperienced, and because—in the process—he completely forgets the "moral drama." He stands typically as a polar opposite to Donissan and Chantal; he is the real Lucifer challenging the priest with the words: "After all, no one here but you and I can take an interest in the soul."

Luc Estang (born in 1911), Bernanos's most gifted disciple, carried the trend of this metaphysical dualism a step further in *Les Stigmates* (1949) and, still more strikingly, in his second novel, *Cherchant qui dévorer* (1951), in which the reader is taken to a theological seminary and made to witness how the students suffer and struggle for the sake of their faith, with little time left to live in the assured happiness of it.

By contrast, the work of Marcel Jouhandeau (born in 1888 in Guéret, Dép. Creuse)—consisting after 40 years of productivity of almost 50 volumes (of which the first was published in 1920)—operates with totally different linguistic devices in the development of its psychomachic vein. Jouhandeau, unlike Bernanos, is no fighter, although this must not be taken to imply that he is not painfully aware of the self-contradictory lack of harmony in the life of the human soul.

In the summer of 1908, Jouhandeau moved from his provincial home to Paris where he took up his studies at the Sorbonne. He became a teacher in the secondary-school system. Beginning in October, 1920, he was a contributor to the *Nouvelle revue française.* In June, 1929, he married the dancer Elisabeth Toulemon. At the wedding ceremony, Gaston Gallimard and Jean Cocteau were the witnesses. Until 1949, the author —who, by the way, is a friend of Ernst Jünger—continued his work as a teacher. From then on, he has been devoting all his time and energy to his fertile literary work which has been entrusted to the care of the publishers Gallimard and Grasset. In his shorter prose pieces (stories, anecdotes, novelettes), which —from the beginning—were produced along with the great novels and numerous essays (*Algèbre des valeurs morales,* 1935; *Essai sur moi même,* 1947) and which have been published in a number of separate anthologies (*Prudence Hautechaume,* 1927; *Les Pincengrain* and *Le Journal du coiffeur,* 1931; *Contes d'enfer,* 1955), Jouhandeau's home country of Chaminadour-Guéret appears depicted in love-hate as the setting of a sort of *Everyman* play.

Jouhandeau's characters—generally fragile in their physical constitution and often susceptible to emotional extravagance and intellectual raving—serve to make visible the workings of a satanic world principle. This entails not infrequently a disruption of the conventional small-town hierarchy (*Fête-Dieu,* 1931). In the double story, *Ma Pureté* (1936), which seems reminiscent of Barbey d'Aurevilly's satanic spiritualism, a careworn old lady relates how her gentle daughter is systematically at work ruining her hated husband. Another form of devilish possessedness is the bloodthirsty frenzy which induces a quiet seemingly insignificant boy to commit murder (*Le Chevaine,* 1936). *La Jeunesse de Théophile* (1921) is a hardly disguised autobiographical novel of development with a setting in Jouhandeau's fictitious city of Chaminadour (to be equated with Guéret). Théophile Binchanteau would like to become a priest. Two women, who exert an influence on his development, embody the world principles of good and evil. Jeanne teaches him an attitude of humility toward God, while Madame Alban—a figure borrowed from the history of Guéret at the turn of the century—seeks, under the cover of pious pretense, to win Théophile for her own egotistic ends and to make of him a priest she can own. Théophile recognizes the danger and breaks away. The high esteem Jouhandeau has for the calling of the priest appears testified to once again in his hagiography of San Filippo Neri (1958).

The motive of the morally unequal sisters, used by Jouhandeau in portraying the decline of a middle-class family in the provinces, connects *Les Pincengrain* (1924) with *Monsieur Godeau intime* (1926). Godeau's position between two women makes clear to him how "different" he is and preserves his narcissism from total collapse. In the thirties, the novelist began "to use as his theme his own household which happened to be of the kind commonly called 'impossible.' "[7] In this series we have *Monsieur Godeau marié* (1933), a work the title of which hardly suggests a psychomachic theme. It was written in the style of Pascal's *Pensées*. Argument calls for counterargument, questions call for answers. The novel form comes close to being meditation and essay. Monsieur Godeau is Jouhandeau himself, his wife Élise the dancer Elisabeth. The focal question is whether Godeau must suffer harm to his soul because he married Élise who lays claim to his whole being. Until he recognizes that Élise is to him a mediatrix of the divine: "Between you and me there is room for things supernatural, or rather, you occupy for me the middle ground between the supernatural and myself." (p. 244). The idea of redemption is formulated still more clearly in a later passage: "Whatever I may do, in the arms of Élise the cross awaits me and on the cross Christ for another marriage." (p. 248). In *Chroniques maritales* (1938), the author continued the self-redemptive process in pointillistic detail. In *De la Grandeur* (1952) he reduced his concept of man to the succinct formula: "In his ignominious extremity man retains nought of his indelible dignity but the presence of God."[8] (p. 108).

François Mauriac (born in 1885 in Bordeaux)—member of the Academy since 1933, awarded the Nobel prize for literature in 1952—specializes in the care and analysis of soul of the wealthy bourgeoisie of southwestern France in the region around Bordeaux, where—thanks to the vineyards and the precious pine resin gathered in the forests—it amasses worldly treasures and, in the process, loses its salvation. Thus Mauriac combines elements of a regional novel with those of the literature of psychomachy.

He established his fame with *Le Baiser au lépreux* (1922). Jean Péloueyre, an ugly young man, an impassioned bookworm, marries a pretty young woman who feels physically repelled by him, a reaction which grows still stronger when Péloueyre falls ill. She overcomes her physical aversion, and kisses her husband the way medieval monks kissed lepers. After his death, she remains faithful to him although she never "knew" him in the biblical sense. This "immured woman" is typical of Mauriac's novels, as is the conflict of the demands of the flesh and its spiritual antagonists. The figure of the "immured" woman appears again in *Génitrix*, a novel of motherly love carried to monomaniac extremes which lead the heroine to a point where she destroys the marriage of her son. In the dual novel, *Thérèse Desqueyroux* (1926) and *La Fin de la nuit*, Mauriac returned once again to the erotic theme of the first of his works mentioned above. Here a highly gifted woman tries to maintain herself and to preserve her self-respect by the side of a coarse-grained husband whose sexuality inspires nothing in her but disgust. Imprisoned in the conventions of marriage, she sees no way of saving herself except through an attempt at murder by poison. At court, she is acquitted because she is covered by her husband. After this episode, he lets her go. Thérèse now goes to Paris. There, fifteen years later, the threads are taken up in *La Fin de la nuit*. Gradually Thérèse understands that no crime will resolve a human conflict. In death, the ray of grace gets through to her.

The murder motif was used again in *Les Anges noirs* (1927). The hero Gabriel imagines that he can put an end to his life of vice by killing a prostitute friend of his.

When, in 1932, Mauriac wrote his great novel *Noeud de vipères*, it became clear that his talent lies less in the portrayal of sensuous aberrations than in that of monomaniac passions—such as misguided motherly love or greed for wealth—with the implicit refusal to yield to grace. This story of the old counselor-at-law, Louis, who provokes those around him through sheer malice and contrariness, who tyrannizes his family and in particular his wife and who, through greed, becomes responsible for the death of his daughter, shows the deep affinity of Mauriac's concept of grace with that of Bernanos. When Louis has managed to ruin his family financially and is about to appoint his illegitimate son in Paris his sole heir, the news of the death of his wife reaches him. This occurrence brings him to his senses. He opens up his heart to grace. Mauriac is so profoundly convinced of the power of grace and of the certainty of its course that he contents himself with merely alluding to the turn of events at the end of the novel. An unsophisticated reader might easily fail to notice it.

L'Agneau (1954) is, so far, Mauriac's latest novel. Here the author succeeded, even more strikingly than in his earlier works, in making symbolically real the process of redemption of sinful man. Mauriac has admitted that in the writing of this work he owed more to Bernanos than ever before. In this novel, Xavier Dartigelongue appears as the counterpart of Chantal in *La Joie*. On his way to a theological seminary in Paris, Dartigelongue observes on the train an obviously unhappy young married couple. He comes to know Jean and Michèle de Mirbel and has high hopes of being able to save them. In the attempt, he gets ever more deeply involved in their marital problems. When finally he leaves precipitously, Jean de Mirbel follows him by car to take him back home and accidentally runs him over. Xavier's death has the same salubrious effect on Jean and Michèle's relationship that Chantal's death had on the Abbé Cénabre. The two young people find the way back to one another. The novel is constructed on a double plane. Its symbolic identifications can be traced in the Bible. Xavier is not only the sacrificial lamb for the sins of Jean and Michèle; he is also the good shepherd following the lost sheep. The book is replete with biblical motifs, symbols, and allusions.

Since Mauriac as a novelist has fallen silent[9] and since Georges Bernanos is dead, Julien Green (born in 1900) is the uncontested leader in the field of the French religious novel. Green was born in Paris as the son of American parents with Irish forebears. At an early time he learned to think of himself as an ethically multifaceted individual. This awareness he transferred as a novelist to his principal figures who are all characterized by the ambivalence of their inner lives. After having served in the French army during the First World War, Green matriculated at the American University of Virginia.

His attempts at painting increased the acuity of his visual sense, to the advantage of his later work as a writer. Early in 1916 Green became a Catholic, but as early as 1919 he again veered away from Catholicism. In 1924, he published a *Pamphlet contre les catholiques de France* whom he accused of no longer taking seriously the psychomachy of good and evil as well as the reality of the demonic principle in the world. After a detour into Buddhist thought, which could not permanently satisfy him, Julien Green finally found his way back to Catholicism in April, 1939.[10]

In this connection, special importance attaches to the novel *Varouna* (1940), for it was begun in May, 1938, and completed during the author's conversion. This tripartite novel takes place in the early Middle Ages in Wales and Scandinavia, then during the Renaissance, and finally in the present. The three sections are thematically interrelated by visionary metempsychoses. In the first section, in particular, the novelist strives to impart to his medieval subject matter a special sheen by means of archaicizing stylistic devices, as for instance when he refers to boats as *nefs*, a term which no longer has that signification and has been replaced by *bateaux*. The action begins when the boy Hoël (from Wales)—who was baptized, without being fully aware of it, by a missionary—is induced by the execution of his parents to start out on an uncertain quest for happiness which takes him far and wide through northern Europe. On his way he meets the power of evil, personified in the figure of a mysterious knight, and its power is to him for the present more palpably real than the workings of the Divine forces. Yet, however superficial and almost accidental his baptism may have been, the effectiveness of baptismal grace does prove itself in the straits of urgent need. When Hoël, overcome by the uncontrollable power of his senses, has murdered a woman, the certainty of having to die by retribution impresses him, after listening to a priest, as though he were allowed to go home to his father. The progressive element in the novel is thus the resolution of uncertain religious concepts into real and immediate knowledge.

This is made additionally clear in the concluding section of the work, when the novelist Jeanne writes the biography of a sixteenth-century Carmelite nun. Through the aesthetic process she establishes for the salvation of her soul the communion of saints. Recollection and dreamlike visualization of the divine are remodeled into precise knowledge. We may conclude that the author retraces thus in his novels his own development.

As we look back over the novels which Green composed before *Varouna*, we clearly see what is new in this latter work. *Mont-Cinère* (1926), a novel set in Virginia toward the end of the nineteenth century, is a somber portrayal of monomaniac passions in the manner of Balzac, albeit mixed with the horror atmosphere of Edgar Allan Poe. The work winds up in the destruction of a home by a conflagration that may be interpreted as an apocalyptic symbol of human catastrophies. The action of *Adrienne Mesurat* (1927) takes place in 1908 in northern France. This is the novel of a repressed passion in a tyranically Puritan family atmosphere where both good and evil are subjected to brutal distortions, until Adrienne Mesurat, in a wild upsurge of rebelliousness, pushes her father down a flight of stairs. Finally, *Léviathan* (1929) treats of the devastating effects of vulgar eroticism. Like a leviathan, the medieval symbol of a horrible collapse, sinful passion dominates events. It has in its throes, particularly, the tutor Guéret who is hoping to win over for himself alone the orphan girl Angèle and then learns that she is being abused by her foster mother, who runs an inn, as a decoy for her establishment. In a mixture of hate and love he maltreats the girl, injuring her severely. Yet Angèle covers him when he is in danger of being apprehended by the police. These early novels of Green's are characterized by a certain religious and moral perversion. Good and evil are misunderstood or criminally interchanged. A point of contact with Mauriac's novels may be seen in the "immured women."

The course which Green took with *Varouna* he pursued further in 1947 with *Si J'étais vous*. With devilish help the hero succeeds in ridding himself of his disliked modest existence and becoming someone else. Dissatisfaction, however, drives him— once the change has begun—from one metamorphosis to the next. After Fabien Especel has run through all possible stations in the realm of human existence, after he has run the gamut of mortal delinquencies and has returned—still dissatisfied—to his original self, death catches up with him. And this fills him suddenly with unimagined joy. The work has surprisingly much in common with the myth of Ahasuerus, the Wandering Jew, in that the possibility of dying appears as the ultimate gift of Grace.

The best book Green has written so far is *Moïra* (1950). The story is based on a news item reporting an incident in the state of New Jersey. Joseph Day, at the age of eighteen goes to an American university not far from his home. The landscape descriptions seem to suggest that Green used here his own sojourn in Virginia as a model. The student takes a room in a boarding house and then goes to sign up for Greek and English. He impresses everyone meeting him as an extremely principled young man. His standards of purity are, indeed, so exaggeratedly strict that he cannot look at Greek statues because they are naked and that he tears up a volume of Shakespeare because he found in it what he considers an offensive passage. Some of his acquaintances dub him "angel" or "pigeon," while others refer to him sneeringly as "the destroying angel." A fellow student, with whom he had a serious fight, calls him "assassin." Awareness of his own well-built body is to Day a moral peril. With disgust he speaks of himself at one time as "sensual," while he notes admiringly, referring to one of his friends, that he is a man "who does not appear to be made of flesh and bones." Religion and piety are to him primarily a matter of keeping the sixth commandment.

The author's diary (published in 1965 as *Mille chemins ouverts*) suggests that Green was guided in this portrayal by his own experiences during the years from 1917 to 1919. The individual's discovery of his own physical existence and strong homoerotic visions of lust are counter-balanced by a strict Bible cult.

Then Moïra appears, the daughter of Day's landlady, a beautiful but depraved creature. Now it will be seen what Day's moralism amounts to. He falls for the girl in practically no time. But after the bacchanal of the very first night his pharisaic scruples already regain their strength. Moïra appears to him as the great whore of whom the Bible speaks, and he sets himself up as a judge and avenger. He chokes the girl to death in bed, buries her, and gives himself up to the police.

The special effect of the novel results from the fact that Green, while presenting his hero as a Catholic, concentrates in this figure all imaginable sectarian aberrations of Christian morality. Joseph Day emerges as the representative of a super-denominational puritanical fundamentalism which judges and condemns instead of practicing charity. Another positive aspect of the work is the truly incredible density of action evolving in a few short days with the relentlessness of a Greek tragedy. Moïra is mentioned for the first time on the fourth page of the book, for Joseph Day occupies her room while she is away. Her mother says, "Look, Moïra forgot her cigarette case." Then: "with her long hand she picked up a small black metal box which was lying on the pillowcase and immediately looked inside." Although Joseph Day knows nothing about the girl except her name, he is quite certain that she must be a depraved creature because she smokes. Then half the novel rolls by before Moïra appears, and in the shortest possible time her and her murderer's fate are sealed. The uncontrollable in him, the "assassin," the animal in him bursts forth.

In the portrayal of the uncontrollable within the human soul —which tears down the delicate partition between good and evil and which it is hardly possible any longer to subject to psychological analysis because in it devilish powers are at work —Green's so far latest work, *Chaque homme dans sa nuit* (1960), goes even a step farther. The themes of grace, redemption, and awe of death interweave in the tapestry of an almost surrealist world, and all the great decisions are made on its dark side. An indelible "stigma of grace" and a growing realization of his own sinfulness cast the 24-year-old Wilfred Ingram into grave conflicts of conscience which are further intensified as he rises to a socially higher and morally more corrupt stratum of society. Before he succeeds in seducing Phoebe Knight, who is the only figure of light in the novel, Ingram is shot to death by Max, a sinister stranger of slavonic background who assumes, in the course of the action, more and more unmistakably the character traits of the devil. Seen in the perspective of Green's total work, this conclusion reflects the consistent determination to maintain the somber atmosphere of aberration and perversion, while light and goodness—as in Mauriac—are granted only a narrow space in the continuity of the action and must rather be deduced. Referring to *Chaque homme dans sa nuit*, Green noted in his diary in June, 1959: "There is in this book in a way a peephole giving us a glance at the abyss we carry within us—fear of sin depriving us of grace, fear of dishonoring intercourse, fear of unchristian death. Each one of us is a house divided unto itself." This sybillic aphorism is a concealed reference to Pascal's *Pensées*.

Green's indebtedness to the Anglo-American Gothic novel likewise continues unchanged. With motifs like that of a lonely house, of criminal assault, of an eerie chiaroscuro, he presents catacomb-like worlds as reflections of corresponding spiritual landscapes under the motto, as it were, of Pascal's "wretchedness of man without God," so that—seen from the standpoint of the characters involved—there is often no way out but insanity or murder. In all this the reader must clearly distinguish between the standpoint of the characters and that of the author, for in the divergence of the two lies time and again the ultimate message. Thus, for instance, while Moïra appears to Joseph Day as the equal of the great whore, to Green she is the eternal Mary Magdalene with a share in redemption no less certain than the share of the righteous. In any event, the religious novel, begun by Bernanos with high hopes in the twenties, was continued by Green with no decline in the level of content and form, and we are certainly justified in claiming for Green a place next to Gide, Proust, Malraux, Martin du Gard, Sartre, Aragon, and Butor among the leading novelists of the first six decades of the twentieth century whose rank is firmly assured.[11]

Measured by standards derived from Green's work, the production of the much more popular Gilbert Cesbron (born in 1913) comes as a sobering falling-off in literary merit. Cesbron is today program director of Radio Luxembourg. He rocketed to fame with his workman's-priest novel *Les Saints vont en enfer* (1952). The book is still interesting as a documentary on the workman's-priest-movement which has meanwhile been cut short by a decree from Rome, but as a literary work of art it is hardly more than trivial entertainment with shortcomings particularly evident in its treatment of the religious aspects of the subject matter. This fact is not changed by the sales figure of 300,000 copies in seven years. The same applies to the film novel *Chiens perdus sans collier* (1954) and the Lourdes book *Vous verrez le ciel ouvert* (1958). Such an author is surely qualified to entertain the masses with religious material, but the tremendous impact of the irruption of the world beyond into ours or the catastrophy of its exclusion and the shining light of the mirror of sanctity are things spoken of far more impressively and unforgettably by writers other than Cesbron.

XI

THE NOVEL OF SOCIETY IN THE TWENTIETH CENTURY

Georges Duhamel, Jules Romains, Roger Martin du Gard,
Henry Poulaille, Louis Aragon, Simone de Beauvoir, Philippe Hériat,
Henri Troyat, Joseph Kessel, Michel de Saint-Pierre,
Maurice Druon, Roger Peyrefitte, Paul Vialar, Roger Ikor,
André Pieyre de Mandiargues, Françoise Mallet-Joris

❧ In the years since 1945, literary criticism has on occasion applied the term *littérature engagée* [literature of commitment] to the works of one or another of the authors discussed in this chapter with the implied classification of Duhamel, Romains, and Martin du Gard as humanists and of Aragon, Poulaille, and Simone de Beauvoir as socialists or communists. Since such categories mean very little in terms of the actual rank of the works involved and since, furthermore, they would tend to make us overlook what these authors have in common with others—that is, the fact that they present a panorama of the society of the twentieth century in, on the whole, historically precise identification—we prefer to dispense with them and use our own classification which will serve us in good stead until literary research[1] discovers a better and more significant arrangement.

The literary début of Georges Duhamel (1884–1966), son of a physician and physician himself, was for the author—in subjective terms—an event of deeply painful implications. With Romains and Vildrac he had established, in the area of lyrical poetry, the doctrine of unanimism and had experienced the happiness which a peaceful human community can offer the individual. Thus Duhamel's reaction to the events of 1914 was doubly sensitive, and its epic manifestation in the war novels *Vie des martyrs* (1917) and *Civilisation* (1918) has a stark immediacy and a strongly personal coloring. After the termination of the war, during which he served in the French Medical Corps, Duhamel joined in passionate dedication the ranks of the protagonists of a world-saving neohumanism, potentiating simultaneously in his literary conception the respect for the individual, whom he had seen perish in the anonymity of mass battles and stripped of human dignity, into a kind of spiritualistic individualism. Society appeared to him now as the sum total of everchanging individuals whose freedom of movement he cherished and nurtured.

In the five-volume cycle *Salavin* (1920–32), the novelist revealed his affection for a fairly insignificant person, while *La Chronique des Pasquier* (1933–45) is an accounting from the author's own life, disguised in the form of a novel, with room for memories from his childhood and his years as a student as well as—by way of historical background—the Dreyfus affair and Duhamel's literary association with Romains and Vildrac. In this work, Duhamel's spiritualistic individualism achieved greater depth through a more emphatic and more precisely detailed portrayal of the psychological multifacetedness and the inner contradictions of the characters. This is what raises the work above the level of, let us say, many a novel of Balzac, even though Duhamel did not succeed in synthesizing from his visualization of mind and soul an irresistably convincing epic continuity. As the family of Raymond Pasquier, a notary in Le Havre, is broken up—in human terms primarily in consequence of the father's moral failures—so the work appears as a disjointed collection of separate descriptions of individual lives. Duhamel's respect for the reactions of man's inner life led him naturally to the problem of the reactions between humanism and metaphysics which is the theme of *Souvenirs du paradis* (1946). Thus Duhamel's work, while representative of the novel of society, is so only in a marginal and, as it were, preliminary way.[2]

Jules Romains (born in 1885), on the other hand, carried his interest in the formation of human groups to an almost mystical degree of penetration and portrayal of societal manifestations.

The author was born in the Plateau Central but grew up in Paris where he was influenced decisively by Léon Brunschvieg under whom he studied philosophy. In 1902 he earned his bachelor's degree in Paris, and in 1904 he changed his name Louis Farigoule to the literary pseudonym of Jules Romains. As he graduated in 1906 from the École Normale, he was already most deeply preoccupied with the idea of a collective soul as a principle of life and a stimulus to aesthetic expression. In this effort he joined forces with his like-minded contemporaries Duhamel, Vildrac and René Arcos. In the course of the First World War, Romains—like his friends—turned to pacifism. The manysidedness of his literary talent is admirable. In 1920 he published an important ophthalmological essay and also the scenario for a film, and in 1923 a *Petit traité de versification*. After Anatole France and Paul Valéry, he became the third president of the French Center of the PEN Club. At the PEN Congress in Berlin in 1926 he delivered an address *Sur le chemin de l'amitié franco-allemande* on which Albert Einstein congratulated him. In 1939 he accepted a diplomatic mission and then fled by way of Portugal to the United States. In 1946 he returned to Paris.

Since 1923 Romains has been at work on his magnum opus, the cycle of novels, *Les Hommes de bonne volonté* (1932–46). With its 27 volumes the work represents the most markedly deconfined novel of society of the first half of the twentieth century. Ideologically it rests on the doctrine of life and art which Romains called unanimism, that is, the idea of a collective soul. The omnipresence of this postulated collective group soul may crystallize at every moment and in any place in new combinations of individuals who have been total strangers prior to that event. "Overcoming the individual, merging in a group soul, meant to Romains in his younger years a divine experience. Next to Rolland's renewal of soul, Gide's 'evasion,' and Proust's *recherche*, it is one of the many forms of the pursuit of happiness in this generation." (H. Gmelin, op. cit. p. 159.) In terms of the form of the novel, this demands a new pattern of action and a new style. Since the work—like many a Spanish and French novel of the eighteenth century—was written in a "parochial perspective," since the sovereignty of the author's viewpoint suffices to assure the greatest possible panoramic comprehensiveness, there is, in theory, no need for the figure of a central hero. The group is the hero. Similarly, precise characterization and strict continuity of action can be dispensed with. The action of the novel turns out to be a kaleidoscopic abundance of, on the whole, consciously incoherent "candid-camera shots." It was in particular the city of Paris that was to be understood as an organism and that was to be given epic reality through the microscopic movements of its "particles." The "local myth" of Zola's *Le Ventre de Paris* reappeared thus in a more comprehensively conceived variant.

The work as a whole covers the period of time from October 6, 1908, to October 7, 1933. Of course, Romains was in his venture sufficiently wise and considerate to eschew the surrealist license of writing away without plan or premise, though the reader still finds it hard enough not to get lost. Some of these volumes do have thematic "centers of gravity." We can group them as social (volumes 7, 13, 19), political (volumes 9, 11, 15), ethical (volumes 5, 6, 24, 25), and erotic (volumes 3, 4, 18, 26). Through volume twelve, the action takes place in France. With volume thirteen, Romains moves on to Rome and then returns to the French battlefields and the Europe of fascism. Pervading the entire work as a unifying atmosphere is a growing sense of crisis, a premonition of the catastrophies of 1914–18 and Hitler's seizure of power. The two friends Jallez and Jerphanion occupy in this milling mass vision a plane in the foreground. Romains' manner of writing may be illustrated by this specimen from the volume of *Le 7 octobre* (1946):

"From its hills, from its mildly raised and sloping plains, Paris goes down to work. Its movements are in a way the same as twenty-five years ago, in a way they are different. As the center has shifted to the West, many intineraries setting out from outlying quarters and from the suburbs have likewise veered toward the setting of the sun. But, above all, the morning stir has gained in breadth and complexity. . . . This is no longer the almost natural trickling of the great city toward its central catch basin."*

This leads us in direct continuity to other circles and cycles of themes and people. The human situation of the workman has greatly deteriorated since 1908 (p. 7). Men's obsession with new things has become unnaturally inflated (p. 8). The credi-

bility and the credulity of man has simultaneously declined
(p. 9). The manager of a factory is introduced (pp. 10ff.); the
political situation in Germany is discussed (pp. 12ff.); a woman
is mentioned who has committed murder (pp. 15ff.). After this
random frame has been viewed, the scene shifts to an automobile salon (pp. 18f.), then to the office of a dentist, then to
the bedroom of a sleeping woman who remains anonymous.
Jallez, one of the foreground figures, appears and telephones
(pp. 24ff.). His girl friend comes to visit him (pp. 31ff.). Now
only, after both theme and style have changed abruptly ten
times within the space of less than thirty pages, the flow of
action assumes for the space of a few pages a somewhat more
condensed coherence.

At the beginning it was Romains's plan to let the novel wind
up with the "men of good will" joining forces in an ideal collective; but conditions after 1918 (and in 1933) destroyed his
optimism. In the preface there still was the passage: "Men of
good will! An old benediction is looking for them among the
many and will find them. May they once again, today or tomorrow, be called together by 'good tidings,' may they find a
sure sign by which to recognize one another, so that the earth
of which they are the salt and the desert may not perish."* In
accordance with the conception, the kaleidoscopic style would
be expected to undergo in the course of the work a process of
structural clarification. But since it became impossible for the
author to allow the inner content of his work to evolve, there
also could be no change in the verbal form throughout these
long twenty-seven volumes. Romains stuck to his program without compromise. To be sure, as a result the artistic value of
the entire cycle was endangered. Most of the limitations and
potentialities of the technique of enumeration and simultaneity
aimed at by Romains were demonstrated at about the same
time by the American naturalist John Dos Passos in his trilogy
USA which was still broader in conception by virtue of its very
subject. Dos Passos did not dispense with the figure of a central
hero and restricted the panorama technique to skillful intermezzi which appear scattered throughout the continuity of the
action.

After this not altogether successful but certainly interesting
attempt to break open the form of the social novel of the nine-

teenth century, Romains did not succeed in producing another truly significant work. *Une Femme singulière* (1957) and *Le Besoin de voir clair* (1958)—to mention but two of the more recent titles—hardly suffice to set off their author from other producers of novels of the dime-a-dozen variety.[3]

Thus we turn to Roger Martin du Gard (1881–1958) as the dominating figure in this sector. He came from a Catholic family of the upper bourgeoisie. He devoted himself at first to archeological studies which may have sharpened his eye for the minute detail. His sense of responsibility as a writer can well be gauged by the fact that he destroyed at least two of his early works, *L'Une de nous* and *L'Appareillage,* when he felt that he could no longer identify himself with their message.

Martin du Gard rose to fame when his former fellow student, Gaston Gallimard, published in 1913 his novel *Jean Barois.* This is an ideological novel, written to a large extent in the form of a dialogue. In the figure of the hero, Jean Barois, Martin du Gard brought together various ideological opposites. Barois is the son of a free-thinking physician of high ethical principles, but is raised by his grandmother in strict adherence to the Catholic dogma until the father manages to lead the sickly boy through a humanistic process of catharsis to confirm and to master the world of earthly realities. From now on Jean Barois sides ideologically with his father. To be sure, the fear persists in him that a future recurrence of his physical weakness might make him seek solace in the teachings of the Church. He therefore states in his will that any possible subsequent change in his attitudes must be considered nul and void, since only those things may be allowed to have validity for his entire life which he recognized as right and true in the strength of his most mature years.

After this novel, in which we find the first inkling of Martin du Gard's typical theme of the dichotomy of France (the *deux France*), the author constructed on the basis of the country's denominational dualism a broad panorama of society. From 1922 to 1940 he worked on the seven volumes of the family novel, *Les Thibault*, which stimulated Duhamel to write the previously mentioned *Pasquier* novel. It is a narrative work of dramatic power and multifariousness of scene and setting. Yet, with all the deconfinement of the dramatis personae and scenae, the center of gravity remains Paris, that is, more precisely, the Rue de l'Université with the home of the Thibaults and the Avenue de l'Observatoire with the home of the de Fontanins. Martin du Gard had learned from Zola—better than any other writer of the twentieth century—what possibilities there are—ready and waiting—in the metaphysical, social, and intellectual dualism of the age for the concerns of a novel which is to become the saga of a family and of a nation. *Les Thibault* is the fresco of two generations of which the younger (reading Gide) comes out with the provocative confession, "Families, how we hate you!"

The delineation of the characters could hardly be subtler. There is, for instance, Oskar Thibault. Outwardly he represents the type of a proud, Catholic-conservative member of the upper bourgeoisie, although the diary he leaves behind at the time of his death reveals a much more differentiated, more humane, more emotionally susceptible personality. His sons, Antoine and Jacques, the real heroes of the novel, grow up—as did Jean Barois—without a mother. The implied lack of security is the beginning of the catastrophy which is the action of the book. Antoine, the elder, finds it easier at first to adjust to the father's manner than Jacques whose manhood friendship with the protestant Daniel de Fontanin is misinterpreted and becomes the topic of rumors, with the result that the father has him confined to a clinic. Antoine, who finds it progressively more difficult to understand his father, frees his brother from the humiliating milieu. It is especially the influence of Daniel de Fontanin's sister Jenny that gradually succeeds in resolving the depression of Jacques who feels that he is rejected and an outcast. But neither his budding love nor his brilliant success in the examinations for admission to the École Normale can fully satisfy him and reconcile him with society. He disappears for a period of three years. Meanwhile Antoine completes his medical training. He discovers Jacques in Switzerland where he is active as a writer and pacifist politician. Antoine succeeds in taking his brother to the deathbed of his father, an episode which Martin du Gard treated as the encounter of a younger age with a vanishing old world. All the prophecies worked into the portrayal of this scene come true when shortly thereafter the First World War breaks out. Jacques has returned to Switzerland in the hope that a general strike of the workers throughout Europe may still be able to reverse the trend toward disaster. In an attempt to drop pacifist pamphlets over the French lines, he crashes with his plane and is shot as a spy. Antoine, working as a physician at the front, is poisoned by gas. He shortens the torment of his condition by taking his own life. The sole survivor of the family is Jean-Paul, son of Jacques Thibault and Jenny de Fontanin.

"Jacques Thibault is the first hero of a French novel to claim the individual's privilege of regarding history as dependent on himself. He falls halfway along the road which leads from the horizon of one man to the horizon of all."[4] Thus the inner deconfinement of the novel is alluded to. The motif of the two unequal families and the two unequal brothers is broadened, introducing into the continuity of action generally human and political aspects of the twentieth century as functional elements.

Stimulated by the family novel of Galsworthy and Thomas Mann, Martin du Gard presented, in the form of a portrait of two families, the portrait of France between 1900 and 1914. What this means in terms of artistic achievement becomes apparent through a comparison with Jules Romains. Martin du Gard kept the evidence of ideological deconfinement between the lines, so that the structure of his novel remained clear-cut. The events pursue their course—as they do in a classical tragedy—to the final annihilation of the heroes. Some flaws in the portrayal of character may be attributed to the excessively long period of composition (eighteen years!). The hopelessness of the world of this novel is not imposed, as it is in Romains, by a relentless course of external events (which the figure of the surviving child at the end of the work does not manage to relieve). It is consistently prepared by numerous descriptions of tormenting experiences of the heroes. A significant detail is that the physician Antoine can finally profit from his art only to the extent that it provides the means by which he can take his own life. In such unredeemable relentlessness lies the greatness of Martin du Gard. The motif of father and son assumes special significance in that it becomes the vehicle through which division and hostilities are introduced. The father punishes one of his sons; the other, as a result, turns against his father. The reconciliation of the family at the deathbed of the older Thibault is purely a matter of form and ceremony, for bridging the gap between the generations is no longer possible. War finally destroys the sons. Denominational differences, determined by social standards, are to be blamed for the fact that Jenny's child has no legitimate father.

Thus this novel does not conceive of life as change in a sense which implies—as Romains saw it—the possibility of betterment, but as a progressive catastrophy. Martin du Gard did not find it possible to relinquish this pessimism. His peasant novel, *Vieille France*, published in 1933, presents—less crudely than Zola's *La Terre* and in more advanced differentiation than George Sand's stories—the panorama of human hardships and human aberrations in a rural community, assigning an essential role to the letter carrier of the village who is presented as a purveyor of rumor and gossip, a dishonest civil servant, a small-time profiteer. The efforts of the priest and those of the enlightened socialist teacher aiming to promote peace and order are of no avail. As yet unpublished are Martin du Gard's correspondence with Gide and Schlumberger as well as his late novel, *Souvenirs du colonel de Maumort*.

It is possible to ask which of the irreconcilable images of France found in Martin du Gard—the conservative Catholic or the liberal protestant, the enlightened socialist or the scientifically atheistic, the politically extremist right or that of leftist orientation—should be regarded as "true," that is, as typical, if only in the sense that it reflects the views of the author, but it is not possible to answer that question. Martin du Gard would certainly have been able to resolve the dilemma, but his art consisted precisely in presenting—through the balanced interplay of his characters—the unanswerability of the question as a powerful reflection of the national tragedy which must arise from lack of comprehension and from the persistence of incompatible opposites.[5] Martin du Gard understood that it is not enough to see the world, to see society, from the point of view of a messianic socialist or communist to have an infallible key to a work of true literary art.

Among the authors to whom the foregoing alludes, only two have become important. One of these is Henry Poulaille (born in 1896 in Paris). He is the son of a workman and became affiliated with the group of literary populists (Lemonnier, Thérive, Dabit) who took up a Russian suggestion of the late nineteenth century and decided to place their art entirely in the service of the working classes and to produce literature of social reform. Poulaille veered farther to the left than any of the others and tried to create a specifically proletarian novel. In the wake of C.-F. Ramuz, he started out in 1925 with the war novel *Ils étaient quatre* and proceeded in the tetralogy, *Le Pain quotidien, Les Damnés de la terre, Pain de soldat,* and *Les Rescapés* (1931–38), to describe the struggles of the proletariat for freedom of work and fair wages in the mining industry of the first two decades of the twentieth century. The impact is not infrequently powerful. *Le Pain quotidien* was dedicated to John Dos Passos. This may provide a cue as to the position of this work in the historical continuity of French literature. The proletarian writer of the twentieth century does not, it appears, sympathize with and continue the form of communism preached by Zola, above all in *Quatre évangiles* and his novels of industry, nor Zola's didactic style, but rather the ideas and the stylistic idiosyncrasies of the best American disciple of Zola.

The initial situation from which the action of *Le Pain quotidien* evolves is an accident which befalls the Parisian anarchist Magneux at his place of work. His wife is expecting a child. Magneux's death unites the residents of a tenement in a human community of conspirators who are united in their political views and stand together in all the vicissitudes of daily life. The climax of the action is a strike in which the workers are defeated but from which socialism emerges in shining superiority. The dialectics of the work can hardly be called convincing. The style of the novel is the language of the construction workers. It is colorfully interspersed with argot and consists of a French which is often condensed and mutilated to the point of incomprehensibility.

The physician and party communist Louis Aragon (born in 1897) is without doubt the most versatile writer to have emerged from the surrealist movement. In 1935 he declared in the manifesto, *Pour un réalisme socialiste,* that he was ready to devote himself exclusively to narrative prose in order to place *le monde réel* in the center of his literary efforts. *Le Monde réel* became the general title of a tetralogy consisting of *Les*

Cloches de Bâle (1935), *Les Beaux quartiers* (1936), *Les Voyageurs de l'impériale* (1942), and *Aurélien* (1944). In this work, which is not a cyclical novel in the strict sense requiring chronological linearity, we are given a chronicle of the French bourgeoisie during the years from 1895 to 1940. The author's objective was to present in epic terms the communist theory of an inevitable rapprochement of the best elements of the upper bourgeoisie to the working classes. The first two volumes give a strongly didactic impression. The one concludes euphorically with the Basel Pacifist Congress in 1912, the other with the entry of the provincial bourgeois Armand Barbentane in a strikers' headquarters in Paris. But Aragon's psychological talent breaks through the self-imposed limitations of an assigned essay in social criticism. The prevalence of female characters in the epic personnel after the time of *Les Cloches de Bâle* is symptomatic of the author's interest in multifaceted psychological portraits. The protagonist of *Les Voyageurs de l'impériale,* Pierre Mercadier, exemplifies—with his unqualified flight from the demands of his family and "good" society—the ethos of the novel of individualism in the Stendhalian tradition. And the delicately differentiated torments of soul in the elegy of love, *Aurélien,* helps the reader forget the thematic motif of undeserved wealth. The all-pervading power of eros, reflecting Aragon's relationship with Elsa Triolet, turns out in a sense to be the only real reality, and all the political and social events appear subordinate to it as mere coincidental trappings.

However, Aragon's mastery of the art of the novel is still more impressively manifest in his (so far) most recent novel, *La Semaine sainte* (1958). Here he demonstrated once again how a good writer grows beyond the limits of his chosen subject and how his material turns into a literary statement only through the formative powers of the artistic process. The Holy Week, to which the title of *La Semaine sainte* alludes, is the historically significant period from March 19 to March 26, 1815. The narrator's point of view is technically on the side of the Bourbons fleeing headlong before the suddenly appearing Napoleon. The work thus begins as a portrayal of the military and political events which led to the Napoleonic episode of the Hundred Days. The center of the stage is occupied by the historical figure of the painter Géricault who wears the king's uniform. The initial impression, to the effect that the book is really very much like Alexandre Dumas's *Les Trois mousquetaires*, must be modified when Aragon blends in wartime events of 1940 and has the figures of his novel appear as vectors of modern experiences. The difficulty and the accomplishment lie in the fact that none of the characters are made to feel and to think in a crudely anachronistic way. The problem is dealt with particularly successfully in the central scene, the "road to Damascus" of Géricault, who encounters at night in the woods a group of conspirators and who is most profoundly moved by their political anxiety and their longing for just a morsel of human happiness. Géricault feels himself linked to them in solidarity. He comes to know "the other" and thus "the real world." We see here the development that has occurred in the work of Aragon. It leads from the moralizing black-and-white technique of the first novels—with morally corrupt employers and morally intact workers—to a psychologically ever more sophisticated differentiation. The climax of this development must be seen, so far, in *Aurélien* and *La Semaine sainte*. There is simultaneously a progressive maturing of style toward a goal for which one is tempted to use a term borrowed from Brecht's poetics, that is, "exotification" [*Verfremdung*]. For Aragon projects the problem of solidarity into a world which is unfamiliar to the modern reader and which attracts him by reason of its colorful liveliness, with the result that the skillfully transvested thesis is accepted as an aesthetic pleasure. This is doubltess the highest form of the didactic novel.[6]

In comparison, the novels of Simone de Beauvoir (born in 1908), the companion of Jean-Paul Sartre, are philosophically and sociologically more direct and less disguised. True, the novel is not the most adequate form for her literary endeavors. If she plays in French cultural life a unique role, she does so by virtue of her philosophical writings, such as *Le Deuxième sexe,* and her volumes of memoirs, such as *Mémoires d'une jeune fille rangée* and *La Force de l'âge*, which are highly informative as source books in cultural history. Here her accomplishment assumes major importance, as she postulates—for the existence of woman within society—the principle of "free recognition" and reveals the specifically feminine dichotomy of "being an object" and of "being a subject."[7]

In 1943, Simone de Beauvoir published her first psychological novel of love, *L'Invitée,* and in 1945 the resistance book, *Le Sang des autres.* One year later came *Tous les hommes sont mortels,* a novel of fate, in which the author undertook to show that the experiences of mankind in the thirteenth, the sixteenth, and the nineteenth centuries were the same. Only those who had in themselves the power to elect and to realize themselves in emancipation from the mass of society have achieved more than mere existence and can be said to have really lived. In 1954, Simone de Beauvoir was awarded the Prix Goncourt for *Les Mandarins.* Here she succeeded, to an unfortgettable extent, in depicting the activities of the existentialist group of Saint-Germain-des-Prés. In the process, the novel became a *roman à clé.* The center of the stage is occupied by the woman neurologist Anne, wrestling with the very problems that Simone de Beauvoir had assigned to modern woman in *Le Deuxième sexe.* The male protagonists are Henri Perron and Robert Dubreuilh in whom informed readers were quick to recognize Camus and Sartre. The differences which Sartre and Camus had in the fifties appear reflected in the work with hardly an attempt at literary disguise when Dubreuilh, that is Sartre, determines to put his periodical *Espoir,* that is, *Temps modernes,* entirely into the service of socialist-communist politics, while Perron, that is Camus, prefers to keep aloof from all party-line entanglements. In the story, *Une Mort très douce* (1964), Simone de Beauvoir was again working with material supplied by her own experiences—her mother's death from cancer. Robert Kanters prophesied in the *Figaro littéraire* of November 12, 1964, that this short prose work, side by side with *Les Mandarins* and the volumes of memoirs would—like Sartre's *Les Mots*—provide future generations with a truer reflection of the vital tenor and the social consciousness of the existentialists than any of their novels of pure fiction. "Autobiographies provide existentialist literature with a second life."[8]

Measured by the standards of the authors so far discussed, no other writer of social novels of the twentieth century has produced a work of commensurate merit. The playwright Philippe Hériat (born in 1898)—whose film scenarios reflected his understanding of the potentialities of the new art at a very early time—sketched out a fresco reaching from 1815 to 1915 in his *La Famille Boussardel* (1944). For Henry Troyat (born in 1911), the Russian background of his family—having spent his childhood in Moscow, he fled in 1920 together with his parents via southern Russia to Istanbul and Venice—provided a never-failing reservoir of memories and literary promptings. In the trilogy, *Tant que la terre durera* (1947-50), Troyat presented a colorful portrayal of the collapse of czarist society in 1917 and of the revolutionary turmoil up to the year 1920. His facts were of course derived exclusively from books and this applies likewise to his more recent tetralogy, *Les Compagnons du coquelicot* (1959), *La Barynia* (1960), *La Gloire des vaincus* (1961), and *Les Dames de Sibérie* (1962), four Russian rural-estate novels of the period between 1814 and 1825, that is, between the Russian entry in Paris to the Decembrist uprising after the death of Alexander I. In these works, the need to rely on secondary sources proved definitely disadvantageous.

Still another French Russian—born, it is true, in Argentina—found his way to the social novel. This is Joseph Kessel (born in 1898). Unfortunately, the social novel is not Kessel's strong point. His first works, *La Steppe rouge* (1922) and *L'Équipage* (1923), were novels of adventure which compare not unfavorably with the early Malraux. Subsequently Kessel abandoned the novel of adventure and gave us in the form of the comprehensive trilogy *Témoin parmi les hommes* and then of the tetralogy *Le Tour du malheur* (1950) a family and a social novel of development and of ethical didacticism. In the figure of Richard Dalleau, whose training in the field of law is utilized by the narrator to stage numerous scenes of social import, Kessel tried to develop the problem of the Don Juan in a late variant of Stendhal's cult of the ego, without—however—achieving in any sense Stendhal-like intellectual and philosophical penetration. Of the same order of quality is *Les Aristocrates* (1954) by Michel de Saint-Pierre (born in 1916), a cousin of Henry de Montherlant. This period novel undertakes to provide an idea of the feudal life of the family of the Marquis de Maubrun, which is aroused to heated turbulence when the widowed Marquis takes a fancy to "a girl without name, without wealth, without family traditions," who happens to be a friend of his daughter. In the sequel to this novel, *Les Nouveaux aristocrates,* the setting is shifted to a Jesuit college.

The best-informed user of subject matter associated with the upper bourgeoisie of modern France is doubtless Maurice Druon. He was born in 1918 in Paris, where he subsequently studied political science. *Les Rois maudits* (six volumes, 1955–60), with accurate descriptions of the dark period of France under Philippe IV and his ill-starred sons with whom the House of Capet died out in 1328, has won for Druon the approval of the historians and the acclaim of a broad public of readers with an interest in healthy entertainment. The so far most successful work of Druon appears to be *Les Grandes familles*, which was awarded the Prix Goncourt in 1948. It was filmed later on with Jean Gabin and Pierre Brasseur. In this work, Druon proved himself a worthy disciple of Balzac, utilizing the conflict of power and love in a portrayal of monomaniac torment. We are shown a somber picture of the élite of France as Druon presents the Upper Ten Thousand in their "struggle of the giants," in family deliberations, in the company of prostitutes, at the stock exchange, and at the gambling table. From Zola and Martin du Gard, the author skillfully took over the two-family motif, represented in his case by the families of La Monnerie and Schoudler.

Roger Peyrefitte (born in 1907), published his first novel, *Les Amitiés particulières*, in 1944. The book is strongly reminiscent of Gide's *Les Faux-monnayeurs*. It is a novel of the ethical readjustments and aberrations characteristic of youth during the years of puberty, but—aside from its psychological orientation—it also reveals a marked propensity for sensationalism. After a series of moral shockers—*Mademoiselle de Murville* (1947), *L'Oracle* (1948)—the author returned with *Les Ambassades* (1955) and *Les Clés de Saint-Pierre* to the novel of now-it-can-be-told reporting on all sorts of secret organizations during the Fourth Republic. This sort of writing can hardly lay claim to being taken seriously as literature, and it seems fitting that *La Fin des ambassades* wound up in a law suit involving Peyrefitte and the former Prime Minister Georges Bidault.

In the mason novel, *Les Fils de la lumière* (1960), Peyrefitte proceeded in his predilection for secret societies but also in his weakness for sensationalism and concessions to the appeal of the police gazette. While the social novel implies the characteristic risk of sinking to the level of the comic-strip technique,

Paul Vialar (born in 1898) strove once again to achieve in the genre, in terms of subject matter, the degree of deconfinement only Balzac had managed to effect before him. Already Vialar's *La Mort est un commencement* (1948) ran to eight volumes. In his *Chronique française du vingtième siècle,* of which six volumes have been published to date, the author plans to complete a pageant of all classes and professions of modern France.

By way of conclusion we mention three novelists whose divergent views of the novel of society may serve to show what breadth this genre can assume and also what difficulties are involved in the attempt to draw a clear line between literature and consumer-oriented fiction. Roger Ikor (born in 1912), a secondary-school teacher living in Paris, took up in his family novel *Le Fils d'Avrom* (1955), which was awarded the Prix Goncourt, the theme of Lacretelle's *Silbermann,* delineating on a broad canvas—with the use of literary devices that are certainly not unworthy of his novel—how a merger of Jewish and French contributions might result in the genesis of a force of European potentialities.[9] André Pieyre de Mandiargues (born in 1909) intermingled in *Le Lys de la mer* (1956) the characteristic traits of the feudal period novel of the kind produced by Michel de Saint-Pierre with the devices of the surrealist approach and the somewhat lax concept of morals of the time of the period of the rococo. It may be taken as the most reliable diagnostic feature of a weak novel of society that it tries to utilize erotic episodes to cover up an inherent lack of interest and epic continuity. *L'Empire céleste* (1958) by Françoise Mallet-Joris (born in 1930), the story of a circle of artists in the Rue d'Odessa on Montparnasse, likewise exemplifies the type. It thrives on allusions and dubious genre scenes of the kind which a certain public regards as innately characteristic of the French novel.

XII

THE REGIONAL NOVEL

Louis Hémon, Jean Hervé Bazin, Jean de La Varende,
André Savignon, Henri Pourrat, Charles-Ferdinand Ramuz,
Jean Giono, André Chamson, Henri Bosco, Marcel Aymé,
Thyde Monnier, Berthe Grimault

❧ The beginnings of the "novel of the sod"[1] go back in France to the eighteenth century when Jean-Jacques Rousseau's demand that man have an organic share in nature initiated a rebirth of the old genre of the idyl which now conceived its motives more realistically, while—somewhat later—Restif de la Bretonne, with the flavor of a lived life in his descriptions of peasant life, initiated the reorientation which was to lead to the brutal portrayal of morals of Zola's *La Terre*. Apart from the works of George Sand and the peasant cycle in Balzac's *Comédie humaine* (and Zola's *La Terre*), the center of gravity of the European regional novel of the nineteenth century lay distinctly outside of France. We find it where Jeremias Gotthelf, Gottfried Keller, Adalbert Stifter, and Theodor Storm worked out the essential contrasts of country and town as their central theme. The fact that this particular form does not account for a major portion of the French novelistic output in the twentieth century either, is possibly to be explained by structural peculiarities of the national literature of France. Specifically the religious novel of Mauriac, Green, and Bernanos, and also —more generally—the works of Rolland and Martin du Gard in their descriptions of rural scenes often utilize the element of nature for purposes of a symbolicistic setting. Here we have perhaps the reason that nature as a motif tends to be regarded as not sufficiently productive to function as the exclusive constitutive dynamic of the regional novel. On the other hand, an exotic freshening of the genre seems difficult, for this involves a domain which has been fully integrated by the novel of adventure.

So it was that Louis Hémon (1880–1913), who wrote his novel *Maria Chapdelaine* (published posthumously in 1915) after having worked for a year and a half as a farmhand in Canada, barred from the outset all elements that might possibly be suggestive of contrived exoticism. The solitude of a Canadian forest and river landscape is the home of the Chapdelaines who wrest from it through hard work the gifts of nature. The only daughter, Maria, emerges unscathed from the bitter experience of disappointment in love, thanks to the strength of the settlers' ethos in her make-up. As nature threatens man, so it also implants in him the capacity for solid and uncomplicated feelings.[2]

In the novel of the Vendée, *Qui j'ose aimer* (1956) by Hervé Bazin (born in 1911), nature completely loses its role of a purveyor of moral strength to man. The book deals with a drama of adultery which proceeds relentlessly without any kind of dependence on, or reference to, the gorgeously rich landscape in the background.

Jean de La Varende (1887–1959) made of his regional novels an expression of his Norman love of country, though his specimens of the genre come close to being historical novels. *Pays d'Ouche* (1936) gives a picture of the peculiarly Norman character at the turn from the eighteenth to the nineteenth century. This stands out even more strikingly in *Le Centaure de Dieu* (1938). The centaur of God is the strong-willed Gaston de La Bare, whom the author presents as the personification of proudly Norman idiosyncrasies in a congenially unspoiled natural setting.

Such almost haughty traits are lacking in the novel of Brittany, *Filles de la pluie* (1924) by André Savignon (born in 1882). The locale is the island of Ouessant. In the wake of Zola's *La Terre*, the novelist strove to depict in this work the heavy passions of lonely island dwellers whose reactions are as impetuous as the surroundings in which they are obliged to live.

As in Hémon and La Varende, ethical tenor and natural milieu appear closely interlinked and functionally congenial.

Still another trend is represented by the roughly fifty novels and stories of Henri Pourrat (1887–1959) with their setting in the Auvergne. This author was less concerned with the possibility of exemplifying and intensifying the emotions of his characters through references to their natural environment than with celebrating nature as the mythical Mother Primeval. Her mysteries, reflected in descriptions of day and of night, occupy in these works the foreground of the events. The most mature and most successful illustrative specimens are to be found in *Les Vaillances, farces et gentillesses de Gaspard des Montagnes* (1922–31), in which Pourrat's visual gifts are particularly striking. "The fields were bathing in a sea of summer. Thick stands of clover everywhere, among the lotus trees, between the warm flagstones around the ruins. Just clover but in vast woolly waves, pale rose and bygone here but yonder fresh of hue like a luscious strawberry, turning crimson, garnet, poppy red."

The merits of Charles-Ferdinand Ramuz (1878–1947), the most important representative of the modern French novel of the soil, have only recently come to be fully recognized and appreciated.[3] This Vaudois is the first writer of French-speaking Switzerland to preserve his literary independence and autonomy, that is, to emulate neither Jean-Jacques Rousseau nor Benjamin Constant nor Edouard Rod who allowed themselves to be drawn completely into French or, more specifically, Parisian cultural life. Ramuz belonged to a group of young French-speaking Swiss, who established in 1904 in Geneva the periodical *La Voile latine*, in which they discussed and commented on their independence from events abroad, their Latin descent, their closeness to the soil, and their sense of obligation to the cultural treasures of the Middle Ages. In keeping with this, three distinct phases characterize the creative career of Ramuz. The first period coincided with a twelve-year stay in Paris winding up in 1914. The early novels are accounts of individual lives and individual destinies. In both composition and style they closely follow the psychological trend of the period around the turn of the century.

The shock of the outbreak of the First World War is reflected in the works of Ramuz by a widening of the horizon and a transition to the analysis of collective destinies. Ramuz's friendship with the musician Igor Stravinsky and his preoccupation with the theories of the painter Cézanne prepared his breakthrough to a new concept of form. The progressive continuity of straightforward reporting became disrupted, and the action appeared dissolved in a series of scenes organized concentrically and, at times, not held together at all by a linear flow of action. The new language seems somehow liturgical and slow-moving. It is replete with meaning and imbued with emanations from the landscape which henceforth became the hallmark of the literary production of Ramuz: the Lake of Geneva and the nearby Alps. The best-known novels of this period are *La Guérison des maladies* (1917), *Les Signes parmi nous* (1919), *Terre du ciel* (1921), *Présence de la mort* (1925), and *La Grande peur dans la montagne* (1926). They all stand in the shadows of gigantic catastrophies engulfing nature and men. Apocalyptic visions of disaster and death and collective fear determine the magically mythical concept of the world. Yet, thematically this second phase in the development of Ramuz winds up in a dead-end road. The attempt to retrace in literary form the ultimate secrets of Christian faith was bound to fail, for Ramuz himself kept aloof and stayed far away from Christianity.

The third phase, marked by a kind of literary conversion, was initiated by the manifesto, *Passage du poète*, which is one of the most original documents composed by Ramuz. It proclaims the writer's renunciation of all myths, especially those of Christian derivation, and makes of this a universal demand valid for all who themselves are lacking the corresponding faith. The manifesto also proclaims Ramuz's renunciation of his earlier preoccupation with collective destinies. From now on the fate of the individual is to be prevalent again. *Farinet ou la fausse monnaie* (1932), *Adam et Ève* (1932), and *Le Garçon savoyard* (1936) are concerned with individuals rooted in the everyday reality of the world of the mountains. All in all, Ramuz's close contact with the soil of his homeland gave him the conviction that it is only in the immediacy of life close to the soil that literature can find a foundation permitting it to depict the drama of human life. Thus Ramuz opened up a perspective exceeding by far the confines of the regional novel.

We have here a major point of difference between Ramuz

and, for instance, Jean Giono (born 1895) who is often (but very unfairly) mentioned in one and the same breath with him. Giono divines nature and strives to identify himself completely with it, while Ramuz's alert mountaineers know from experience that they cannot put a blind trust in the powers of the soil. Giono, whose homeland is the south of France, is essentially idyllic; Ramuz knows of demons and of evil. It is wiser, Ramuz and his characters feel, to assume toward nature an attitude of watchfulness rather than one of ecstatic abandonment. Indeed, it is significant and perhaps decisive that the Provence is Giono's world.

Giono was born in the valley of the Durance in southern France and grew up among herdsmen and peasants. Giono's first works—presented as a trilogy of Pan consisting of *Colline* (1929), *Un de Baumugnes* (1929), and *Regain* (1930)—reflect the author's endeavor to impart to the realistic village novel, by means of nature hymns, the dimensions of the epic. This restoration is reminiscent of the pagan endeavors of the Parnasse in the nineteenth century, but Giono does not look for antiquity in the distant past. Instead he traces, in the soil of the Provence, emanations of a pagan world which Christianity was able to cover up but not to kill. As the hunter Panturle lays settler's claim to a stretch of land in deserted Aubignane and as he founds there a family unconcerned with authority and church, we sense that we read, on a symbolic level, of the archaic transition from nomad to settler.

Giono's language operates with anaphoras, triple chords, and paratactic sentence links, achieving an artful primordiality of expression. "The squadron of clouds slipped its moorings. It made a big, long convoy of clouds sailing northward. It kept going. With it, one felt the earth swell with all the rains and life revive in the grass."* In the Christmas plays of the herdsmen, Giono discerns Pan's omnipresence (*Présentation de Pan,* 1930). In *Jean le Bleu* (1932) we have Giono's account of his own youth, borne by a pagan ethics. The forces of nature and, above all, the emotion-laden intellectual experience of antiquity, joining forces in a congenially conceived myth of the earth, arouse in Jean—as the highest principle of life—a form of sensualism which considers itself answerable only to the forces of the soil and of the blood.

Starting with a description of a real landscape in the Provence, the book *Le Serpent d'étoiles* (1933) rises to the level of a lyrical epic of the cosmos in which nine herdsmen represent the forces of nature, exhorting man not to take heed of the ethical doctrine of Christianity. "Live by the laws of trees and beasts . . . and sing of the glory of being naked, sing of the pride of being naked."

Thus Giono's thinking and its literary precipitate reached a point of development beyond which there was nowhere to go. In fact, in *Le Hussard sur le toit* (1951), the novelist found his way—to the surprise of his readers—to the realm of the historical novel, abandoning what had been his and only his. In 1965, Giono's novel *Deux cavaliers de l'orage* appeared, a Cain-and-Abel story from the early decades of the present century, which Luc Estang characterized in the *Figaro littéraire* contemptuously as "a western from the Hautes Collines." To be sure, all this does not affect Giono's importance in terms of the return of the Provence into French literature. His development is symptomatic on two scores: It marks the failure of all pagan renewals and of the novel of the soil in general.[4]

Apart from Giono, four novelists derived essential stimuli from the Provence, if it is permitted to include the area of the Cevennes in the linguistic domain of Provençal. It was in the Cevennes that André Chamson (born 1900), during the early phase of his productive career, placed three novels to which occasional Provençal inserts imparted a peculiar stylistic local color. These are *Roux le bandit* (1925), *Les Hommes de la route*, and *Le Crime des justes* (1928). The first is a novel of adventure in which the landscape is hardly more than a backdrop. The second and third are pictures of morals describing the deleterious effect of excessive wealth on an ethically intact form of rural life and the struggle of a village community against an individual family. Thus Chamson brought together elements from the novel of the soil and the novel of society. His later works rejoined the mainstream of the sociological and the historical novel.[5]

The novels of Henri Bosco (born in 1888) are of a completely different bent. Bosco's father came from the Piedmont and his mother from the Provence. For some ten years after the First World War, Bosco lectured on comparative literature at the

University of Naples. Through the magic realism of his novels he became a bucolic singer of the glories of the Provence but did not follow Giono in the effort to unearth pagan myths and restore them to life. With *Le Mas Théotime* (1942), Bosco introduced himself as a sensitive delineator of the mythical forces of the locale which serve to motivate and to heal fateful events in the lives of the people of Théotime Farm. *Le Jardin d'Hyacinthe* (1946) is a pastoral novel in which the central figure is a foundling girl, "who perhaps passed through Paradise without remembering it, for there is about her a garden fragrance of flowers and of fruit, unequaled by the fragrance of any other girl on earth." In keeping with this characteristic passage, the story is emphatically a fantastic novel in which unlikely things are made to come true.

In the novels of Marcel Aymé (1902-67), the elements of the Provençal and rural and of the fantastic are joined by a third component, a sturdy bit of "esprit gaulois." In 1933, *La Jument verte* appeared, a peasant novel harking back to the seventies of the past century, with the author using the description of a supposedly green stud to cause wild and daring confusion. In addition, we must note that in Aymé the link between nature and man is so close that the dividing line between moral decree and animal behavior is totally obliterated. With *Gustalin* (1937) and *La Vouivre* (1943), Aymé comes close to the mythical exaltation of Giono. After twelve years of silence, Aymé published *Les Tiroirs de l'inconnu,* a burlesque detective story in which the scene shifts from the Provence to Paris.

It is one of the ironies in the world of the intellect that the woman who is least concerned with her literary affiliation, that is, Thyde Monnier (1887–1967), has managed through her voluminous output of novels to impress many readers outside of France as being typically representative of the Provence. Except for her earliest novels of womanhood (*La Rue courte, Annonciata*), Thyde Monnier constructed her later books— especially *Le Pain des pauvres* (1939) and *Fleuve* (1942)—as light-weight love stories in which the landscape of the Provence, Marseille, and the Rhône valley are at best a picturesque backdrop for superficially depicted human encounters. As so often in second-rate novels of society, depth of artistic endeavor is replaced by a liberal sprinkling of risqué details.

With the novels of the peasant girl Berthe Grimault (born in 1943), which Eliezer Fournier revises for her (*Beau clown; Tuer son enfant*), the regional novel of the immediate past reverts, finally, to preliterary realms of scandalmongering in a rural setting.

XIII

THE NOVEL OF THE ABSURDITY OF
EXISTENCE

*Henri Michaux, Jean-Paul Sartre, Albert Camus, Raymond Queneau,
Pierre Gascar, Jean Genet, Nathalie Sarraute, Samuel Beckett*

❧ The truly uncanny breadth, which the novel of the absurd
has evolved in France in the course of the two or three decades
since the thirties,[1] may be accounted for by three major factors
revealing simultaneously the genesis of the atmosphere of
horror and also of spiritual lethargy which this form of the novel
produced in the most unexpected situations. The experiences
of the First World War instilled in many writers after decades
of pondering the conviction that the one lesson incontrovert-
ably to be derived from the reality of the current cultural crisis
had to be that gruesome senselessness rules world events instead of logic and humaneness. Under the influence of André
Breton's surrealist manifestos after 1924, in which non-logic,
seen as the positive original category of man's power of thought,
was elevated to the rank of a primary literary force—with
Freud and Jung supplying the terminology and the methodology of such introversion on psychiatric grounds—induced not
a few writers to present conventional subjects and themes in
the distorted form of daydreams, in which a frequent re-
kneading of facts remembered (as the analysts assure us) winds
up in the absurd. The stories, *Thomas l'imposteur* (1923) and *Les
Enfants terribles* (1929) by Jean Cocteau (1889–1963) bear wit-

ness to the power of such preoccupations. Finally, since the end of the twenties, the works of the Prague writer Franz Kafka became known in French translations, confirming the as yet hesitant endeavor to think of the world as a maze in which the individual is condemned to the labors of Sisyphus. The increasingly sensitive awareness on the part of individual writers of the incommensurate in the relationship between man and world could easily be raised to a higher power of fixed macabre ideas. Portrayal of the absurd signifies thus primarily that countersense, the incommensurate, the fixed ideas (which, of course, need not be taken as highly personal confessions of the author) determine the demeanor and the reactions of the characters in literary works.

The first French-writing author to strike out in this direction was the Namur Walloon Henri Michaux (born in 1899), who began his career under the impression of the works of Lautréamont and Hellens. So far literary criticism has recognized Michaux at best as a lyrical poet, but it was he who in 1930 and 1938 published fragments and two preliminary versions of a mythical novel of the absurd, *Un Certain Plume*, in which anyone who has read Franz Kafka—*Die Verwandlung, Der Prozess*, or *Das Schloss*—recognizes a reflection of Kafka's philosophy. Michaux did know Kafka.

A simple individual by name of Plume—symbolic of his insignificance—gets himself enmeshed (without being guilty, though not without baseless and hence absurd guilt complexes) in senseless social and legal dependence on his environment, until the world around him assumes to his mind a gargoylishly transcendental appearance. It "transcends," that is, it "goes beyond" both his understanding and his being in every possible way, but it never precipitates in the form of a consistent metaphysics. In this world God has been annihilated. Whether the prevailing chaos has resulted from this annihilation is not quite clear. Plume's figure impresses us as particularly tragic since Michaux evidently conceived it as an "Everyman" figure. The novel was unfortunately never completed.[2]

The next in line after Michaux in the series of novelists of the absurd is the writer-philosopher Jean-Paul Sartre. He was born on June 21, 1905, in Paris and entered the École Normale Supérieure in 1924. The rational intellectualism of that institution shaped his entire subsequent demeanor, both as a creative writer and as a thinker. In 1928 he took his degree and began teaching philosophy in Laon. From 1931 to 1936 he lived in Le Havre (except for the intervening period which he spent in Berlin). The following year he went to Neuilly where he stayed until 1941. During the Second World War he served with the French Armed Forces and was taken prisoner. From 1944 on he has been active as a writer without other professional ties and is regarded in France as the founder of existentialism, a philosophical movement which is consciously antirationalist in the information it purports to provide on the existence of man. In 1946, Sartre established his own leftist party, the "Rassemblement Démocratique Révolutionnaire," which, however, never managed to get off the ground. In the fifties, Sartre traveled extensively in the company of Simone de Beauvoir, both for pleasure and study. In the course of these travels he spent some time in Cuba. In the fall of 1964 he was awarded the Nobel Prize for Literature, which he turned down with an explanatory reference to his sympathies for the policies of the Eastern Block.

Sartre's fame as a narrative prose writer is based on the works *La Nausée* (1938), *Le Mur* (1939), and the tetralogy *Les Chemins de la liberté* (1945 ff.) of which only the first three volumes have been completed. Sartre's themes are the world of things, the relationship between the I and the You, and socialist idealism. It would seem that the importance of these works lags behind that of Sartre's plays and philosophical essays. One also has the impression that his art as a narrator has not been gaining strength over the years but has rather tended to grow progressively paler. Yet, all this cannot change the fact that no other figure on the literary scene of France during the years from 1944 on can be compared with him in terms of predominance and impact. The postwar generation of Europe is preoccupied with Sartre as it is with no other writer, with the possible exception of Albert Camus.

La Nausée has a brief preface written in fictitious accordance with the philological principles governing critical editions. The "editors" inform the reader that the present work consists of the papers of the scholar Antoine Roquentin in precisely the form in which they were found after his death. The reader is told that Roquentin, up to the time of his death, lived in Bouville where he was engaged in historical studies. Footnotes sprinkled over the first pages of the work skillfully uphold the fiction. Bouville is Le Havre. To a certain extent, Antoine Roquentin may be identified with the novelist himself. The work was written after Sartre—and this is a documented fact —had discovered and read an article on disgust in the Year-book for Philosophical and Phenomenological Research (Vol. X, 1929). The work, written in the form of a diary, treats of Roquentin's dwindling interest in his historical studies in Bouville and of the inroads made by absurd incidents in his hermit's life as well as of the disgust they provoke in him. In an entry dated January 29, 1932, he notes, referring to a parti-cular encounter, how things to him are losing their objective being, their "at-hand-ness" (Heidegger) and how their appear-ance seems "blocked" to him by something ugly. "Then there was his hand, like a huge white worm in my hand ... it seemed to me that I was filled with lymph or lukewarm milk."* The following day Roquentin reports how the crisis is mounting. On the way to the library, he explains, "I meant to pick up a piece of paper lying on the ground and could not do it ... I had the feeling that I was no longer free ... we must not allow things to touch us, for they are not alive. I fear touching them as though they were living beasts."* Then Roquentin recalls how he once picked up a stone at the beach. It was smooth on top and dry and solid, but underneath it was sticky and moist. "It was a sweetish disgust ... a kind of repulsive sensation in my hands."

Incommensurability and fixed ideas thus introduce the absurd experience of nausea. The disgust evoked by the stone returns in still keener form in a similar experience later on, involving a root the proliferation of which enables it to slip out of its "at-hand-ness." Now Roquentin recognizes that "nausea" and awareness of the "too much" are related. The style of the novel becomes progressively more seismographic. Roquentin's relationship to the world around him has been re-duced to an ever alert and simultaneously frightened pursuit of what is nauseating, until he finally interrupts his work and leaves Bouville.

But then—and the parallel to the conclusion of Proust's *A*

la Recherche du temps perdu is striking—an aesthetic phenomenon surprisingly opens up the possibility of redemption from
the seemingly hopeless situation. Repeatedly Roquentin hears
the hit tune, "Some of these days." "When the voice broke
forth from the silence, I felt how my body grew hard, and the
disgust was up and away." The tune represents to him the
ultimate in perfection imaginable. "It does not exist, for it has
nothing that is too much. Everything else is too much in relation
to it. It is. And I, too, have wanted to be."* Yet he remains condemned to exist.

In *La Nausée* the artistic problem consisted for Sartre above
all in the resolution of a philosophically more or less precise
program in novelistic situations. He used for the purpose the
form of the individualistic novel of consciousness. As he presents Roquentin who of a sudden—while walking down some
unattractive, mathematically straight street—begins to feel at
ease, as he shows how Roquentin isolates himself against everything vital and avoids all "abundance," how he probes his way
from the world of effusion of human intercourse to the world
of things (though even these impress him as not sufficiently hard
and hence as nauseating), the effect is indeed that a world picture of existentialist philosophy is turned into aesthetic reality.
For the early Sartre of *La Nausée*, the equation is valid: To
exist is to sense that one exists [*se sentir exister*]. That is the
sensation of the "too much." It instills disgust, and disgust is
the consciousness of the absurd. To be sure, it is also a fact that
later on the playwright Sartre, especially under the ideological
pressure of the Communist party, abandoned these beginnings
to a very large extent. Still, a point to be emphasized remains
that Sartre's nihilism rests on an aesthetic basis (compare also
L'Imagination, 1936, and *L'Imaginaire,* 1940). Things real are
never beautiful; the concept of beauty can only be referred to
the imaginary (*L'Imaginaire,* p. 242). This axiom is identical
with what *La Nausée* wants to say.

The unqualified honesty and the radical individualism of
Sartre's early creative period remain characteristic of *Le Mur.*
La Nausée refers with its motto to Céline, but *Le Mur* bears
even more clearly the imprint of influences of the author of
Voyage au bout de la nuit. Céline and Sartre are agreed in their
aversion against people who can find happiness only through

a clearly defined and neatly labeled identification with a religious group, a social class, a professional guild. The burden of being made to depend on one's neighbor is the topic of *La Chambre*, one of the five stories in the volume *Le Mur*. The story *Hérostrate*, in the same volume, treats of total freedom. Paul Hilbert, who hates everything human, decided—after the model of the Greek Herostratus (who set the temple of Ephesus on fire)—to achieve a sinister kind of fame by killing a number of people. Yet, as he is about to shoot six people in the street, the first shot fills him with panic and fear, and he runs away. The intended meaning is difficult to grasp. Clear is again Sartre's hate of things physical, but the story appears more clearly as a parody of the "gratuitous act" which Gide had celebrated in *Les Caves du Vatican*. Sartre rather agrees with Nietzsche that only individualistic nihilism in its true form can be creative and goal-conscious.

In *L'Intimité*, the most daring and most provocative piece of writing ever to have been published by Sartre, the author transposes the problem of the "too much" into the sphere of homoeroticism. *L'Enfance d'un chef*, finally—a sketched-out novel of education and, in a sense, a summary of Sartre's themes—can be regarded as a good introduction to his world of thought. The fact that the hero is the son of an entrepreneur affords Sartre an opportunity to introduce elements of social criticism. As Lucien feels attracted initially more by the world around him than by his own conceptions, Sartre discusses on a narrative plain the central problem from *L'Être et le néant*, the contrast of "being within oneself" (=existing) with "being for oneself" (=having the freedom of conceiving nothingness by virtue of one's own powers), in such a way that everything physical and vital appears denigrated as a disturbance of the "being for oneself." Scholastic training reinforces in the hero the hellish experience of "the other." But instead of deriving a lesson from this experience, Lucien grows ever more deeply into his existence "within himself," developing the greatest non-virtue that Sartre's world knows, "bad faith" which is the premise for all dishonesty and all dissoluteness of thought. He feels himself called upon to become the true chief (although he adjusts his entire life on the basis of the reactions of others) when he acquires through his antisemitism the respect of a certain political group. Now, in the terminology of Sartre, he is a *salaud*, a "swine."

The autobiographical work *Les Chemins de la liberté*—including *L'Age de raison* (1945), *Le Sursis* (1945), and *La Mort dans l'âme* (1949)—was conceived as a novel of love and of ideas and simultaneously as a literary reflection of the era of the thirties and forties. In the person of the teacher of philosophy, Mathieu, the work introduces a figure which in many respects may be identified with the novelist himself. In the very exposition we learn that Mathieu's companion, Marcelle, reproaches him with placing his "lucidity" over every other experience. "It is to liberate yourself, to enable you to regard yourself and to judge yourself. That, basically, is your ideal: to be nothing." Mathieu's counterpart is Daniel, whom Marcelle marries in the end. He exists "within himself." The absurd does not enter his consciousness. He requires pre-established forms. So he finds his way from homosexuality to the ethics of catholicism. In this he is not motivated by inmost religious considerations, but he is pursuing his quest for the label. The second and the third volumes are not very satisfying. Written in the multifaceted style of Jules Romains and John Dos Passos (which does not really come off), *Le Sursis* is a novel of the political *brisance* of a week of crucial significance to the world (September 23 to September 30, 1938), while *La Mort dans l'âme* represents Sartre's dutiful contribution to the literature of the occupation of France and the budding resistance. Sartre's neo-humanist theory during this period of his creative career, that "nothing can be for us without being for all," lacks the power of an aesthetically convincing statement. Here the novelist finds himself confronted with the necessity of refurbishing Mathieu's abstracting reason (which prevented him from taking part on the republican side in the Spanish Civil War) and of devolving from it the principles of behavior obligating the individual to the community and the group. In the process he ascribes the highest ethical significance to the terrorism of his hero who joins the resistance when the "phony war" has come to an end (*La Mort dans l'âme*, p. 193). Freedom now manifests itself in action.

Thus this work leaves a most multifarious impression. This results, on the one hand, from the ideological maturation which led the author in the course of one decade from a provocative individualism to a socialist form of idealism and, on the other hand, from the progressive broadening of the form of the novel, with the style of the diary giving way to the kaleidoscopic style of universally human preoccupations. To be sure, in the later years meaning and form diverge more often than the idea of a work of art can withstand unscathed.[3]

After 1944 Sartre hardly missed an opportunity to extol to the French public the one writer whom he regarded as the most important contemporary, the Algerian Frenchman Albert Camus (1913–60). He thus referred the public to a figure that cannot fail, both in human and in literary terms, to instill in us the highest interest and esteem. Camus was born on November 7, 1913, in Mondovi near Bône in Algeria as the son of a workman. When, after great material hardship, he had acquired the degree of licencié in literature at the University of Algiers, tuberculosis prevented him first from continuing his studies and then from joining the armed forces. During these years Camus was greatly interested in the stage and organized a company of actors. In 1939 he went to Paris. Five years later, he became editor-in-chief of the daily *Combat*. In 1952 he clashed with Sartre in the matter of the Russian concentration camps. In 1957 he was awarded the Nobel Prize for Literature in Stockholm. On January 4, 1960, he was killed in an automobile accident on his way to Paris in a car owned by Michel Gallimard. In his pocket, a railway ticket was found. It is as though his own death was meant to confirm the absurd existence of the figures of his novels. A short time before, Camus had stated that his work had only just began. He left behind twenty book-length works, including twelve volumes of essays, letters and addresses, four plays, and four short novels or stories. Seven plays and novels written in other languages had been adapted by him for the French stage. About a dozen studies on his work had appeared in book form while he was still alive, including several thoroughly informed appraisals.[4] A markedly autobiographical novel, *La Mort heureuse*, begun around 1936, has never been published (cf. *Carnets*, p. 24).

The four volumes of narrative prose, which are of particular interest to us in the present context, are *L'Étranger* (1942), *La Peste* (1947), *La Chute* (1956), and *L'Exil et le royaume* (1957).

Some of Camus's essays are of interest to the reader and student of his narrative prose. These include, in particular, *L'Envers et l'endroit* (1936), *Noces* (1938, Second Edition 1950), *Le Mythe de Sisyphe* (1943), *L'Homme révolté* (1951), and *L'Été* (1954). The place of Sartre's socialist idealism is occupied in Camus by a credible humanism of action; the preoccupation with the world of things has been replaced by the Mediterranean myth of a cast-proud rationalism; instead of fixed ideas of the absurd there appears a gradual triumph over contingency and incommensurateness in the world. It follows that we must not try to understand Camus on the basis of his most widely read book, *La Peste*, but rather by starting out from his story, *L'Étranger*, and the essays, *L'Envers et l'endroit, Noces,* and *L'Été*. Here we find statements relative to Camus's life in Algiers such as: "I find it enough to live with all my body," and "[Life] is the cultic center, and has the admiration of the body." (*Noces,* pp. 22 and 58). It is hard to imagine a wider gulf than that which separates us here from Sartre's *La Nausée*. Camus opposes this magnificient existence to "the night of Europe, the winter in men's faces." (*L'Été,* p. 144). It is in the world of light that Camus located an absurd tragedy when, in 1937, he wrote *L'Étranger*, the first-person narrative of the Algerian Frenchman Meursault, who feels little or nothing when his mother dies, but who shortly thereafter proves good-natured enough to write for Raymond, who is an acquaintance of his, a farewell letter to his, that is, Raymond's Arabic girl friend. This is the exposition. Then Raymond and Meursault happen to meet the girl's brother at the beach, and they come to blows. A while later Meursault returns to the place and shoots the Arab to death. Why? Before the reader can figure out the answer, he is struck by the plethora of metaphors in this passage which is written in an abruptly changed style. Especially the light of the sun is referred to figuratively as a blade (of a knife or a sword). Later on Meursault explains in court, in keeping with this, "I killed him because of the sun." Unless we wish to interpret this medically as suggesting that Meursault suffered a sunstroke—which, we can be sure, is not what Camus had in mind—we can only see in that answer an admission of the absurd which can take hold of men. Since it derives from nature, which Meursault loves, he understands neither the language of the prosecutor nor that of the prison priest, whose purpose it is to make him "see" what he has done and to make him repent. Meursault, however, clings only the more tenaciously—especially in the presence of the priest—to his deed which he continues to uphold. The absurd is fate and cannot be bargained with.

Compared to this, *La Peste* goes even a step farther. The conceit of the story as a chronicle intensifies the illusion of credibility and simultaneously imposes on the author the necessity of proceeding by simple chronological reporting. The evidently intended simplicity of the level of style helps to focus attention entirely on the philosophical breadth of *La Peste*. The nature-given "feeling of the absurd" is here raised to an intellectual "notion of the absurd." Once risen to the level of consciousness, the absurd becomes the object of rational analysis and of humanistic countermeasures. The plague befalls the city of Oran. At first it kills rats; then it attacks humans. Camus—and let us remember that the label of chronicle was applied to the book by the author himself—probes here in a town of average people the behavior of substance-endowed personalities in a state of emergency. While the Jesuit priest, Paneloux, regards the epidemic as a token of the deserved wrath of God, the physician Bernard Rieux keeps working as the leader of a group of courageous men and women to stem the tide of the scourge, an effort which is finally crowned with success. It has been suggested that these events can be interpreted as mirroring the German invasion of 1940 and the French resistance. But this approach fails to touch the core of the work which is organized as a philosophical novel around the dual theme of the absurd and the upright [*honnêtete*], as Rieux's demeanor is called. In *La Peste*, Camus discovered man as a sacrificial offering, and he placed himself spontaneously at the side of it. Although, at the end of the work, Rieux foresees that the plague will return, he does fight. It is on this basis that we must understand Camus's characterization of Rieux' behavior: "Man, in his absurdity, cannot but exhaust himself."*

This applies also to the hero of the short novel, *L'Hôte*, which forms part of *L'Exil et le royaume*. The Algerian teacher Daru has been singled out by the French police to deliver into their hands an Arab clan murderer. But Daru—having spent a night with the murderer—leaves it up to him to flee or to give himself up to the police. What the Arab's decision finally is, we are not told. When Daru gets back to his schoolhouse, he finds on the blackboard a message threatening his life. Thus a sinister "star of misunderstanding" rules over the happenings in this short novel. The educated Arab Daru, ethnically and socially isolated both from his people and from the representatives of the colonial power, is driven by the law into a situation which admits of no rational solution. "Man in his absurdity can only exhaust himself." The principles of "solitary" and of "solidarity" no longer add up to a harmonious resolution.

In *Le Mythe de Sisyphe* (1943), Camus undertook an attempt to provide the phenomenon of the absurd for his novels with an ideologically precise substructure. First we read the thesis: "The divorce of man and his life, of the actor and his stage, is the very essence of the experience of the absurd."* This is clearly applicable to Meursault, a little less so to Daru, and least to Rieux. Camus chose the myth of Sisyphus as an illustration because it is so frequently cited as the most desolate exemplification of the curse of human existence. This makes Camus's interpretation the more surprising. "The gods had condemned Sisyphus to roll forever a rock to the top of a hill from where its own weight made it forever slide back down again. They had reasoned, with some justification, that there is no punishment more terrible than work which is useless and without hope."* With a second simile, taken from the Bible, Camus relates Sisyphus's state to mankind as a whole: "These are our nights of Gethsemany." (p. 166). But, Camus continues: "Happiness and the absurd are two children of the same earth." (p. 167). This explains Meursault's unprotesting acceptance of the absurd. Applied to Rieux and Daru, the equation leaves a remainder which can no longer be fully accounted for. In this we may see evidence of an ideological development. Indeed, the two figures—Rieux and Daru—were drawn after the time of the Sisyphus essay. Rieux undertakes to fight the absurd in trying to stem the epidemic, and Daru does so by refusing to be a mere tool in the hands of the colonial regime, although this refusal may cost his life. The prototype of both Rieux and Daru is Sisyphus, as Camus by now has come to think of him: "It is there that all the silent joy of Sisyphus lies. His fate is his own. His rock is his. In the same way, when man in the absurd reflects on his torment, he makes all idols fall silent. And as the universe has of a sudden been forced back into its silence, the thousand wondrous little voices of the earth speak up. Unconscious and secret appeals, invitations from all faces, these are the necessary reverse and the prize of victory. There is no sun without shade, and we must know the night. Man in the absurd says yes, and his effort no longer wants an end. If there is a personal destiny, there is none superior to it or at least only one which he regards with contempt as immutable. For the rest, he knows himself master of his life. . . . The struggle uphill as such suffices to fill a man's heart. We must think of Sisyphus as happy."*

With these "glad tidings" *Le Mythe de Sisyphe* concludes, and it was only consistent when Camus wrote in *L'Homme révolté*, as a comment on the myth of Prometheus which in this world view rounds out the interpretation of Sisyphus: "Man is the only being which refuses to be what it is." That is Rieux's achievement. A diary entry from the year 1936 reads similarly: "Commit yourself. Then, accept with the same energy the yes or the no." (*Carnets*, p. 38). In a revolt which is simultaneously metaphysical—being a revolt against the priest Paneloux—and directed against society, he annuls the absurd ever anew in a feeling of solidarity with all those who are made to play the role of sacrificial offerings. It is this relentless effort that must be emphasized. Now the proximity of Camus and Gide becomes clear: The revolt against the gods and the humanistic appeal of *Thésée*, of *Le Mythe de Sisyphe*, and of *La Peste*—all three published in the forties—are mutually supplementary.

The evolution of Camus, author of *L'Étranger*, to the level of the Camus who wrote *La Peste* is now completely clear. The savagely radiant power of the world of the Mediterranean, to which Meursault ecstatically abandons himself ("happiness and the absurd are two children of the same earth"), turns out to be for Rieux, and in a certain sense also for Daru, the bearer and the support of a higher humanity. This is the only vulnerable point in Camus. If these powers of a landscape are rated so highly and if—as can hardly be gainsaid—it is a fact that they cannot be made accessible to all mankind, then it follows that an ethics based on them cannot lay claim to being a universal goal. The very same objection we raised in an earlier context against Barrès.

But in his most recent great novel, *La Chute*, Camus demanded of himself an exacting reckoning and conscientiously cast doubt on every form of philosophical self-assurance. The work—like *L'Étranger*—is conceived in the form of a monologue. Through it, the Judge Penitent Jean-Baptiste Clamence provides for an anonymous interlocutor a moral portrait of himself. (*Juge-pénitent*, here rendered as "Judge Penitent," is a neologism; only *juge pénal* exists.) The irony which pervades the book cannot be fully decoded until we learn more about Camus from as yet unpublished letters, diaries, and conversations. With their help we shall perhaps find out whether Clamence meant his confession to represent an (unsuccessful) approach to metaphysical problems or whether he merely meant to report—half nihilisticaly, half cynically—how at one time in his life he failed morally when he did not prevent the suicide he witnessed on the Pont des Arts in Paris. Critics have objected that *La Chute* is not successful as a work of epic prose since Camus nowhere suggests or justifies any kind of sympathy with Clamence. But if the purpose was to describe critically how he himself rose from less than modest beginnings to the position of a literary figure of the first order, then his procedure can only be welcomed. *La Chute* has indeed little in common with Camus's earlier works, unless we see a connection in the ever-recurring symbolism of light. As a moral invective, the work in fact need have but little bearing on what preceded it.

To be sure, it is tragic that the creative work of the novelist Camus had to break off as it did, especially since we know that he was planning to show in a cycle of novels of Nemesis—to be called *Le Premier homme*—that the absurd existence under the myths of Sisyphus and Prometheus could be, as it were, transfigured, could be divested of the fixed ideas they now entail, and that it would be possible to provide for actively striving man a world of moderation and of happiness.

The atheism of Camus may be objected to and criticized on philosophical grounds. The fact remains—a fact of basic importance—that this novelist achieved and exemplifies the highest form of humanistic world mastery which a non-

Christian can achieve. Through his endeavor on behalf of the conditio humana, he joined, as a prose narrator and essayist, the ranks of the French moralists who, beginning with Montaigne, have been striving indefatigably to fathom the question of man and of his relationship to metaphysics, to the state, and to society. And Camus ascribed to man greater dignity than Sartre did; nor did he try to lull him to sleep with false existentialist assurances. The death of Camus in 1960 and Sartre's silence as a novelist have made possible (and necessary) our interim stock-taking of the achievements of the novel of the absurd. The balance sheet does not look very encouraging. Neither Queneau nor Gascar, Genet, Sarraute, nor Beckett can fill the gap with full qualifications. It appears that the years from 1938 to 1957 were the golden years in the history of this genre.

Raymond Queneau from Le Havre (born in 1903) began his career as a clerk in a banking institution and advanced to the position of editor of the *Encyclopédie de la Pléiade* published by Gallimard. Since 1951 he has been a member of the Académie Goncourt. In his novels—*Pierrot mon ami* (1942), *Le Dimanche de la vie* (1959), and, especially, *Zazie dans le métro* (1959)—he succeeded, while giving preference to motifs of the suburbs, in presenting the concept of the continuity of time as a built-in factor apt to impress upon us the irrationality of existence. Queneau's precise knowledge of Flaubert—he wrote, on three occasions, prefaces to *Bouvard et Pécuchet*—appears to have attuned him to the absurd. For Zazie, a schoolgirl from the suburbs, a one-day visit in Paris invests everything (as it did for Flaubert's clerk) with ultimate significance. For only knowledge of everything can overcome the apparent impenetrability of things. But the day passes, and the yield of it remains nil. When Zazie, that night, is asked, "You did see the métro?," she answers—though she had spent most of her time underground—"No!"—"But then, what did you do?"—"I have grown older." This precocious answer of a child covers up the despair involved in the recognition that both experience of time and genuine consciousness are irrelevant. To be sure, feats of stylistic acrobatics, operating in this novel with bits of argot that are too contrived to be readily decipherable, conceal the underlying tenor, but the question, "What can a fellow be really

sure of?" is representative of Queneau's pessimism. Furthermore, it was not precisely a stroke of genius that the author
chose a girl from the suburbs as his mouthpiece, expecially since
he tends to digress in the telling of his story.[5]

The cognitional impotence in Queneau—that is, impotence
on an intellectual level—has its counterpart in Pierre Gascar
(born in 1916) in the form of an emotional variant of pessimism.
Gascar's early stories show their derivation from Maupassant's
realism of compassion. We mention *Les Meubles* (1949) and
Visage clos (1951). Subsequently, however, Gascar wrote novels
of a pitiless world of executioners. The absurd, as he managed
it, represented less the substance and content of consciousness
(as holds true in Sartre and Camus) but emanated much rather
from the total gestalt of the situation. In the stirring book, *Les
Bêtes* (1953), Gascar makes short shrift of the late-romantic
image of the animal (as it appears, for instance, in Rudyard
Kipling's *Jungle Book*), showing the reactions of animals at the
slaughterhouse or under the hail of bombs, not in order to de-
lineate them as creatures of interest to the minds and emotions
of man but as suffering fellow creatures with the function, as
it were, of opening man's eyes to the meaninglessness with
which he has filled the world. The stories of internment, *Le
Temps des morts* (1953) and *Les Femmes* (1955), are gruesome
interpretations of the same idea. It is regrettable that Gascar
shifted his course in 1958 with *La Barre au corail* to fall in line
with the traditional love novel with an exotic local color. His
most recent novel, *Les Moutons de feu* (1963), deals—duly disguised—with the problems of current politics and has much in
common with Gracq's *Le Rivage des Syrtes*.

The brutality of Gascar's novels, however, is mild in comparison with what Jean Genet (born in 1910) expects his
readers to stomach. The disparate veers off into the shocking
and the risqué; the fixed idea of the absurd degenerates in
lustful wallowing in an ethical and spiritual chaos; and the
anti-rationality of non-reason provides a welcome excuse for
trying to frighten the bourgeois by pleading the cause of the
abnormal in terms of law and in terms of morals. When Sartre
in 1952 broke with Camus, Genet became his new protégé. He
praised his supposed qualities in a voluminous preface to the
Gallimard edition of Genet's works. It is quite enough to read

Notre-Dame-des-fleurs (1951), which was written in prison, to understand that Genet, who spent a considerable portion of his life behind bars, considers human society exclusively as a platform for things criminal. With Genet, the work of the Marquis de Sade appears revived on a more macabre plane. *Notre-Dame-des-fleurs* reflects, in a sense, a spirit of hero worship of criminals and homosexuals whose pictures the author kept pinned to the wall of his cell. This imparts to the novel two levels of tension. There is Genet himself, pondering and mulling while waiting for his trial, and then there is Genet the biographer of imaginary criminals. Sartre called this—and meant the phrase to be laudatory—"a black mass." He was fascinated by the absurd splits of consciousness—"if she felt 'woman,' she thought 'man' "—but no reader will find it pleasing that such gangster literature is allowed, by dint of piling disgust on disgust, to claim that it can provide information on the absurd in human existence and that in doing so it is in fact given the endorsement of established authorities.

Nathalie Sarraute (born in 1902), Russian by birth, published in 1938, the year of Sartre's *La Nausée*, the volume *Tropismes*. The title is derived from the Greek word *tropos* and refers to organic proliferations induced by physical, physiological, or chemical stimuli. The metaphor serves the writer to depict life as a series of miniature struggles and neuralgias, seemingly elicited by absurd stimuli. In keeping with this, *Portrait d'un inconnu* (1948) represents a sort of psychological short-hand description of three inner-life landscapes which are being probed down to their last crannies, particularly below and behind deceptive façades, with inner contradictions and disharmony of the subjects providing virtually throughout the major affective motivation. In her programmatic manifesto, *L'Ère du soupçon* (1956), Sarraute paid tribute to Dostoevski and Kafka and—more especially—to Camus, the author of *L'Étranger,* because here for the first time in the history of the French novel a hero had "professed his allegiance" to the absurd. *Les Fruits d'or,* which in 1963 was awarded the International Literature Prize, is an attempt to derive new vitality for the psychological novel from the technique of the radio play. Compared to *Portrait d'un inconnu,* this newer work seems refreshing through the undertone of satire directed against literary cliques.

In the works of Samuel Beckett, an Irishman from Dublin writing in French (born in 1906), the novel of the absurd has reached its ultimate confines. To be sure, Genet went the limit with his arsenal of monstrosities, but his language hardly exceeds the stylistic chaos already familiar from Céline. In Beckett, however, the world seen as a maze and human deeds seen as the torment of Tantalus have the unending monologue and the moribund moan as their specific physiognomy of speech. In *Molloy* (1951), a crippled vagabond talks about his vain attempts to find his mother, whose name he has forgotten, until he perishes while traveling through the land. Now a man named Moran makes the case his own and thereby becomes Molloy. The reader must not look for much logical explanation. He will sense, however, that obscure and dark myths of earth and motherhood time and again force Molloy to start out afresh and that the principle of failure underlies all events like a fixed idea of original sin.

The novels *Malone meurt* (1952) and *Comment c'est* (1960) carry the same motif of failure to the next higher level of religious, introspectively human, and social complexities. Malone is lying on his squalid bed trying to take stock of his present condition. But the situation exceeds what language can cope with. At this point, *Comment c'est* takes over. A man, helplessly crawling through muck, looks for his brother and neighbor. He finds him in the person of Pim, but soon their companionship breaks up again. The fable in this novel is nothing more than an existentialist-oriented behavioralistic study, with the ordinate "I" and the coordinate "non-I." The I reaches out with its tentacles for the non-I which is not a genuine you. The tentacle metaphor, used previously with pivotal functions by Nathalie Sarraute, is best suited to characterize the mollusk-like events. And as tentacles stretch out, collide, are hurt, retract, repeating the same maneuver with the monomania of a fixed idea, so proceeds Beckett's language. *Comment c'est* is a punctuation-exempt monologue in which emphasizing repetitions permit at times the isolation of segments and residues of meaning. As the hero in his absurd situation is unable to see things clearly, so the style is unable, nor meant to be able, to clarify the events for the reader. The absurd has been potentiated to a state of permanent opacity.

Be it that authors like Beckett lack the insight of Sartre and of Camus or be it that the spirit of the age finds former ideas of the world's senselessness insufficiently tragic, insufficiently distorted, and hence correspondingly unqualified to express what prevails, in any event, the novel of the absurd is about to destroy itself through the instrument of its language.[6]

XIV

THE NOVEL OF THINGS

Alain Robbe-Grillet, Raymond Roussel, Michel Butor,
Claude Simon, Claude Mauriac, Robert André

❧ At this point—marking the beginning of our concluding chapter, which is to deal with the "novel of phenomenological realism" or, more succinctly, the novel of things—the reader must realize what ethical buoyancy Camus had his heroes derive from the surrounding landscape and what affective charge characterizes the world of things in Sartre. He must go back by still another generation and recall how Proust was able to focus the events of the phenomenal world in the autistic consciousness of the individual and how, even before Proust, Huysmans as a representative of the *fin de siècle* was unable to accept reality in any form other than that of the distorted reflection in the sophisticatedly decadent mind of a religious and raving aesthete, in order to be prepared to recognize what is new in the novelists who were fond of labeling their output aggressively as "anti-novel," "new novel," or "non-literature," that is to say, in Robbe-Grillet, Butor, Simon, and Claude Mauriac.

To guard against all possible later misunderstandings, we must emphasize from the outset that the two most important representatives of the group—Robbe-Grillet and Butor—differ strikingly both in their conception and execution of the novel.

On the other hand, it is also remarkable that in the years 1956 and 1957, when the last novels of Camus marked the closing of the circle for the philosophical novel of the absurd, that is, of the absurdity of existence, both Robbe-Grillet and Butor were already on hand with their major works. Such remarkable continuity has been characteristic of French literature for close to a thousand years.

Alain Robbe-Grillet (born in 1922) is a native of Brest. He is an agronomist. After the war he worked for the National Institute of Statistics and Economic Studies. Beginning in 1951, his professional work took him to the French colonies in Africa and the Antilles. Today he works as a reader for the publishing house of the Éditions de Minuit. He established himself as the spokesman of the new movement through two theoretical essays in the *Nouvelle revue française* (1956, No. 43; 1958, No. 70). The models he cited were Joyce, Faulkner, and Kafka. By these references he did not—to be sure—establish a striking differentiation between himself and Camus or Sartre. However, he simultaneously objected to the anthropocentric orientation of the novel in its earlier forms. Long before Robbe-Grillet, it is true, a novel had once appeared with the subtitle, "without a hero." This was William Makepeace Thackeray's *Vanity Fair*, but Robbe-Grillet transformed the ironic play with the devices a scientifically trained geometer has at his disposal into a revolutionary theory of the novel: Things have surfaces and nothing but surfaces; they are neither man's mirror nor his moral support. It is, therefore, inadmissible to symbolize them. And the novelist can therefore no longer have recourse to metaphor, for metaphors fuse in a most unseemly manner spheres of being which cannot possibly be thought of as contiguous. A hero can no longer exert an influence on the world around him. On the contrary, his entire demeanor depends on constellations of things whose master he may no longer be unqualifiedly assumed to be. It follows that he is no longer an entity as a character, for his behavior must adjust itself from case to case to the milieu, and ethical programs can no longer be implemented.

Since the hero is no longer able to establish himself as the master of things, since he can only probe them as he tries to make his way through the maze of their presence (a way which is all there is to his existence), it follows that all manifestations of a psychological variety are relegated to a secondary rank. Condemned to impotence through materially real fixed ideas, man turns into a *"voyeur."* In the novel, *Le Voyeur* (1955), which followed the somewhat earlier detective story *Gommes* (1953), Robbe-Grillet made quite clear how much he owed in style and technique to the detective story. In personal conversations, Robbe-Grillet has also professed that his somewhat precious style is a reflection of his admiration for Raymond Roussel (1877–1933), whose novels *La Doublure* (1897) and *La Vue* (1902) attracted little attention before André Breton praised their hairsplittingly precise style.

In *Le Voyeur*, the reader accompanies a watch dealer to a small island where this businessman expects to find a virgin market for his cheap merchandise. He works out for himself a timetable which he himself is unable to follow and which the reader has great difficulties in keeping track of, especially when evident gaps intervene. In one such the watch dealer murders a little girl who is guarding her herd. This, however, is not made known to us until the murderer grows uncertain of himself and once again works through his timetable to verify his alibi and remembers, in doing so, that there was an eyewitness to the crime. The technique fits the subject extremely well.

But how can Robbe-Grillet depict jealousy, which after all depends in its very essence on premonition, suspicion, and supposition? How can he operate in this area without psychological perspectives? *La Jalousie* takes the reader to a house in the center of a banana plantation. (It is significant that the German edition of this work helps the reader with a road map.) On the porch outside the house, three individuals are sitting, a man and his wife who live there and a house guest. They are sitting there most of the time. The guest's name is Frank. The woman's name is A. . . . The husband remains anonymous. He, the "hero," must derive from the arrangement of things and movements the motives underlying his jealousy, using—as it were—the eyes of the author or the reader to read his conclusions as one reads from a diagram. In the process, the world turns to him into a mass of uncertain clues—chairs standing close together, glances falling or exchanged, a letter sticking out of a coat pocket—and all the while he himself is little more than a stagehand in the play that is going on. The author's omniscience (of yesteryear's novels) is no more. In this kind of narrative prose three-dimensional space assumes functions which leave no room for a point of view specific to the author. Monotonous repetition is the stylistic device used to document the all-pervading ignorance. The author and reader see at all times neither more nor less than the husband too, can see, and his morbid jealousy must be inferred from the attention he pays to every last detail: "She takes a few steps inside the room, walking across to the big chest of which she opens the top drawer. She fingers through some papers in the right half of the drawer, bends down to see better what is farther back, and pulls the drawer still a little farther toward her." (p. 14).

But it is not only in the reader's awareness that the world of things—contrary to Robbe-Grillet's program—gradually changes into a world of expression. Thirteen times in succession the jealous husband's glances land on a spot on the wall of the room where the house guest had crushed one evening a poisonous millipede, and the incident with its hygienic motivation is potentiated by sheer repetition into a fixed idea in the husband's mind who feels that he is helpless and useless like a fifth wheel on the wagon. Yet another occurrence rises clearly to the status of symbolic significance, again representing the helplessness, the total recourselessness of the jealous husband in the world surrounding him. Somewhere on the plantation the Negro workers are singing endlessly the same song whose meaning, however, keeps escaping him. "The sounds, with all their obvious repetitions, appear to follow no musical pattern. They do not combine to form a tune, to form a melody, to form a rhythm." (p. 194f.) The world falls disparately apart into its elements, and its elements are things. There is no harmony, there is no structure. The non-being of both is postulated a priori, and the observer's reason cannot reconstruct them.

With *Dans le labyrinthe* (1959), man—as Robbe-Grillet sees him—sinks further (if sinking further is possible) toward the level of zero. Yet there is evidence of a development of sorts in the creative resources of the author. The trivial triangle of *La Jalousie* has been replaced in *Dans le labyrinthe* by a rendezvous which does not take place. Robbe-Grillet makes of the

central figure—the soldier (or is it deserter?) Henri Martin—
the prototype of the anti-hero. Soldierdom and non-heroism—
the one as an accidental rank and the other as the world's
situation—are meant to clash. Henri Martin walks through an
anonymous town which he does not know and which is awaiting the arrival of likewise anonymous enemy troops. Referring
this to 1940 will not help the reader in any way. Martin is looking for a street the name of which has slipped his mind. It seems
that it is the street where the family of a fallen comrade of his
is living. He has with him in a tin box his dead friend's belong-
ings which he wants to return. Since, speaking over the
telephone, he did not clearly hear the name of the street, he
never reaches his goal. The city turns for him into a maze. The
brutally naked geometric array of streets reveals gradually all
the demoniac powers of which the world of dead things is possessed. Then Henri Martin gets help from a boy who is at home
in the city. "But it was still snowing at the time, in dense flakes,
and the footprints of the guide, no sooner made, began to lose
their precision, filling out rapidly and turning more and more
unrecognizable as the distance between the soldier and him
increased until their very presence began to be most doubtful
—a faint depression hardly perceptible in the uniformity of the
surface."[*] But thus the constellation of things, denied or not,
does assume a deeper significance. Snow and snow-filled footprints turn into tokens of human blindness and impotence. The
category of "surface" is released from its mathematical confines and turns into the symbol of an ultimate absurdity which
is completely lacking in the ethos of performance characteristic
of the figure of Sisyphus in Camus and which is equally lacking in anything reminiscent of Sartre's endeavor to achieve a
"being for himself." Also, Henri Martin's involvement in the
maze is prepared by a fall and failure of intellectual implications. He did not catch the name of the street. It is in the same
way that Samuel Beckett's Molloy forgot the name of his
mother. Both for Molloy and Henri Martin the failure to recall
means death.

In the course of the six years from 1953 to 1959, Robbe-
Grillet evolved—out of his beginnings as a writer of detective
stories—an existentialist image of Everyman with Kafka-like
implications. The monotonous and yet somehow captivating

police-gazette style increased in breadth and in detail. In terms of the underlying philosophy, we are back again where we were with Michaux's *Un Certain Plume*.

With a publication of the year 1962, entitled *Instantanés*, Robbe-Grillet reverted once again, in stricter compliance, to his own literary principles of the fifties. *Instantanés* presents true "snapshots," random scenes, visualized and described in accordance with the "aesthetics of the surface." There is only surface, and what is not surface cannot be visualized. What is not visible and hence describable does not exist. To be sure, we cannot fail to note—and recognize as a stylistic stratagem— that the perspective of the narrator and that of an assumed anonymous observer are by no means identical. In *Le Manne- quin* (pp. 9-13), a plain room is described in great detail. Then comes the concluding sentence: "But, at present, all those things cannot be seen because of the coffee pot."

La Maison de rendez-vous (1965) suggests through its struc- ture that Robbe-Grillet would still be able to write a detective story. The fact that the action is placed in Hong Kong is not a concession to the appeal which the exotic has in terms of enter- tainment. The accumulation of things unfamiliar is to a large extent in keeping with Flaubert's stylistic pursuit in *Salammbô*. The subject matter, which has little bearing on the author's per- sonal life—managed with all the comic-strip clichés of Far-East undercover agents, smugglers, and prostitutes (see, for instance, p. 13)—forces Robbe-Grillet to concentrate his attention on the whodunit technique of his own choosing. The flashbacks, the repetitions and corrections, which are required to make up for earlier memory lapses of the fictitious narrator, do produce a labyrinthine tension, but this is exclusively a matter of stylistic heaves. The influence of the technical devices of the film, as represented for instance by Godard, cannot be doubted. The suggestion is confirmed by the fact that Robbe-Grillet himself has done work as a scenario writer. Examples are *L'Année der- nière à Marienbad* and *Trans-Europe Express*.

In 1957, the critic André Rousseaux wrote in the *Figaro littéraire* with reference to Michel Butor: "It has been a long time since last such a writer appeared, so new, so strong, so fully master of his astonishing art as to be able to advance very far into the mysteries of life." Another critic, writing in *Combat*, stated more concretely: "In him we hear an echo of Proust, Joyce, and Virginia Woolf." Indeed, through Butor the French novel of things establishes a link in world literature with the works of James Joyce, Virginia Woolf, or Alfred Döblin. Especially of the first-named, for behind immense, chaotic accumulations of motifs from the world of things, the Irishman Joyce had age-old myths loom up, and this technique appears again in Butor.

Michel Butor was born in 1926 near Lille. He studied literature and philosophy at the Sorbonne and began his career as a teacher in Egypt. He subsequently became lecturer for French at the University of Manchester and then again secondary school teacher in Saloniki and Geneva. He has on occasion, not without justification, been dubbed the "professor errant." At present he is, like Robbe-Grillet, reader for the publishing house of the *Éditions de minuit.*

In a number of lectures Butor has outlined his conception of the novel. In lieu of the "commitment" of the Sartre novel and the principle that "it must serve something," the new novel—according to Butor—demands a more critical relationship to the world of things. He advises the novelist to learn from the "poet-critic" Baudelaire. What was meant by these theoretical utterances (which—by the way—were formulated much more conservatively than Robbe-Grillet's corresponding statements) is apparent from Butor's novels of which four have so far been published. They are: *Passage de Milan* (1954), *L'Emploi du temps* (1956), *La Modification* (1957), and *Degrés* (1960). In all of them Butor proved himself above all past master in the delineation of local myths. *Passage de Milan* is the novel of a six-story apartment house. The contrived restriction of the author's viewpoint that was characteristic of Robbe-Grillet's *La Jalousie* has again been abandoned. The novelist once again has "his" world, as Romains and Dos Passos had theirs in their panoramic displays. To be sure, the disorder of things and their displacement demand an organizational and selective effort on the part of the author. It is in this sense that the introduction must be read as a challenge: "The Abbé Ralon was leaning out of the window. All around there was Paris, separated from him by a false wall of haze and smoke of the color of iodine tincture, of chestnuts, and of old wine. . . ." As a typical element of the narrative manner of the novel of things, we do have a complete lack of distance: The time of the action and the time of the narration coincide. Metaphor and comparison, the most important stylistic figures in terms of their power to impart meaning, are used liberally by Butor. This again distinguishes him from Robbe-Grillet. Thus the major difference between the two "novels of houses," *La Jalousie* and *Passage de Milan*, may be found—apart from Butor's larger circle of personages—particularly in the fluency of his language. In lieu of the almost Cartesian catenation of thought in Robbe-Grillet and his police-report style, we find here a conscious receptiveness of language to lyrical elements.

In *L'Emploi du temps* this is even more evident. The subject is identical with that of Robbe-Grillet's *Dans le labyrinthe*: the individual in the maze of the world. The action takes place in the fictitious town of Bleston in England which shows a certain resemblance to Manchester. The hero and narrator is a Frenchman by name of Jacques Revel. He has accepted a position with a local firm under an agreement binding him for one year. He starts out by buying a map of Bleston, for he wants to learn as quickly as possible to find his way around. And from this seemingly insignificant detail, reminiscent of a tourist's mannerism, the real plot evolves. For to Revel the unknown, grimy industrial town with its ugly monotony assumes little by little the character of a monster which demands of him, with unrelenting insistence, a continuous "labor of fact-finding and of search." Revel keeps a detailed record of everything he does. Wherever there are passages of description in the novel, they reflect an intense preoccupation with the world of things. The reader misses in this Robbe-Grillet's focused segments, the detailed descriptions of parts of a body never allowed to come into view. The perspective of "lying-in-ambush" is not a requirement in Butor. His reality is rather that of a blank square waiting for the ordinates and coordinates to be drawn in. So the conquest of the world begins, in a sort of stock-taking, with a huge pile of things that must be sorted and arranged. Here is a sample from *L'Emploi du temps*: "It was for the first time that I saw the oval table of varnished mahogany, the three place mats with their yellowed lace borders, the white-and-blue Chinese cups with their teapot, the opalescent standard lamp that was not to be lighted that day (that Saturday, October 20), the two copper plates in their frilly frames (a cattle boat and a landscape of Oceania and some fallen king, fleeing, in his mantle, his crown on his head, through a thick forest full of wolves with shining eyes)."*

At first blush one might conclude, erroneously, that this novel is in its core a novel of education, for the hero, eager to learn, turns to the smallest, seemingly indifferent detail. Yet the pre-eminence of the micrological approach, the detective-like endeavor to get to the root and meaning behind the deceptive façade of things does point to something quite different. As Jacques Revel knows that his sojourn in Bleston is restricted to one year, he works out for himself a time schedule in order to establish systematically the "at-hand-ness" of the things surrounding him. But there is in Butor, in addition, something unmistakably idiosyncratic. The labyrinth in Robbe-Grillet was a topos of the literature of the absurd which in turn had taken it from Mannerism imparting to it an existentialist meaning. In Butor the maze is a resurrected form of the Cretan labyrinth where the Minotaur is lurking. At this point in the action the veil is dropped which so far concealed the mythological background. Now Revel recognizes that his labors are like those of Theseus, and this gives him strength. In his British girl friends —helpful Ann and seductive Rose—he recognizes Ariadne and Phaedra (pp. 173–175).

It seems possible that James Joyce's novel *Ulysses* (1922) and —more certainly—Gide's *Thésée* induced Butor to present a new treatment of the great myth of errancy of Greek antiquity. He felt encouraged in this by the depth psychology of Jung which regards myths as archetypal collective concepts outside of all time. In a later passage Butor underlined this point: "Thus the primary succession of days of old comes to us only through a multitude of others, ever changing, with every occurrence evoking the echo of earlier ones in which it has its beginnings, its explanation, or its homologue." (p. 294). Revel admits how a tapestry with Theseus motifs suggested to him the idea that he should re-examine and re-evaluate his attitude toward Bleston, and how—on the other hand—he has come to recognize between a representation of Cain in a church window and the murder of a well-known writer of detective stories links and relations which a positivistic approach fails to grasp. As Revel achieves full certainty of such mythical interdependences, his consciousness acquires a new dimension. It is of no avail to work out a time schedule for the destruction of the labyrinth and the Minotaur. Precisely as Theseus continues to exist as an archetype, so too must the Cretan labyrinth go on existing forever in ever-changing configurations. Furthermore, Theseus is conceivable only in confrontation with the labyrinth, not without it. "Of a sudden the accumulated fatigue of months, of a sudden the fatigue of you, Bleston, has descended upon me, clinging to me like the throws of a wet shroud" (p. 297). And quite logically and consistently, his departure is felt to be "a deliverance." The lesson of the novel—whatever Butor's philosophical and didactic intentions may have been—the lesson of the novel is that the strength of a single human being does not suffice to annihilate a myth. This remains clear despite all contrary asseverations in Butor's literary self-appraisal. A confrontation of Butor's work with Camus's *Le Mythe de Sisyphe* is interesting. Revel's time schedule has the sole function of allowing him a more intense preoccupation with the "surface," which then turns out to be an infinite sequence of strata in depth.

So the novel reflects in its thought content a carefully worked-out structure. Its outer form is correspondingly rich. Butor prefers lengthy hypotactic sentences which allow him to operate with a dense network of factual references and allusions. On the other hand, he likes to enrich his style—especially in landscape and milieu descriptions which are often used to introduce a new chapter—with lyrical elements such as metaphor, simile, inner rhyme, alliteration, and assonance : "The last clouds resembling firebrands, resembling the broad low branches of a flaming forest about to die down but swept away again and rekindled by the fury of the storm, the last clouds roll over the shining roofs that glisten, like moist glue, from the last rain and over the smokestacks of Dew Street, while the lid of the skies begins once more to open up over this immense field, already profoundly, exquisitely drenched and tinctured with water, where still some spirals of vapor and smoke drag on, all covered with petals of an overly abundant orchard with millions of flights of heavy-winged silent bees. . . ."*

After the *fin-de-siècle* doctrines of style, the novel has again struck out on its way to the "poem in prose."

Parallel to the Theseus myth in *L'Emploi du temps*, we have as the central idea in *La Modification* the myth of Rome. Butor's special affinity for local myths is beautifully apparent in his travel diary *Génie du lieu* (1959), especially in the passages describing Istanbul and Córdoba. Both *L'Emploi du temps* and *La Modification* close on the same note of resignation. In the latter, Louis Delmont, manager of the Paris branch of an Italian typewriter manufacturer, leaves on a day in November from the Gare de Lyon for a trip to Rome. He intends to break with his wife Henriette in order to begin a new life with his mistress in Rome. In the course of the rail trip, which lasts twenty-four hours, Delmont changes his mind. It seems hard to imagine a less trivial theme. Yet it is precisely the paucity of the skeleton of action that allows the author to render to his heart's content all the desired minutiae and all the fragments of thought of the "interior monologue" going on in his hero in the state of half-sleep induced in him by the monotonous motion of the train.

Delmont tackles the "mission" which he had assigned to himself with the same verve as Revel, yet—like Revel —he fails. To be sure, in his case the motive forces are not mythical in kind but simply psychological. He realizes that his love for Henriette was once just as passionate as his current love for Cécile and that the fascination of Rome has contributed to his remembering his friend as more unusual than she actually is. A technical novelty in *La Modification* is the use of the second person plural instead of the conventional first and third person singular. "You [i.e., *vous*] have put your left foot on the brass fluting and with your [i.e., *votre*] right shoulder you [i.e., *vous*] try in vain to push the sliding frame a little farther away." The procedure is too contrived to yield fully the desired effect, which is doubtless to raise Delmont's reactions to a supra-individual plane by making the reader, as it were, responsible for it.

L'Emploi du temps marks clearly the high point in Butor's work so far. Neither *La Modification* nor the school novel *Degrés* can surpass it. *Degrés* was published in 1960, but it would seem to have been written before that time, for both

in style and subject matter the work shows close affinities with
Passage de Milan. It represents a demystified unanimism,
though toward the end, Butor allows us to doubt again the previously implied omniscience of the author. The time of the novel
comprises a few weeks of school late in the fall of 1954 at the
Lycée Taine in Paris. The geography and history teacher Vernier (Butor, we recall, was himself a teacher) tries to present
a report of life at school, covering the simultaneity of class
events as well as private occurrences in the lives of the teachers
and students of one of the upper forms and giving the impression, as it were, of longitudinal and latitudinal sections
through a beehive and its combs. In a procedure quite different
from that of the formally comparable village-spire perspective
in Lesage's *Diable boiteux,* the author endeavors to show factual and psychological occurrences without taking any sort of
interest in the social panorama. Vernier fails in this maze, he
collapses: after Revel-Theseus, we now have Vernier-Icarus.

It seems too early to decide what will come in future of
Butor's position in the French novel. Is he going to occupy a
rank comparable to that held, for instance, by Uwe Johnson in
recent years in Germany? In any event, with *Mobile. Étude
pour une représentation des États-Unis* (1962) and *Réseau
aérien* (1963) he struck out on a course which may easily take
him away from literature as an art. *Mobile* was dedicated to the
American painter Jackson Pollock, the leader of the so-called
informal and radically tachistic school of painting. There is a
connection between this dedication and the style of the work
which utilizes as well unanimistic effects, such as Jules Romains
or John Dos Passos had employed sparingly, as also fragmen-
tary utterances of a sweeping kind which one is tempted to
call surrealist for the purpose of representing a pluralist reality
suggestive of a bird's-eye view. There is little here to remind us
of Butor's successful novels of the past but the language which
continues to stress sound-painting effects: "Dark night of
Cordova, Alaska, the extreme north, the extreme proximity of
the terrible, the abominable, the unimaginable land."

If apart from Robbe-Grillet and Butor other authors, following their model, tried their hand at the novel of things, there
was little reason to expect any kind of outstanding performance.
Claude Simon (born in 1913) followed consciously in the foot-

steps of Butor with his novel *Le Vent* (1957). Everyday occurrences are mythologized and deprived of their historical factualness. The style is characterized by a remarkable predilection for lengthy sentences which are carried to a contrived extreme. There are instances, for example in the story *L'Attentat* (in the *Nouvelle revue française* of March, 1962), in which one can no longer be certain of the subject.

Claude Mauriac (born in 1914), son of François, described in *Le Dîner en ville* (1959) an evening party, obliging the reader, as it were, to sit down with the other eight men and women around the table and to try to sort out the fragments of conversation in order to keep the speakers halfway apart. We have here a radical exaggeration of the technique first introduced by the Goncourts and subsequently utilized on occasion by Thomas Mann and Georges Bernanos, that is, the technique of letting the characters speak and to entrust to the reader the task of their identification. But Claude Mauriac goes so far in this that his novel might just as well be broadcast as a radio play, and, indeed, the resulting possibility of an acoustic differentiation would accrue to the profit of the work. In *L'Agrandissement* (1936), the author undertook to utilize the theories of Unamuno and Pirandello in regard to the author's dialogue with his creatures, generating a hybrid genre of novel-essay or essay novel. Non-literature is a "cultured pearl." Creation and insight are illusions. Literary creation becomes preoccupation with the ineffable.

If a tentative schematic hierarchy is wanted, it may be suggested that Roussel, Robbe-Grillet, and Claude Mauriac are interrelated by the fact that they share a number of traits, while Butor and Simon have in common—apart from literary parallels—their all-pervading interest in archetypes. There can be no doubt but that Butor's "new novel" is deeper in thought than all the others. Whether he can maintain his position at the top in future, no one can foretell. In fact, it is perhaps significant that in the area of the French novel it is entirely impossible to prophesy by prognostic extrapolation. At all times, from the beginnings of the nineteenth century on, in Senancour, Constant, Balzac, Stendhal, Flaubert, Zola, Huysmans, and Proust, seemingly ultimate possibilities of form and meaning were fully exploited, and yet, there followed a subsequent development along the road of still greater deconfinement.

If, by way of conclusion, we mention a work by Robert André (born in 1920), better known from his reviews in the *Nouvelle revue française*, we do so in order to show how French literature has already begun to metabolize the novel of things critically and thus to modify it. André's *Un Combat opiniâtre* (1960) is at first blush a story of chess. The experienced reader, however, recognizes that the description of a professional visit of the accountant Marcel Lambert in a small town in the Vosges mountains, where he, a passionate chess player, enjoys every evening a match with local people, reflects technical devices and leitmotifs of the novel of things. That Robert André introduces his hero as an accountant is almost conventional. The husband in *La Jalousie*, the eye-witness in *Le Voyeur*, the soldier in *Dans le labyrinthe*, Jacques Revel in *L'Emploi du temps*, are check-list accountants and strive to reveal. The motif of the ever-increasing eeriness of the town is reminiscent of *L'Emploi du temps* and *Dans le labyrinthe*. The Ariadne figure of Odile, who takes the stranger by his hand, corresponds to the boy in *Dans le labyrinthe* and to Ann (=Ariadne) in *L'Emploi du temps*. It is quite amazing what a powerful tradition the novel of things has been able to establish within the short space of a few years. But the oppressive power of the world of things, which used to force the heroes to unheroic failure or at least to resignation, is canceled out by this author. It is like a rejoinder to *La Modification* when Marcel Lambert shapes a love affair as he wants it. To be sure, it is no unmitigated joy for us to note that the novel of things comes to be questioned by a hyper-virility which does have Montherlant as at least one of its ancestors. In any event, the decisive point is the phenomenon that precisely these devices are used to proclaim the end of the dictatorship of things over man's free will of free decision.[1] It is certain that the "new novel"—thanks, especially, to the indefatigable lecture activity of Robbe-Grillet, Butor, and Claude Simon, both in France and possibly still more intensely in other countries— has managed to lay claim to a position of leadership in French narrative literature and to obtain a full hearing for its ideals which amount basically to ideological abstention and a profound distrust of all forms of "philosophy of life" (Sarraute, *L'Ère du soupçon!*) and of all stylistic dependence on pseudo-absolutes. This is what is new when we think back to Balzac, Stendhal, and Zola, and also to Green and Aragon. Aragon, in particular, in *La Mise à mort* (1965), a novel-essay abounding in digressions and subjective comments suggestive of a literary last will and testament, and also Robert Pinget in *L'Inquisitoire* (1962) or Jean-Marie Gustave Le Clézio in *Le Procès-verbal* (1963) are about to take over, and simultaneously to overtake the surface technique of the novel of things.

In his monograph, *Où va le roman?* (1962, pp. 286 and 288), Pierre de Boisdeffre wrote: "The history of the novel from the seventeenth century to the present has been a history of acquisition." On the other hand, the modern novel of things is, in Boisdeffre's words, *"littérature débarrassée."* In our introductory remarks we coined for the development of the French novel throughout the nineteenth and twentieth centuries the keynoting term of "deconfinement" which encompasses both the tendencies mentioned by Boisdeffre. Deconfinement is a dynamic process kept alive by the novelist's conscientious reappraisal of his genre. It presupposes a vital relationship to the past. While in Germany no novelist would think of formulating a new theory of the novel on the basis of his rejection of Fontane, in France the "new novel" starts out by suspending the Balzac type in narrative prose. We, outside of France, may find this somewhat farfetched, but it is precisely this attitude which justifies ever new hopes and an ever new confidence in the future of the French novel.

NOTES

%

INTRODUCTION

1. See, especially, the following works, which will be found useful as general introductions and comprehensive surveys.—O. Walzel (Ed.), *Handbuch der Literatur-Wissenschaft. Die Romanischen Literaturen des 19. und 20. Jahrhunderts,* two volumes, Potsdam, no year.—Covers the material up to 1945; V. Klemperer, *Die moderne französische Prosa,* Leipzig, 1948; M. Girard, *Guide illustré de la littérature française moderne 1918–49,* Paris, 1949; P. de Boisdeffre, *Une Histoire vivante de la littérature française d'aujourd'hui 1939–1964,* Paris, 1964 (fifth edition); B. M. Bémol, *Essai sur l'orientation des littératures de langue française au XXᵉ siècle,* Paris, 1960; G. Prampolini, *Storia universale della letteratura,* seven volumes, Turin, 1960 (third edition); *Dizionario universale della letteratura contemporanea,* five volumes, Milan, 1959–63; Cl.-E. Magny, *Histoire du roman français depuis 1918,* Paris, 1950; H. Peyre, *The Contemporary French Novel,* New York, 1960; K. A. Horst, *Das Spektrum des modernen Romans,* Munich, 1960; G. Picon, *Panorama de la nouvelle littérature,* Paris, 1960 (third edition); G. Zeltner-Neukomm, *Das Wagnis des französischen Gegenwartsromans,* Hamburg, 1960; G. Krause, *Tendenzen im französischen Romanschaffen des 20. Jahrhunderts,* Frankfurt on the Main, 1962; P. de Boisdeffre, *Où va le roman?,* Paris, 1962; R.-M. Albérès, *Histoire du*

roman moderne, Paris, 1962; M. Turnell, *The Novel in France,* Harmondsworth, 1962; M. Nadeau, *Le Roman français depuis la guerre,* Paris, 1963; N. Frye, *Anatomy of Criticism,* Princeton, 1957; R. Wellek and A. Warren, *Theory of Literature,* New York, 1963 (third edition)—with a comprehensive bibliography; G. Lukács, *Die Theorie des Romans,* Berlin, 1920 (Neuwied, 1963, second edition); *Zur Poetik des Romans,* edited by V. Klotz, Darmstadt, 1965; P.-H. Simon, *Histoire de la littérature française au XXᵉ siècle,* two volumes, Paris 1965 (eighth edition); W. Engler, *Französische Literatur im 20. Jahrhundert,* Berne-Munich, 1968.

2. H. P. Thieme, *Bibliographie de la littérature française de 1800 à 1930,* Paris, 1933-, three volumes—with supplements by S. Dreher and M. Rolli for 1930–39 and M. Drevet for 1940–49; H. Talvert and J. Place, *Bibliographie des auteurs modernes de langue française 1801ff.,* Paris, 1928ff.—See also the running bibliographical lists in *Revue d'histoire littéraire de la France* (RHLF) and *Beihefte zur Zeitschrift für romanische Philologie* (ZRPH); O. Klapp, *Bibliographie der französischen Literaturwissenschaft,* Frankfurt, 1960ff.— five volumes published so far. To be consulted for information on the most recent publications: *French VII Bibliography; critical and biographical references for the study of contemporary French literature,* New York, 1955ff.

3. R. Jauss, "Non vitae, sed scholae—eine kritische Nachlese," *Praxis des neusprachlichen Unterrichts,* VIII, 1961, pp. 1–5; J. v. Stackelberg, "Die Misere der französischen Literaturgeschichte in Deutschland," *Germanisch-Romanische Monatsschrift,* XLV, 1964, pp. 349–60.

I. THE NOVEL OF INDIVIDUALISM

1. On this probem in general, cf. Nicolas Ségur, *Histoire de la littérature européenne,* volume IV, Neuchâtel and Paris, 1951. —On Nietzsche and his significance for French literature, cf. Julius Wilhelm in *Beiträge zur romanischen Literaturwissenschaft,* Tübingen, 1956, pp. 124–40.

2. W. P. Friederich, *Outline of Comparative Literature,* Chapel Hill, 1954, pp. 255f.

3. Cf. André Monchoux, *L'Allemagne devant les lettres françaises. De 1814 à 1835,* Paris, 1953.

4. On this approach, cf. Paul van Tieghem, *Le Préromantisme,* Paris, 1924; A. Monglond, *Le Préromantisme français,* Paris,

1930–32; D. Mornet, *Le Romantisme en France au 18ᵉ siècle,* Paris, 1912; Pierre Moreau, *Le Classicisme des romantiques,* Paris, 1932; *Le Romantisme,* Paris, 1957; Auguste Viatte, *Les Sources occultes du romantisme,* Paris, 1928; Pierre Martino, *L'Époque romantique en France,* Paris 1944; L. Eméry, *L'Âge romantique,* Paris, 1958; R. Giraud, *Mensonge romantique et vérité romanesque,* Paris, 1961; M. Iknayan, *The Idea of the Novel in France: The Critical Reaction 1815–1848,* Geneva, 1961.—These scientific concepts have been utilized in the Garnier, Gallimard (Pléiade), and Droz (*Textes littéraires français,* TLF) editions. In the case of authors whose works are available in one of these three series, their use is to be recommended.

5. On the antiromantic attitude, cf. Nisard, *Manifeste contre la littérature facile,* 1834; the writings of Charles Maurras; and Hugo Friedrich, *Das antiromantische Denken im modernen Frankreich,* Munich, 1935.

6. A. J. George, *The Development of French Romanticism,* Syracuse (University Press), 1955, pp. 47–57 and 135–52; F. Lion, *Der französische Roman im 19. Jahrhundert,* Zurich, 1952.

7. Cf. the published doctoral dissertation by Irene Schäfer, *Oberman. Lettres publiées par E. P. Senancour,* Zurich, 1955.

8. A good initial introduction to this work will be found in Albert Béguin, *L'Âme romantique et le rêve,* Paris, 1946 (second edition), pp. 330ff.; less impressive is the Senancour article by Picon in *Histoire des littératures,* volume III, pp. 1013ff. The first comprehensive discussion was that by Levallois in 1897. The standard treatment is still A. Monglond, *Le Journal intime d'Oberman,* Grenoble and Paris, 1947.—Cf. also F. Baldensperger, *Le Mouvement des idées dans l'émigration française,* two volumes, Paris, 1924; and M. Raymond, *Senancour. Sensations et révélations,* Paris, 1966.

9. Moreau, *Le Romantisme,* pp. 26ff.—On the incompleteness of Madame de Staël's concept of Germany, cf. Monchoux, op. cit., p. 44.—The most comprehensive contribution to date to the study of Madame de Staël, in which the earlier literature is carefully utilized, is the book by Christopher Harold, *Mistress of an Age,* Indianapolis, Ind., 1960.

10. A. Le Breton, *Le Roman français au XIXᵉ siècle,* Paris, 1901; G. Rudler, *La Jeunesse de Benjamin Constant,* Paris, 1909; E. Herriot, *Madame Récamier et ses amis,* Paris, 1924; D. Berthoud, *Constance et grandeur de Benjamin Constant,*

Lausanne, 1944; Ch. du Bos, *Grandeur et misère de Benjamin Constant,* Paris, 1946; Arnold de Kerchove, *Benjamin Constant ou le libertin sentimental,* Paris, 1950.

11. M. Markowitch, *Chateaubriand en Russie,* Mélange Baldensperger, Paris, 1930.

12. The three novels are now accessible in a single volume published by Garnier in 1958.

13. The work has been discussed within the framework of the Moorish novel by M. J. Chaplyn, *Le Roman mauresque de Zayde au Dernier Abencérage,* Paris, 1927, pp. 135ff.

14. This problem has been placed in a wider context by Ch. Schlötke-Schröer, "Das Raum-Zeiterlebnis in der französischen Frühromantik," *Zeitschrift für französische Sprache und Literatur,* LXVII, 1957, pp. 202–20.

15. Comprehensive discussions will be found in P. Moreau, *Chateaubriand,* Paris, 1927 (especially pp. 102ff.); Marcel Duchemin, *Chateaubriand,* Paris, 1938; André Maurois, *Chateaubriand,* Paris, 1938; Joan Evans, *Chateaubriand,* London, 1939; Michel Robida, *Chateaubriand,* Paris, 1948; Maurice Levailland, *Le Véritable Chateaubriand,* Oxford, 1951.—For Chateaubriand's subjective excitement about Christianity and the myth of the New World, cf. also his more epic works, *Les Martyrs* (1809) and *Les Natchez* (written 1797, published 1826).

16. John Davis, *Walter Kennedy,* London, 1808.

17. This holds true, for instance, for Levaillant, *Neuf siècles de littérature française,* Paris, 1958, "Le Romantisme," pp. 369–591.—Older works are those by Levallois (1872) and Séche (1904). The most recent contributions are those by André Billy, *Sainte-Beuve,* Paris, 1952; A. G. Lehmann, *Sainte-Beuve,* Oxford, 1961; and R. Grimsley, *Romantic Melancholy in Sainte-Beuve's "Volupté,"* Festschrift for P. M. Jones, Manchester, 1961, pp. 144–62.

18. On the style of Vigny's narrative works, cf. A. Junkersdorff in *Arbeiten zur romanischen Philologie,* volume 39, 1936. Comprehensive studies are by F. Baldensperger, *Alfred de Vigny,* Paris, 1912; R. de Traz, *Alfred de Vigny,* Paris, 1928; and Henri Guillemin, *M. de Vigny, homme d'ordre,* Paris, 1956.

19. G. Picon, *Histoire des littératures,* volume III, pp. 1021ff.

20. Cf. the succinct sketch by P. Hazard, *Lamartine,* Paris, 1925, pp. 96ff.; also H. Guillemin, *Lamartine,* Paris, 1940.

21. Studies of George Sand's life and work are: René Doumic, *George Sand,* Paris, 1909; M. L. Pailleron, *George Sand,* three volumes, Paris, 1938–42; and E. Thomas, *Sand,* Paris, 1959.

22. René Doumic, op. cit., p. 101.

23. Whether the contrast of red and black may be taken to represent revolution and restoration, the military and the clergy, or the fields in roulette has not been settled.

24. K. Wais, *Französische Marksteine von Racine bis Saint-John Perse,* Berlin, 1958, pp. 97–128.

25. F. M. Albérès, *Le Naturel chez Stendhal,* Paris, 1956, pp. 343ff.

26. K. Wais, *An den Grenzen der Nationalliteraturen,* Berlin, 1958, p. 119–42.

27. Cf., especially, Madame Bardèche, *Stendhal romancier,* Paris, 1947, pp. 355–432.

28. The beginnings of the preoccupation with Stendhal are marked by Mérimée's book, *Henri Beyle,* Paris, 1874. The movement got really underway with Paul Bourget's *Essais de psychologie contemporaine,* Paris, 1883. In 1908, Paul Léautaud wrote an introduction to *Les Plus belles pages de Stendhal.* There followed Léon Blum's *Stendhal et le beylisme,* Paris, 1914. The earliest scholarly analysis of Stendhal was Martino's *Stendhal,* Paris, 1914. This was followed by Paul Hazard, *Stendhal,* Paris, 1927; Alain, *Stendhal,* Paris, 1935; Jean Prévost, *La Création chez Stendhal,* Paris, 1942; and Maurice Bardèche, op. cit. Henri Martineau presented three studies during the years from 1950 to 1953. Other contributions were Claude Roy, *Stendhal par lui-même,* Paris, 1952; A. Caraccio, *Stendhal, l'homme et l'œuvre,* Paris, 1952; Georges Blin, *Stendhal et les problèmes de la personnalité,* Paris 1954, and *Stendhal et les problèmes du roman,* Paris, 1958. Also the previously cited work by F. M. Albérès, *Stendhal,* Paris, 1956, as well as V. Del Litto, *La Vie intellectuelle de Stendhal (1802–1821),* Paris, 1959; Jean Dutourd, *L'Âme sensible,* Paris, 1959; L. Maranini, *Nascita di un personaggio: Lamiel. Studi in onori de V. Lugli e D. Valeri,* Venice, 1961, pp. 621–43; H. R. Jauss, "Nachahmungsprinzip und Wirklichkeitsbegriff in der Theorie des Romans von Diderot bis Stendhal," in *Nachahmung und Illusion,* Munich, 1964, pp. 157–78.

29. Victor Klemperer, *Geschichte der französischen Literatur im 19. und 20. Jahrhundert,* Berlin, 1956, volume II, pp. 157ff.: "Gobineau."—Cf. also Ernest Seillière, *Le Comte de Gobineau et l'aryenisme historique,* Paris, 1903; Ludwig Schemann, *Gobineau,* Paris, 1913–16; and L. Thomas, *Arthur de Gobineau inventeur du racisme,* Paris, 1941.

II. THE NOVEL OF SOCIETY

1. On Prosper Mérimée, cf. A. Filon, *Mérimée*, Paris, 1898; I. Poikowsky, *Prosper Mérimée*, Geneva, 1910; G. H. Johnstone, *Prosper Mérimée, a Mask and a Face*, London, 1926; J. W. Hovenkamp, *Mérimée et la couleur locale*, Paris (dissertation), 1928; F. Bac, *Mérimée inconnu*, Paris, 1939; Marquis de Luppé, *Mérimée*, Paris, 1945; P. Léon, *Mérimée et son temps*, Paris, 1962.

2. On Dumas, cf. Ch. Glinel, *Alexandre Dumas et son œuvre*, Reims, 1884; H. Parigot, *Alexandre Dumas père*, New York, 1901; M. Constantin-Weyer, *L'Aventure vécue de Dumas père*, Geneva, 1944; J. Charpentier, *Alexandre Dumas*, Paris, 1947; H. Clouard, *Alexandre Dumas*, Paris, 1955; A. Maurois, *Alexandre Dumas*, Paris, 1956.

3. On the impact of Sir Walter Scott, cf. W. P. Friederich, *Outline*, pp. 309ff., and A. Monchoux, *op. cit.*, p. 93; on the historical novel in general, cf. Baldensperger, in *Rev. de litt. comparée*, January, 1927.

4. Cf. A. Mouret, "Note sur une source du Roman de la momie de Th. Gautier," in *Rev. d'hist. litt. d. l. France*, volume 5, 1899, pp. 362–66; on Gautier in general, cf. Spoelberch de Lovenjoul, *Hist. des œuvres de Th. Gautier*; Maxime du Camp, *Th. Gautier*, Paris, 1890; R. Jasinski, *Les Années romantiques de Th. Gautier*, Paris, 1929.

5. On Hugo's life's work and, in particular, his novels, cf. E. Biré, *Victor Hugo*, three volumes, Paris, 1883–94; A. Bellesort, *Victor Hugo, essai sur son œuvre*, Paris, 1929; F. Gregh, *Victor Hugo*, Paris, 1934; A. Viatte, *Victor Hugo et les illuminés*, Paris, 1951; H. Guillemin, *Victor Hugo, l'homme et l'œuvre*, Paris, no year; Le Perche, *Victor Hugo*, Paris, 1958 (Poètes d'aujourd'hui 27); G. Piroué, *Victor Hugo, romancier*, Paris, 1963.

6. Cf. Pierre Angrand, "Genèse et fortune des Misérables," *Rev. d'hist. litt. d. l. France*, 1960 (3), pp. 334–44.

7. Cf., in general, P. Martino, *Le Roman réaliste sous le Second Empire*, Paris, 1913. Martino discusses the period from 1833 to 1870. Edouard Maynial, *L'Époque realiste*, Paris, 1931 (anthology and introduction); R. Dumesnil, *Le Réalisme*, Paris, 1936; E. Maynial, *L'Époque réaliste et naturaliste*, Paris, 1945; M. Greiner, *Die Entstehung der modernen Unterhaltungsliteratur*, Hamburg, 1964.

8. Cf. P. Eudel, *L'Œuvre de Champfleury*, Paris, 1891, and Dumesnil, *Réalisme*, pp. 15–24.

9. Cf. R. Zellweger, *Les Débuts du roman rustique*, Paris, 1941.
10. Cf. H. Friedrich, *Drei Klassiker des französischen Romans (Stendhal, Balzac, Flaubert)*, Frankfurt on the Main, 1966 (fifth edition), pp. 91ff.—General surveys are: H. Heiss, *Balzac. Sein Leben und Werk*, Heidelberg, 1913; E. R. Curtius, *Balzac*, 1923, Berne, 1951 (second edition); A. Billy, *Vie de Balzac*, two volumes, Paris, 1944; M. Bardèche, *Balzac romancier*, Paris, 1943; A. Béguin, *Balzac visionnaire*, Geneva, 1946; Stefan Zweig, *Balzac*, Paris, 1950; B. Guyon, *La Création littéraire chez Balzac*, Paris, 1951; G. Lukács, *Balzac und der französische Realismus*, Berlin, 1952; F. Marceau, *Balzac et son monde*, Paris, 1955; F. Lotte, *Dictionnaire biographique des personnages fiftifs de la Comédie humaine*, Paris, 1952; G. Picon, *Balzac par lui-même*, Paris, 1956; J. Borel, *Personnages et destins balzaciens*, Paris, 1958; M. Butor, "Balzac et la réalité," *Nouvelle revue française*, Paris, 1959; Herbert J. Hunt, *Balzac's Comédie Humaine*, London, 1959; *L'Année balzacienne*, 1960ff.; G. Delattre, *Les Opinions littéraires de Balzac*, Paris, 1961; F. Brunetière, *Honoré de Balzac*, Paris, no year; A. Maurois, *Prométhée ou la vie de Balzac*, Paris, 1965.
11. N. Atkinson, *Eugène Sue et le roman-feuilleton*, Paris, 1930; J.-L. Bory, *Sue*, Paris, 1962.
12. The beginning of Flaubert studies goes back to Paul Bourget's *Essais de psychologie contemporaine*, previously mentioned as having initiated a wave of interest in Stendhal. Somewhat later came E. Faguet, *Gustave Flaubert*, Paris, 1893, presenting Flaubert under a strictly dualistic aspect of romanticism and realism, while A. Thibaudet, *Gustave Flaubert*, Paris, 1922 (second edition, 1935), analyzed Flaubert's historical development. Cf. also R. Dumesnil, *Gustave Flaubert*, Paris, 1932, and *Flaubert, l'homme et l'œuvre*, Paris, 1947; E. Maynial, *Flaubert*, Paris, 1943; R. Lehmann, *Die Formelemente des Stils von Flaubert*, Marburg, 1911; E. Pfändtner, *Die Frau im französischen Roman von Emma Bovary bis zur Gegenwart*, Berlin (dissertation), 1949; the essay on Flaubert in Friedrich's *Drei Klassiker* (op. cit.)—presenting the novelist primarily in his successful struggle to free himself from his romantic liabilities; R. Herval, *Les Véritables origines de Madame Bovary*, Paris, 1957; Jacques Suffel, *Flaubert*, Paris, 1958; A. Y. Naaman, *Les Débuts de Flaubert et sa technique de la description*, Paris, 1962; J. Bruneau, *Les Débuts littéraires de Flaubert, 1831–1845*, Paris, 1962.—Complete editions which can be recommended (the Pléiade edition is an anthology) are

the two-volume edition brought out by Le Seuil and the fourteen-volume edition (including the correspondence) brought out by Rencontre, Lausanne.

13. On Maupassant, cf. E. Maynial, *La Vie et l'œuvre de G. de Maupassant*, Paris, 1906; H. Gelzer, *G. de Maupassant*, Heidelberg, 1926; R. Dumesnil, *G. de Maupassant*, Paris, 1933; Knud Togeby. *L'Œuvre de Maupassant*, Copenhagen/Paris, 1954; André Vial, *G. de Maupassant et l'art du roman*, Paris, 1954; Paul Morand, *Vie de Guy de Maupassant*, Paris, 1942; J. Halperin, *Maupassant der Romancier*, Zurich, 1961; A.-M. Schmidt, *Maupassant par lui-même*, Paris, 1962.

14. L. Séché, *J. Vallès*, Paris, 1886; A. Zevaès, *Jules Vallès, son œuvre*, Paris, 1932; G. Fink, *Jules Vallès*, Berlin (dissertation), 1931; G. Gille, *J. Vallès*, Paris, 1941; V. Brombert, *The Intellectual Hero* (Vallès and others), Philadelphia/New York, 1961.

III. STORIES OF FANTASY AND THE FANTASTIC NOVEL

1. Cf. Sainte-Beuve's introduction to the new edition of the *Œuvres complètes*, Paris, 1839, pp. i–xl; W. Ungewitter, *Xavier de Maistre, sein Leben, seine Werke*, Berlin, 1892; A. Berthier, *Xavier de Maistre*, Saint-Étienne, 1921; E. Henriot, *Courrier littéraire, 19e siècle*, vol. I, Paris, 1948.

2. Kurt Wais, *Das antiphilosophische Weltbild des französischen Sturm und Drang 1760–1789*, Berlin, 1934.

3. P.-G. Castex, *Le Conte fantastique en France de Nodier à Maupassant*, Paris, 1950.—This study represents an improvement over the older J. H. Retinger, *Le Conte fantastique dans le romantisme français*, Paris, 1908.

4. J. Larat, *La Tradition et l'exotisme dans l'œuvre de Charles Nodier*, Paris, 1923; W. Mönch, "Nodier und die deutsche und englische Literatur," *Romanische Studien*, XXIV, 1931.— Nodier has been discussed with unusual understanding by A. Béguin in *L'Âme romantique et le rêve*, Paris, 1946 (second edition), pp. 336–45, and in "Poésie de la présence," *Les Cahiers du Rhône*, November, 1957, vol. XXXIX, pp. 169–75. —Cf. also R. Maixner, *Nodier et l'Illyrie*, Paris, 1960; W. Engler, "Der Mythos vom verlorenen Paradies bei Charles Nodier," *Antaios IV* (March, 1963), pp. 521–35.

5. K. Wais, "Le Roman d'artiste: E. T. A. Hoffmann et Balzac," (lecture and discussion), in *La Littérature narrative d'imagination*, Paris, 1961, pp. 137–55.

6. E. Starkie, *Petrus Borel, His Life and Time,* London, 1953; also two articles by J.-L. Audin and D. Marc in *Les Petits romantiques français,* special issue of *Cahiers du Sud,* Paris, 1949, pp. 74ff.

7. Cf., as an introduction and literature survey, Julius Wilhelm's contribution in *Beiträge zur romanischen Literaturwissenschaft,* Tübingen, 1956, pp. 81–102. Also: A. Marie, *Gérard de Nerval, le poète et l'homme,* Paris, 1914; A. Béguin, *Gérard de Nerval,* Paris, 1945; J. Richer, *Gérard de Nerval et les doctrines ésotériques,* Paris, 1947.

8. Cf., in this connection, W. Engler, "Die Metamorphosen in den Chants de Maldoror von Lautréamont," *Antaios III* (1962). Still unsurpassed is G. Bachelard, *Lautréamont,* Paris, 1940.

9. M. Daireaux, *Villiers de l'Isle-Adam,* Paris, 1935; P.-G. Castex, "Villiers de l'Isle-Adam au travail," *Revue des sciences humaines,* LXXIII (1954), pp. 175–97.

IV. THE NATURALISM OF JULES AND EDMOND DE GONCOURT AND OF ÉMILE ZOLA

1. A particularly enlightening contribution to the discussion of the problem is Kurt Wais, "Zur Auswirkung des französischen naturalistischen Romans in Deutschland," in *An den Grenzen der Nationalliteraturen,* Berlin, 1958, pp. 215–36. Cf. also P. Cogny, *Le Naturalisme,* Paris, 1963.

2. Cf. O. Walzel, *Die Geistesströmungen des 19. Jahrhunderts,* 1924; F. Brunetière, *Le Roman naturaliste,* Paris, 1883.

3. In Coriolis's reaction, an element of anti-Semitism appears, and Manette derives cruel pleasure from this "Aryan-Semitic encounter" (Charpentier edition, 1910, p. 420).

4. The *Journal* was published in 22 volumes from 1956 to 1959. "Texte établi et annoté par Robert Ricatte (Monaco)." Noteworthy contributions to the Goncourt literature are, especially, F. Fosca, *E. et J. Goncourt,* Paris, 1941; R. Ricatte, *La Création romanesque chez les Goncourts (1851–1870),* Paris, 1953; R. Ricatte, *La Genèse de "La Fille Elisa,"* Paris, 1959; R. Baldick, *The Goncourts,* London, 1960.

5. The list of volume titles in *Les Rougon-Macquart, histoire naturelle et sociale d'une famille sous le Second Empire* is: *La Fortune des Rougon* (I); *La Curée* (II); *Le Ventre de Paris* (III); *Conquête de Plassans* (IV); *La Faute de l'abbé Mouret* (V); *Son Excellence Eugène Rougon* (VI); *L'Assommoir* (VII); *Une Page d'amour* (VIII); *Nana* (IX); *Pot-bouille* (X);

Au Bonheur des dames (XI); *La Joie de vivre* (XII); *Germinal* (XIII); *L'Œuvre* (XIV); *La Terre* (XV); *Le Rêve* (XVI); *La Bête humaine* (XVII); *L'Argent* (XVIII); *La Débâcle* (XIX); and *Le Docteur Pascal* (XX).

6. Good introductions to the works of Zola are P. Martino, *Le Naturalisme,* and Ch. Beuchat, *Histoire du naturalisme français,* Paris, 1949.—Cf. also B. Diederich, *Émile Zola,* Leipzig, 1898; S. Lemme, *Zur Entstehungsgeschichte von Émile Zolas Rougon-Macquart und den Quatre Evangiles,* Halle, 1913; C. Francke, *Émile Zola als romantischer Dichter,* Marburg, 1914; Henri Barbusse, *Émile Zola,* Lagny-sur-Marne, 1932; Heinrich Mann, *Zola,* Paris, 1939; G. Robert, *Zola,* Paris, 1952; special issue of *Europe,* November/December, 1952; M. Bernard, *Zola par lui-même,* Paris, 1956; G. Walter, *Émile Zola,* Munich, 1959; R. Ternois, *Zola et son temps,* Paris, 1961; H. S. Gershman and K. B. Withworth, *Anthology of Critical Prefaces to the Nineteenth Century French Novel,* Missouri, 1962; J. Dubois, *Romanciers français de l'instantané au 19e siècle,* Brussels, 1963; H. Guillemin, *Présentation des Rougon-Macquart,* Paris, 1964.

V. NARRATIVE PROSE OF THE FIN DE SIÈCLE

1. On the period as a whole and inherent problems of structure, cf. A. Baillot, *L'Influence de Schopenhauer en France (1860–1900),* Paris, 1927; A. Billy, *L'Époque 1900,* Paris, 1951; K. Jäckel, *Richard Wagner in der französischen Literatur,* Breslau, 1932.

2. M. Cressot, *La Phrase et le vocabulaire de J.-K. Huysmans. Contribution à l'histoire de la langue française pendant le dernier quart du XIXe siècle,* Paris, 1938.

3. On Barbey d'Aurevilly, cf. E. Grélé, *Barbey d'Aurevilly,* Cannes (thesis), 1904; A. Zevaès, *J. Barbey d'Aurevilly,* Paris, 1924; H. Quéru, *Le Dernier grandseigneur: J. Barbey d'Aurevilly,* Paris, 1946; J.-P. Séguin, *Blbliographie de Barbey d'Aurevilly,* Paris, 1950.

4. On Daudet, cf. Lucien Daudet, *La Vie d'Alphonse Daudet,* Paris, 1941; J.-H. Bornecque, *Années d'apprentissage d'Alphonse Daudet,* Paris, 1951.

5. On Barrès, cf. A. Thibaudet, *La Vie de Maurice Barrès,* Paris, 1921; E. R. Curtius, *Maurice Barrès und die geistigen Grundlagen des französischen Nationalismus,* Bonn, 1921; H. Brémond, *Maurice Barrès,* Paris, 1924; R. Lalou, *Maurice Barrès,* Paris, 1950.

6. On Fromentin, cf. C. Renaud, *La Genèse de "Dominique,"* Grenoble, 1939; V. Giraud, *Eugène Fromentin,* Paris, 1945; K. Wais, *Marksteine* (op. cit.), pp. 223–44; J. Monge, "Un Précurseur de Proust: Fromentin et la méthode affective," *Revue d'histoire littéraire de la France,* LXI, 1961, pp. 564–88; A. R. Evans, *The Literary Art of Fromentin,* Baltimore, 1964.

7. P. Schneider, J. *Renard par lui-même,* Paris, 1956; L. Guichard, *Renard,* Paris, 1961.

8. On Bourget, cf. E. Seillière, *P. Bourget, psychologue et sociologue,* Paris, 1937; J. Saueracker, "Bourget und der Naturalismus," *Sprache und Kultur der germanischen und romanischen Völker,* XIII, Breslau, 1936.

9. On Bourges, cf. A. Lebois, *Les Tendances du symbolisme à travers l'œuvre d'Elémir Bourges,* Paris, 1953, and *La Genèse du Crépuscule des dieux,* Paris, 1954.

10. On Loti, cf. N. Serban, *Pierre Loti, sa vie, son œuvre,* Paris, 1924; G. Hirschmann-Gunzel, *Der Todesgedanke bei Lotis Romanen,* Hamburg, 1930; E. Schweikert, *Pierre Loti und André Gide,* Munich, 1932; R. de Traz, *Pierre Loti,* Paris, 1958.

11. Cited after Keith G. Millward, *L'Œuvre de Pierre Loti et l'esprit "fin-de-siècle,"* Paris, 1955, p. 318.

12. On Anatole France, cf. Ch. Maurras, *Anatole France, politique et poète,* Paris, 1924; A. Bönsch, "Anatole France und das 18. Jahrhundert," *Sprache und Kultur der germanischen und romanischen Völker,* XVI, Breslau, 1938; J. Suffel, *Anatole France,* Paris, 1946; J. Marvaud, *France—écrivain français,* Paris, 1962.

13. On Huysman, cf. A. Thérive, *J.-K. Huysmans,* Paris, 1924; H. Bachelin, *J.-K. Huysmans. Du naturalisme littéraire au naturalisme mystique,* Paris, 1925; H. M. Galliot, *Explication de J.-K. Huysmans,* Paris, 1954.

14. Cf. Guy Chastel, *J.-K. Huysmans et ses amis,* Paris, 1957, especially pp. 285ff.

15. On Bloy, cf. St. Fumet, *Mission de L. Bloy,* Paris, 1935; J. Steinmann, *L. Bloy,* Paris, 1956. Cf. also H. K. Weinert, *Dichtung aus dem Glauben,* Hamburg, 1948 (second edition; with comprehensive bibliography on the catholic revival).

VI. THE NOVEL OF "REALIZATION"

1. By way of introduction to the twentieth-century novel, cf. R. Lalou, *Le Roman français depuis 1900,* Paris, 1941 (eighth edition, 1960); Cl.-E. Magny, *Histoire du roman français*

depuis 1918, Paris, 1950; Ch. Bruneau, *La Prose littéraire de Proust à Camus,* Oxford, 1953; Henri Peyre, *The Contemporary French Novel,* 1955; M. Turnell, *The Art of Fiction,* London, 1959; and P. de Boisdeffre, *Où va le roman?,* Paris 1962.

2. On Marcel Proust, cf. André Maurois, *A la Recherche de Marcel Proust,* Paris, 1949; E. R. Curtius, *Marcel Proust,* Berlin, 1952; H. R. Jauss, *Zeit und Erinnerung in Marcel Prousts "A la Recherche du temps perdu,"* Heidelberg, 1955; L. Guichard, *Introduction à la lecture de Proust,* Paris, 1956; E. Köhler, *Marcel Proust,* Göttingen, 1958; J. Chaix-Ruy, "Les Thèmes de la 'Recherche du temps perdu' dans le roman autobiographique de Proust 'Jean Santeuil,'" *Revue de la Méditerranée,* XXI (1961), pp. 241–53; Ph. Kolb, "Proust et Ruskin. Nouvelles perspectives," *CahAIEFr,* June 1960, pp. 259–73.—On the Proust-Ruskin relationship, cf. especially Proust's letters of January 21, 1900, March, 9, 1903, July 29, 1903, and February 9, 1905, as well as the letter to Robert de Montesquiou which is difficult to date but may have been written in November or December, 1912. Cf. also J. v. Stackelberg, *Drei Dichter als Kritiker: Gide, Proust, Valéry,* Göttingen, 1965.

3. On Nietzsche's influence on Gide, cf. G. Bianquis, *Nietzsche en France,* Dijon, 1929; R. Lang, *André Gide und der deutsche Geist,* Stuttgart, 1953; J. Wilhelm, "Nietzsches Wirken auf das zeitgenössische Frankreich," in *Beiträge zur romanischen Literaturwissenschaft,* Tübingen, 1956, pp. 124–40.

4. On *La Porte étroite,* cf. especially the relevant essay by K. Wais in *Französische Marksteine von Racine bis Saint-John Perse,* pp. 311–27.

5. On André Gide generally, cf. L. P. Quint, *André Gide,* Paris, 1932; P. Archambault, *L'Humanité d'André Gide,* Paris, 1950; R.-M. Albérès, *L'Odyssée d'André Gide,* Paris, 1951; P. Ch. Berger, *André Gide, Mensch und Werk,* Coburg, 1949; P. Lafille, *André Gide romancier,* Paris, 1954; J. Schlumberger, *Madeleine et André Gide,* Paris, 1956. On Gide's reception abroad, enlightening information may be found in his correspondence with Rainer Maria Rilke (*Correspondance 1909–1926,* Paris, 1952) and the special issue of the *Nouvelle revue française* (Hommage à André Gide), Paris, 1951, with contributions by Thomas Mann, Ernst Jünger, Hermann Hesse, John Steinbeck, G. Ungaretti, and others. Recent additions to the Gide bibliography are J.-J. Thierry, *Gide,* Paris, 1962, and A. Naville, *Bibliographie des écrits de Gide (1891–1952),* Paris, 1962.

6. On Montherlant as a novelist, cf. E. Meriel, *Henry de Montherlant,* Paris, 1936.

7. On Radiguet, cf. K. Goesch, *R. Radiguet,* Paris (thesis at the Sorbonne), 1955.

8. On Françoise Sagan, cf. G. Hourdin, *Le Cas Françoise Sagan,* Paris, 1958; G. Mourgue, *Françoise Sagan,* Paris, 1958.

VII. THE NOVEL OF DEVELOPMENT

1. In general, cf. Fritz Martini, "Der Bildungsroman," DVJB, XXXV, 1961, pp. 44–63. On Rolland, cf. especially J. Robichez, *Romain Rolland,* Paris, 1961, which is the most thorough study to date, providing a good bibliography and information on the whereabouts of Rolland's numerous unpublished manuscripts. In addition, we mention W. Ilberg, *Der schwere Weg, Leben und Werk Romain Rollands,* Schwerin, 1955; and M. Krampf, *La Conception de la vie héroique dans l'œuvre de Romain Rolland,* Paris (thesis at the Sorbonne), 1956.

2. On Arland, cf. J. Duvignaud, *Arland,* Paris, 1962.

3. On Chardonne, cf. G. Guitard-Auviste, *La Vie de Jacques Chardonne et son art,* Paris, 1953.

4. On Colette, cf. J. Larnac, *Colette, sa vie, son œuvre,* Paris, 1951; M. Le Hardouin, *Colette,* Paris, 1956.

5. In general, cf. G. Bachelard, *La Poétique de la rêverie,* Paris, 1960, and more specifically on Alain-Fournier, Chr. Dedeyan, *Alain-Fournier et la réalité secrète,* Paris, 1948; J.-M. Delettrez, *Alain-Fournier et Le Grand Meaulnes,* Paris, 1954; Cl. Borgal, *Alain-Fournier,* Paris, 1955; A. Béguin, "Alain-Fournier," in *Poésie de la présence, Les Cahiers du Rhône,* November, 1957, pp. 187–97; J. Rivière, "L'Agenda inédit d'Alain-Fournier," *Figaro littéraire,* March 5, 1964.

6. On Larbaud, cf. F. Contreras, *Valery Larbaud et son œuvre,* Angers, 1930; E. Maurer, *Die Unruhe bei Valery Larbaud,* Zurich, 1936; G. Jean-Aubry, *Valery Larbaud, sa vie et son œuvre,* Monaco, 1949; N. Erné, "Die französische Novelle im 20. Jahrhundert," *Antares,* I, 5, 1954, pp. 15–21.

7. On Hellens, cf. *Le Dernier disque vert—hommage à Franz Hellens,* Paris, 1957; A. Lebois, *Franz Hellens,* Paris, 1963.— On the Belgian novel in French in general, cf. G. Charlier and J. Hanse *Histoire illustrée des lettres françaises de Belgique,* Brussels, 1958, particularly pp. 251ff., and also Prampolini, op. cit., vol. 6 (third edition, 1961), pp. 363ff. (on Belgian, Swiss, Canadian, and Central-American literature in French).

VIII. THE WAR NOVEL

1. On the war novel in general, cf. J. Augée, *L'Image du combattant dans le roman de guerre français et allemand (1914–1918)*, Paris (thesis), 1955.

2. On Barbusse, cf. L. Spitzer, *Studien zu Henri Barbusse*, Bonn, 1920; A. Vidal, *Henri Barbusse, soldat de la paix*, Paris, 1953.

3. On Dorgelès, cf. A. Dubeux, *Roland Dorgelès, son œuvre*, Paris, 1930.

4. On Psichari, cf. W. Becherer, *Ernest Psichari in seiner psychologischen Entwicklung*, Jena (dissertation), 1933; Jean Peyrade, *Psichari, maître de grandeur*, Paris, 1947.

5. Cf., in this connection, R.-M. Albérès, *L'Aventure intellectuelle du XXᵉ siècle*, Paris, 1959, p. 17.

6. On Malraux's life, cf. especially J. Rühle, *Literatur und Revolution*, Cologne, 1960, pp. 318ff.

7. For example in G. Zeltner-Neukomm, *Das Wagnis des französischen Gegenwartsromans*, Paris, 1960, pp. 31–39.

8. On Malraux in general, cf. G. Picon, *André Malraux*, Paris, 1952; P.-H. Simon, "André Malraux ou le défi de la mort," in *L'Homme en procès*, Neuchâtel, 1950, pp. 29ff.

9. On Saint-Exupéry, cf. E. A. Racky, *Die Auffassung vom Menschen bei Antoine de Saint-Exupéry*, Wiesbaden, 1954; P. Chevrier, *Saint-Exupéry*, Paris, 1958; M. Migeo, *Saint-Exupéry*, Paris, 1958.

10. On Vercors, cf. W. Möller, *Vercors' Werk*, Berlin (dissertation), 1954.

11. On Céline, cf. R. Poulet, *Entretiens familiers avec Louis-Ferdinand Céline*, Paris, 1958.

12. On Gracq, cf. P. de Boisdeffre, *Une Histoire vivante de la littérature d'aujourd'hui*, Paris, 1960, pp. 298ff.

IX. THE NOVEL OF ADVENTURE

1. On Carco, cf. P. Chabaneix, *Francis Carco*, Paris, 1949.

2. On Simenon, cf. G.-A. Martius, *Die Bedeutung der Maigretromane von Georges Simenon im Rahmen der modernen Detektivliteratur*, Göttingen (dissertation), 1954; A. Parinaud, *Connaissance de Georges Simenon*, Paris, 1957.

3. On Morand, cf. G. Guitard-Auviste, *Paul Morand*, Paris, 1956. Quotation page 47.

4. On Benoit, cf. L. Chaigne, *Pierre Benoit*, Paris, 1934.

5. On Giraudoux, cf. Cl.-E. Magny, *Histoire du roman français depuis 1918*, op. cit., pp. 146–68; G. Meister, *Gestalt und*

Bedeutung der Frau im Werk Jean Giraudoux, Basel, 1951; J. Toussaint, *Jean Giraudoux,* Paris, 1953; R.-M. Albérès, *Esthétique et morale chez Jean Giraudoux,* Paris, 1957; J. Th. Coleman, *Le Monde illusoire de Jean Giraudoux,* Pittsburgh (dissertation), 1961.

X. THE RELIGIOUS NOVEL

1. Cf., in this connection, "Le Roman catholique," in M. Bémol, *Essai sur l'orientation des littératures de langue française au XXᵉ siècle,* Paris, 1960, pp. 213ff.; T. Hitchen, *Le Problème du mal dans les romans de Mauriac, Bernanos et Green,* Liverpool, 1959.
2. Cf., on the religious novel in general, J.-L. Prévost, *Satan et le romancier,* Paris, 1954, and *Le Roman catholique a 100 ans,* Paris, 1958; P.-H. Simon, *La Littérature du péché et de la grâce,* Paris, 1957.
3. These articles by Bernanos have been collected and published by A. Rousseaux under the title of *Français, si vous saviez,* Paris, 1961. They are particularly significant with respect to the relationship of Bernanos to Mauriac and Charles de Gaulle.
4. Cf., on Bernanos in general, E. Lefèvre, *Georges Bernanos,* Paris, 1927; L. Estang, *Présence de Bernanos,* Paris, 1947; G. Picon, *Bernanos,* Paris, 1948; A. Béguin, *Georges Bernanos, études, souvenirs et documents,* Paris, 1949; H. Urs von Balthasar, *Georges Bernanos,* Cologne, 1954; G. Gaucher, *Le Thème de la mort dans les romans de Bernanos,* Paris, 1955; M. Estève, *Le Thème de l'amour dans les romans de Bernanos,* Paris, 1958.
5. Cf., in this connection, J.-L. Prévost, *Le Prêtre, ce héros de roman,* 2 vols., Paris, 1952–53.
6. H. Urs von Balthasar, *Georges Bernanos,* Cologne, 1954, p. 397.
7. A. Blanchet, *La Littérature et le spirituel,* Paris, 1959, vol. I, pp. 177–89: "Jouhandeau."
8. Cf., on Jouhandeau in general, Jean Gaulmier, *L'Univers de Marcel Jouhandeau,* Paris, 1959; J. Cabanis, *Jouhandeau,* Paris, 1959.
9. Cf., on Mauriac in general, Ch. Du Bos, *François Mauriac et le probléme du romancier catholique,* Paris, 1933; A. Fillon, *François Mauriac,* Paris, 1936; G. Hourdin, *Mauriac romancier chrétien,* Paris, 1953; A. Léonhard, *François Mauriac ou la psychologie du pécheur,* Liége, 1951; J. Robichon, *François Mauriac,* Paris, 1953.—An important publication, by reason

of its autobiographical content, is *Mémoires intérieurs,* Paris, 1959. A recent addition to the Mauriac bibliography is B. Roussel, *Mauriac,* Paris, 1965.

10. On Green's relations to catholicism, cf. in particular Ch. Moeller, *Littérature du XXe siècle et christianisme,* Paris, 1954, volume I, pp. 302–70.

11. Cf., on Julien Green in general, H. Lauresne, *Deux romanciers de la solitude morale: George Eliot et Julien Green,* Paris, 1928; M. Eigeldinger, *Julien Green ou la tentation de l'irréel,* Paris, 1947; A. Fongaro, *L'Existence dans les romans de Julien Green,* Rome, 1954; J. Wilhelm, "Betrachtungen über das Journal von Julien Green," in *Festschrift für Fr. Neubert,* Berlin, 1956, pp. 481–93; P. Brodin, *Julien Green,* Paris, 1957; Germaine Brée and M. Guiton, *An Age of Fiction, The French Novel from Gide to Camus,* New Brunswick, 1957, pp. 101ff.; J. Sémolué, *Julien Green ou l'obsession du mal,* Paris, 1964.

XI. THE NOVEL OF SOCIETY IN THE TWENTIETH CENTURY

1. On the social novel of the twentieth century in general, cf. W. Lacher, *Le Réalisme dans le roman contemporain,* Geneva, 1940 (especially pp. 153–64 and 209–40); H. Gmelin, *Der französische Zyklenroman 1900 bis 1945,* Heidelberg, 1950; A. Junker, "Zur Spiegelung unserer Zeit in der französischen Litteratur des 20. Jahrhunderts," *Die neueren Sprachen,* X, 1961, pp. 153–69.

2. On Duhamel, cf. L. Wehrli, *Mensch und Stil im Werk Georges Duhamels,* Wädenswil, 1937; P.-H. Simon, *George Duhamel ou le bourgeois sauvé,* Paris, 1946; I. Scheller, *Das Generationsproblem bei Jules Romains, Georges Duhamel und André Maurois,* Tübingen (dissertation), 1953.

3. On Romains, cf. A. Cuisenier, *Jules Romains et les Hommes de bonnes volonté,* Paris, 1954; A. Figuéras, *Jules Romains* (Poètes d'aujourd'hui), Paris, 1951; M. Berry, *Jules Romains,* Paris, 1953; Leo Spitzer, "Der Unanimismus Romains' im Spiegel seiner Sprache," in *Stilstudien II,* Munich, 1961, pp. 208–300.

4. P. Daix, *Réflexions sur la méthode de Roger Martin du Gard,* Paris, 1957, p. 81.

5. On Martin du Gard, cf. H. C. Rice, *Roger Martin du Gard and the World of the Thibaults,* New York, 1944; R. Lalou, *Roger Martin du Gard,* Paris, no year; J. Brenner, *Martin du*

Gard, Paris, 1961; I. Dimic, *La Crise psychologique dans le roman du XXe siècle. De Martin du Gard au nouveau roman,* Strasbourg (dissertation), 1961.

6. On Aragon, cf. Cl. Roy, *Aragon,* Paris, 1945; H. Juin, *Aragon,* Paris, 1960; R. Garaudy, *L'Itinéraire d'Aragon,* Paris, 1961.

7. The best discussion of these problems will be found in H. Nahas, *La Femme dans la littérature existentielle,* Paris, 1957.

8. On Simone de Beauvoir, cf. G. Gennari, *Simone de Beauvoir,* Paris, 1959; D. Wasmund, *Der Skandal der Simone de Beauvoir,* Munich, 1963; S. Julienne-Caffié, *Simone de Beauvoir,* Paris, 1966.

9. On Ikor, cf. G. Krause in *Tendenzen im französischen Romanschaffen des 20. Jahrhunderts,* Frankfurt on the Main, 1962, pp. 82–115.

XII. THE REGIONAL NOVEL

1. On the regional novel in general, cf. G. Roger, *Situation du roman régionaliste,* Paris, 1951; K. Zerenner, *Der französische Bauernroman des 20. Jahrhunderts,* Jena (dissertation), 1952; G. Roger, *Maîtres du roman du terroir,* Paris, 1959; E. v. Jan, *Französische Literaturgeschichte in Grundzügen,* Heidelberg, 1962 (fifth edition), pp. 308–14.

2. On Hémon and Hervé Bazin, cf. A. McAndrew, *L. Hémon, sa vie et son œuvre,* Paris, 1936; J. Anglade, *Hervé Bazin,* Paris, 1962.

3. On Ramuz, cf. W. Günther, *C.-F. Ramuz, Wesen, Werk, Kunst,* Berne, 1948; A. Tissot, *C.-F. Ramuz, ou le drame de la poésie,* Neuchâtel, 1948; E.-M. Nagel, *Die Dichtungstheorie von C.-F. Ramuz und ihre Darstellung im Werk,* Tübingen (dissertation), 1960.

4. On Giono, cf. J. Pugnet, *Jean Giono,* Paris-Brussels, 1955.

5. On Chamson, cf. E. Bendz, *André Chamson, un aspect récent de son œuvre,* Paris, 1952.

XIII. THE NOVEL OF THE ABSURDITY OF EXISTENCE

1. Cf., in general, M. Goth, *Kafka et les lettres françaises 1928–1955,* Paris, 1956; P.-H. Simon, *L'Homme en procès,* Neuchâtel, 1958; H. H. Holz, *Der französische Existentialismus,* Speyer, 1958; H. Barnes, *Literature of Possibility,*

Lincoln (Nebraska), 1959; G. A. Zehm, *Historische Vernunft und direkte Aktion. Zur Politik und Philosophie Jean-Paul Sartres,* Stuttgart, 1964.

2. On Michaux, cf. Winfried Engler, *Henri Michaux. Das Michauxbild 1922–1959,* Tübingen (dissertation), 1960, photo reproduction, 1964.

3. On Sartre, cf. M. Beigbeder, *L'Homme Sartre,* Paris, 1947; R.-M. Albérès, *Jean-Paul Sartre,* Paris, 1953; I. Murdoch, *Sartre, Romantic Rationalist,* Cambridge, 1953; J. Möller, *Absurdes Sein. Auseinandersetzung mit der Ontologie Jean-Paul Sartres,* Stuttgart, 1959; F. Jameson, *Sartre, The Origins of a Style,* London, 1961; M. Craneston, *Sartre,* Edinburgh-London, 1962.—In 1964, Gallimard published Sartre's *Les Mots,* which is the story of his youth and his first literary attempts. The reflections contained in this publication with respect to the "sincerity" of the adolescent are informative with respect to Sartre's literary work. It appears that it was in particular his grandfather, Charles Schweitzer, who established in him, as it were, the certainty that he was destined to become a writer. "Being an imaginative child, I became a knight in shining armor whose exploits were going to be books, real books" ["Enfant imaginaire, je devenais un vrai paladin dont les exploits seraient de vrais livres" (p. 141)].

4. On Camus, cf. W. M. Frohock, *Camus. Image, Influence and Sensibility,* Yale (French Studies), 1949; A. Maquet, *Albert Camus ou l'invincible été,* Paris, 1955; Germaine Brée, *Camus,* New York, 1959; Ph. Tody, *Albert Camus, 1913–1960,* London, 1961; special issues of *Nouvelle revue française, Table ronde,* and *Preuves,* 1960; A. Noyer-Weidner, "Das Formproblem der 'Pest' von Albert Camus," GRM, VIII, 1958, pp. 260–85, and "Camus im Stadium der Novelle," ZFSL, LXX, 1960, pp. 1–38; R. Thieberger, "Albert Camus. Einführung in sein dichterisches Werk," *Beihefte DNS,* 1961; Anne Durand, *Le Cas Albert Camus,* Paris, 1962; M.-G. Barrier, *L'Art du récit dans L'Étranger d'Albert Camus,* Paris, 1962.

5. J. Bens, *Queneau,* Paris, 1962.

6. R. Federmann, *Journey to Chaos. Samuel Beckett's Early Fiction,* Berkeley and Los Angeles, 1965.

XIV. THE NOVEL OF THINGS

1. Cf., in general, Claude Mauriac, *L'Alittérature contemporaine,* Paris, 1958; G. Zeltner-Neukomm, *Das Wagnis des fran-*

zösischen Gegenwartsromans, Hamburg, 1960; P. A. G. Astier, *Le Nouveau roman. Analyse et critique d'un renouvellement du genre romanesque (1955–1960),* Providence (Brown dissertation), 1961; E. Bouvier, *Les Lettres françaises au XXᵉ siècle,* Paris, 1962; J. Cruickshank (ed.), *The Novelist as Philosopher. Studies in French Fiction 1935–1960,* London, 1962; M. Nadeau, *Le Roman français depuis la guerre,* Paris, 1963.—On Robbe-Grillet and Butor, cf., in particular, Y. Guers, "La Technique romanesque chez Robbe-Grillet," *French Review,* XXX, 1961/2, pp. 570–77; K. Wilhelm, "Der 'Nouveau Romancier' Alain Robbe-Grillet," ZFSL, LXXII, 1962, pp. 169–85; F. C. St. Aubin, "Butor and the Phenomenological realism," *Studi Francesi,* VI, 1962, pp. 51–62; L. Spitzer, "Quelques aspects de la technique des romans de Butor," *Archivum Linguisticum,* XIV, 1962, pp. 49–76; P. Bürger, "Zeit als Struktur und Schicksal. Versuch über einen Roman von M. Butor (L'Emploi du temps)," *Die Neueren Sprachen,* VI, 1963, pp. 269–75; R.-M. Albérès, *Butor,* Paris, 1964, B. Morrissette, *Les Romans de Robbe-Grillet,* Paris, 1963; W. Leiner, "Begriff und Wesen des Anti-Romans in Frankreich," *Zeitschrift für französische Sprache und Literatur,* LXXIV, 1964, pp. 97–129; J. Roudaut, *Michel Butor ou le livre futur,* Paris, 1964.—Robbe-Grillet's theoretical writings have been made conveniently available as *Pour un nouveau roman,* Paris, 1963.

APPENDIX OF FRENCH
QUOTATIONS

[Page 13] Chateaubriand, *René* (Garnier Edition, pp. 184ff.):
"Je ne puis, en commençant mon récit, me défendre d'un mouvement de honte. La paix de vos coeurs, respectables vieillards, et le calme de la nature autour de moi, me font rougir du trouble et de l'agitation de mon âme.

"Combien vous aurez pitié de moi! Que mes éternelles inquiétudes vous paraîtront misérables! Vous qui avez épuisé tous les chagrins de la vie, que penserez-vous d'un jeune homme sans force et sans vertu, qui trouve en lui-même son tourment, et ne peut guère se plaindre que des maux qu'il se fait à lui-même? Hélas, ne le condamnez pas; il a été trop puni!

"J'ai coûté le vie à ma mère en venant au monde; j'ai été tiré de son sein avec le fer. J'avais un frère que mon père bénit, parce qu'il voyait en lui sons fils aîné. Pour moi, livré de bonne heure à des mains étrangères, je fus élevé loin du toit paternel.

"Mon humeur était impétueuse, mon caractère inégal. Tour à tour bruyant et joyeux, silencieux et triste, je rassemblais autour de moi mes jeunes compagnons; puis, les abandonnant tout à coup, j'allais m'asseoir à l'écart, pour contempler la nuit fugitive, ou entendre la pluie tomber sur le feuillage."

[Page 29] Stendhal, *La Chartreuse de Parme* (Garnier Edition, p. 298):
"Mais enfin, à son inexprimable joie, après une si longue attente et tant de regards, vers midi Clélia vint soigner ses oiseaux. Fabrice resta immobile et sans respiration, il était debout contre les énormes barreaux de sa fenêtre et fort près. Il remarqua qu'elle ne levait pas les yeux sur lui, mais ses mouvements avaient l'air gêné comme ceux de quelqu'un qui se sent regardé ... Quoique, suivant toute apparence, elle veillât sur ses actions avec le plus grand soin, au moment où elle s'approcha de la fenêtre de la volière, elle rougit fort sensiblement. La première pensée de Fabrice, collé contre les barreaux de fer de sa fenêtre, fut de se livrer à

l'enfantillage de frapper un peu avec la main sur ces barreaux, ce qui produirait un petit bruit, puis la seule idée de ce manque de délicatesse lui fit horreur."

[Page 44] Balzac, *Père Goriot*: "À nous deux maintenant."

[Page 48] Balzac, *La Cousine Bette* (Garnier Edition, pp. 68f.):
"Elle se vengeait sur ce jeune homme de ce qu'elle n'était ni jeune, ni riche, ni belle. Puis, après chaque vengeance, elle arrivait, en reconnaissant ses torts, en elle-même, à des humilités, à des tendresses infinies. Elle ne concevait le sacrifice à faire à son idole qu'après y avoir écrit sa puissance à coups de hache ... Quant à ce malheureux jeune homme à pensées élevées, méditatif, enclin à la paresse, il offrait dans les yeux, comme ces lions encagés au Jardin des plantes, le désert que sa protectrice faisait en son âme. Le travail forcé que Lisbeth exigeait de lui ne défrayait pas les besoins de son cœur. Son ennui devenait une maladie physique, et il mourait sans pouvoir demander, sans pouvoir se procurer l'argent d'une folie souvent nécessaire."

[Page 55] Flaubert, *Madame Bovary*:
"Emma avait la tête penchée sur l'épaule droite. Le coin de sa bouche, qui se tenait ouverte, faisait comme un trou noir au bas de son visage; les deux pouces restaient infléchis dans la paume des mains; une sorte de poussière blanche lui parsemait les cils, et ses yeux commençaient à disparaître dans une paleur visqueuse qui ressemblait à une toile mince, comme si des araignées avaient filé dessus."

[Page 57] Flaubert, *L'Éducation sentimentale* (Garnier Edition, Paris, 1958, p. 108):
"Frédéric alla de l'estaminet chez Arnoux, comme soulevé par un vent tiède et avec l'aisance extraordinaire que l'on éprouve dans les songes. Il se trouva bientôt à un second étage, devant une porte dont la sonnette retentissait; une servante parut; une seconde porte s'ouvrit; Madame Arnoux était assise près du feu. Arnoux fit un bond et l'embrassa. Elle avait sur ses genoux un petit garçon de trois ans, à peu près; sa fille, grande comme elle maintenant, se tenait debout, de l'autre côté de la cheminée."

[Page 77] Goncourts (Diary):
"Un des caractères particuliers de nos romans, ce sera d'être les romans les plus historiques de ce temps-ci, les romans qui fourniront le plus de faits et de vérités vraies à l'histoire morale de ce siècle."

[Page 79] Zola, *Les Rougon-Macquart* (Preface):
"L'hérédité a ses lois . . . Je tâcherai de trouver et de suivre, en résolvant la double question des tempéraments et des milieux, le fil qui conduit mathématiquement d'un homme à un autre homme."

[Page 79] Zola, *Les Rougon-Macquart* (Preface):
"La lente succession des accidents nerveux et sanguins qui se déclarent dans une race . . . et qui déclarent, selon les milieux, chez les individus de cette race, les sentiments, les désirs, les passions, toutes les manifestations humaines, naturelles et instinctives, dont les produits prennent les noms convenus de vertus et de vices."

[Page 82] Zola, *Les Rougon-Macquart* (Pléiade Edition, vol. I, Paris, 1960, pp. 633f.):
"C'était la marée, c'étaient des beurres, c'était la volaille, c'était la viande. Des volées de cloche passaient, secouant derrière elles le murmure des marchés qui s'ouvraient. Autour de lui, le soleil enflammait les légumes. Il ne reconnaissait plus l'aquarelle tendre des pâleurs de l'aube. Les coeurs élargis des salades brûlaient, la gamme du vert éclatait en vigueurs superbes, les carottes saignaient, les navets devenaient incandescents, dans ce brasier triomphal. (. . .) La mer continuait à monter. Il l'avait sentie à ses chevilles, puis à son ventre; elle menaçait à cette heure de passer par-dessus de sa tête. Aveuglé, noyé, les oreilles sonnantes, l'estomac écrasé part tout ce qu'il avait vu, devinant de nouvelles et incessantes profondeurs de nourriture, il demanda grâce, et une douleur folle le prit, de mourir ainsi de faim, dans ce Paris gorgé, dans ce réveil fulgurant des Halles."

[Page 86] Unidentified writer (*Voltaire,* May 4, 1886):
"Etre fin-de-siècle, c'est n'être plus responsable; c'est subir d'une façon presque fatale l'influence des temps et du milieu; c'est prendre tout simplement sa petite part de lassitude et de la corruption générales; c'est pourrir avec son siècle et déchoir avec lui."

[Page 100] Huysmans, *À Rebours* (Bibliothèque Charpentier, p. 72):
"Dans l'odeur perverse des parfums, dans l'atmosphère surchauffée de cette église, Salomé, le bras gauche étendu, en un geste de commandement, le bras droit replié, tenant à la hauteur du visage, un grand lotus, s'avance lentement sur les pointes, aux accords d'une guitare dont une femme accroupie pince les cordes. La face recueillie, solennelle, presque auguste, elle commence la lubrique danse qui doit réveiller les sens assoupis du

vieil Hérode; ses seins ondulent et, au frottement de ses colliers qui tourbillonnent, leurs bouts se dressent; sur la moiteur de sa peau les diamants, attachés, scintillent; ses bracelets, ses ceintures, ses bagues crachent des étincelles; sur sa robe triomphale, couturée de perles, ramagée d'argent, lamée d'or, la cuirasse des orfèvreries dont chaque maille est une pierre, entre en combustion, croise des serpenteaux de feu, grouille sur la chair mate, sur la peau rose thé, ainsi que des insectes splendides aux élytres eblouissants, marbrés de carmin, ponctués de jaune aurore, diaprés de bleu d'acier, tigrés de vert paon."

[Page 109] Proust, *À la Recherche du temps perdu* (Pléiade Edition, vol. I, Paris, 1959, pp. 4f.):

"Quelquefois, comme Eve naquit d'une côte d'Adam, une femme naissait pendant mon sommeil d'une fausse position de ma cuisse. Formée du plaisir que j'étais sur le point de goûter, je m'imaginais que c'était elle qui me l'offrait. Mon corps qui sentait dans le sien ma propre chaleur voulait s'y rejoindre, je m'éveillais. Le reste des humains m'apparaissaient comme bien lointains auprès de cette femme que j'avais quittée, il y avait quelques moments à peine; ma joue était chaude encore de son baiser, mon corps courbaturé par le poids de sa taille. Si, comme il arrivait quelquefois, elle avait les traits d'une femme que j'avais connue dans la vie, j'allais me donner tout entier à ce but: la retrouver, comme ceux qui partent en voyage pour voir de leurs yeux une cité désirée et s'imaginent qu'on peut goûter dans une réalité le charme du songe. Peu à peu son souvenir s'évanouissait, j'avais oublié la fille de mon rêve."

[Page 112] Proust, *Le Temps retrouvé* (vol. II, p. 28):

"Mais cette découverte que l'art nous pouvait faire faire n'était-elle pas au fond celle de . . . ce qui nous reste d'habitude à jamais inconnu, notre vrai vie, la réalité telle que nous l'avons sentie et qui diffère tellement de ce que nous croyons que nous sommes emplis d'un tel bonheur, quand le hasard nous en apporte le souvenir véritable?"

[Page 120] Gide, *Thésée* (p. 12):

"Sache montrer aux hommes ce que peut être et se propose de devenir l'un d'entre eux. Il y a de grandes choses à faire. Obtiens-toi."

[Page 162] Bernanos, *Sous le soleil de Satan* (pp. 170f):

"Celui qui, noué des deux mains à la pointe extrême du mât, perdant tout à coup l'équilibre gravitationnel, verrait se creuser et s'enfler sous lui, non plus la mer, mais tout l'abîme sidéral, et bouillante à des trillions de lieues l'écume des nébuleuses en gestation, au travers du vide que rien ne mesure et que va traverser sa chute éternelle, ne sentirait pas au creux de sa poitrine un vertige plus absolu. Son coeur battit deux fois plus furieusement contre ses côtes, et s'arrêta. Une nausée souleva ses entrailles. Les doigts, d'une étreinte désespérée, seuls vivants dans son corps pétrifié d'horreur, grattèrent le sol comme des griffes. La sueur ruissela entre ses épaules. L'homme intrépide, comme ployé et arraché de terre par l'énorme appel du néant, se vit cette fois perdu sans retour. Et pourtant, à cet instant même, sa suprême pensée fut encore un obscur défi."

[Page 164] Bernanos, *Journal d'un curé de campagne*:
"Ma paroisse est dévorée par l'ennui, voilà le mot. Comme tant d'autres paroisses! L'ennui les dévore sous nos yeux et nous n'y pouvons rien ... Mais que pèsent nos chances, à nous autres, qui avons accepté, une fois pour toutes, l'effrayante présence du divin à chaque instance de notre pauvre vie ... Calculer nos chances, à quoi bon? On ne joue pas contre Dieu."

[Page 179] Romains, *Le 7 octobre* (p. 6):
"De ses collines, de ses plaines faiblement surélevées et penchantes, Paris descend au travail. Son mouvement est un peu le même qu'il y a vingt-cinq ans, un peu autre. Comme le centre a bougé vers l'ouest, beaucoup d'itinéraires, à partir des quartiers périphériques et des faubourgs, se sont inclinés aussi du côté du couchant. Mais surtout ce remuement matinal a gagné en ampleur et en complication ... Il ne s'agit plus du ruissellement quasi naturel d'une grande ville vers sa cuvette centrale."

[Page 180] Romains, *Les Hommes de bonne volonté* (Preface):
"Les Hommes de Bonne Volonté! Une antique bénédiction va les chercher dans la foule et les recouvre. Puissent-ils être encore une fois, un jour et l'autre, rassemblés par une 'bonne nouvelle' et trouver quelque sûr moyen de se reconnaître, afin que ce monde, dont ils sont le mérite et le sel, ne périsse pas."

[Page 196] Giono, *Regain* (p. 233):
"L'escadre des nuages a largué les amarres, ça a fait un grand et long charroi de nues qui montaient vers le nord. Ça a duré; à mesure, on sentait la terre qui se gonflait de toutes ses pluies et la vie réveillée de l'herbe."

[Page 203] Sartre, *La Nausée*:
"Et puis il y avait sa main comme un gros ver blanc dans ma main . . . Il me semblait que j'étais rempli de lymphe ou de lait tiède."

[Page 203] Sartre, *La Nausée*:
". . . J'ai peur d'entrer en contact avec eux tout comme s'ils étaient des bêtes vivantes."

[Page 204] Sartre, *La Nausée*:
"Elle n'existe pas, puisqu'elle n'a rien de trop: c'est tout le reste qui est trop par rapport à elle. Elle est. Et moi aussi j'ai voulu être."

[Page 209] Camus, *La Peste*:
"L'homme absurde ne peut que s'épuiser."

[Page 210] Camus, *Le Mythe de Sisyphe* (p. 18):
"Ce divorce entre l'homme et sa vie, l'acteur et son décor, c'est proprement le sentiment de l'absurdité."

[Page 210] Camus, *Le Mythe de Sisyphe* (p. 163):
"Les dieux avaient condamné Sisyphe à rouler sans cesse un rocher jusqu'au sommet d'une montagne d'où la pierre retombait par son propre poids. Ils avaient pensé avec quelque raison qu'il n'est pas de punition plus terrible que le travail inutile et sans espoir."

[Page 210] Camus, *Le Mythe de Sisyphe* (pp. 167f):
"Toute la joie silencieuse de Sisyphe est là. Son destin lui appartient. Son rocher est sa chose. De même, l'homme absurde, quand il contemple son tourment, fait taire tous les idoles. Dans l'univers soudain rendu à son silence, les mille petites voix émerveillées de la terre s'élèvent. Appels inconscients et secrets, invitations de tous les visages, ils sont l'envers nécessaire et le prix de la victoire. Il n'y a pas de soleil sans ombre, et il faut connaître la nuit. L'homme absurde dit oui et son effort n'aura plus de cesse. S'il y a un destin personnel, il n'y a point de destinée supérieure ou de moins il n'en est qu'une dont il juge qu'elle est fatale et méprisable. Pour le reste, il se sait le maître de ses jours . . . La lutte elle-même vers les sommets suffit à remplir un coeur d'homme. Il faut imaginer Sisyphe heureux."

[Page 222] Robbe-Grillet, *Dans le labyrinthe* (p. 118):
"Mais la neige tombait encore, à ce moment-là, en flocons serrés, et les empreintes du guide, à peine faites, commençaient aussitôt à perdre leur précision et se comblaient rapidement, de plus en

plus méconnaissables à mesure que la distance augmentait entre le soldat et lui, leur simple présence ne tardant pas à devenir à son tour très douteuse, dépression à peine sensible dans l'uniformité de la surface."

[Page 225] Butor, *L'Emploi du temps* (pp. 51f):
"C'était pour la première fois que je voyais la table ovale en acajou verni, les trois napperons bordés de dentelle jaunie, les tasses chinoises avec leur théière, blanches et bleues, la lampadaire en opaline, qui ne devait pas être allumé ce jour-la, ce samedi 20 octobre, les deux grandes gravures en taille douce, dans leurs cadres à rang de perles (un bateau à roues dans un paysage d'Océanie, et je ne sais quel roi déchu, s'enfuyant, drapé dans son manteau, couronne en tête, à travers une épaisse forêt pleine de loups aux yeux lumineux)."

[Page 227] Butor, *L'Emploi du temps* (p. 125):
"Les derniers nuages semblables aux brandons, aux grandes branches basses embrasées d'une forêt qui achève de se consumer, emportés, attisés par un ouragan furieux, les derniers nuages roulent au-dessus des toits brillants, gluants de la dernière pluie, et des cheminées de Dew Street, tandis que le couvercle du ciel recommence à s'entrebailler sur cette immense prairie profondément, exquisement mouillée, teinte d'eau, où traînent quelques spirales de vapeurs et de fumées, toute couverte de pétales d'un surabondant verger, et des millions de vols de silencieuses abeilles aux ailes alourdies . . ."

INDEX OF NAMES

(Roman numerals in parentheses refer to chapter headings.)

Index

Index

Index

INDEX OF TITLES

(Works which the reader is likely to look for under their translated titles are listed, with proper cross references, both in the original and in English.)

Index

Index

Notre-Dame des désemparés (Murciaux), 143

Notre-Dame-des-fleurs [Our Lady of the Flowers] (Genet), 215

Nouveaux aristocrates, Les (Saint-Pierre), 189

Nouveaux contes cruels (Villiers de l'Isle-Adam), 71

Nouveaux prétextes (Gide), 116

Nouvelle Héloïse, La (Rousseau), 8

Nouvelles confidences, Les (Lamartine), 19

Nourritures terrestres (Gide), 115, 140

Novembre [November] (Flaubert), 53

Noyers de l'Altenburg, Les [The Walnut Trees of Altenburg] (Malraux), 140

Numa Roumestan [Numa Roumestan] (Daudet), 90

Oberman [Oberman] (Senancour), 6, 10, 12, 24

Oiseaux s'envolent et les fleurs tombent, Les (Bourges), 95

Old Goriot (Balzac), see Père Goriot

On the Dream (Vould), 110

On the Marble Cliffs (Jünger), see Auf den Marmorklippen

Or, L' [Sutter's Gold] (Cendrars), 152

Oracle, L' (Peyrefitte), 190

Ordre, L' (Arland), 130f.

Other Voices, Other Rooms (Capote), 134

Our Lady of the Flowers (Genet), see Notre-Dame-des-fleurs

Outsider, The (Camus), see Etranger

Où va le roman (Boisdeffre), 232

Pain de soldat (Poulaille), 185

Pain des pauvres, Le (Monnier), 198

Pain quotidien, Le (Poulaille), 185

Paludes [Marshlands] (Gide), 114, 120

Pamphlet contre les catholiques de France (Green), 170

Pantagruel (Mérimée), 33

Papa Pasquier (Duhamel), see Chronique des Pasquier

Papesse Jeanne, La (Jarry), 103

Paris-Timbouctou (Morand), 152

Paroisse morte, La (Bernanos), 161, 165

Parzival (Wolfram), 127

Pasquier Chronicles, The (Duhamel), see Chronique des Pasquier

Passage de Milan (Butor), 224f., 229

Passage du poète (Ramuz), 195

Passengers of Destiny (Aragon), see Voyageurs de l'impériale

Passing Time (Butor), see Emploi du temps

Pastoral Symphony, The (Gide), see Symphonie pastorale

Paul et Virginie [Paul and Virginia] (Saint-Pierre), 11, 19, 35

Pays d'Ouche (La Varende), 193

Peau de chagrin [Wild Ass's Skin] (Balzac), 52, 68

Péché de Monsieur Antoine, Le (Sand), 41

Pêcheurs d'Islande [An Iceland Fisherman] (Loti), 96

Penguin Island (France), see Ile des pingouins

Pensées [Thoughts on Religion] (Pascal), 161, 167, 174

Père Goriot [Père Goriot; Old Goriot] (Balzac), 43, 45f., 50, 62

Perish in Their Pride (Montherlant), see Célibataires

Peste, La [The Plague] (Camus), 207ff., 211

Petit chose, Le (Daudet), 90

Petite Fadette, La [Little Fadette] (Sand), 41

Petit prince, Le [The Little Prince] (Saint-Exupéry), 143

Petit traité de versification (Romains), 178

Petits poèmes en prose (Baudelaire), 33, 38

Philosophical Studies (Balzac) see Etudes philosophiques

Physiologie du mariage [The Physiology of Marriage] (Balzac), 49

Picture of Dorian Gray, The (Wilde), 99

Pierre et Jean [The Two Brothers] (Maupassant), 62

Pierrette [Pierrette] (Balzac), 46

Pierrot mon ami [Pierrot] (Queneau), 213

Pilote de guerre (Saint-Exupéry), 144

Pincengrain, Les (Jouhandeau), 166f.

Pipe d'opium, La (Gautier), 68

Piping Hot (Zola), see Pot-bouille